Managing Media Businesses

Mike Rosenberg • Philip H. Seager
Editors

Managing Media Businesses

A Game Plan to Navigate Disruption and
Uncertainty

Editors
Mike Rosenberg
IESE Business School
Barcelona, Spain

Philip H. Seager
IESE Business School
Barcelona, Spain

ISBN 978-3-319-84798-6   ISBN 978-3-319-52021-6   (eBook)
DOI 10.1007/978-3-319-52021-6

Cover design by Samantha Johnson

Printed on acid-free paper

This Palgrave Macmillan imprint is published by Springer Nature
The registered company is Springer International Publishing AG
The registered company address is: Gewerbestrasse 11, 6330 Cham, Switzerland

Who: To media and entertainment executives everywhere, but especially the Media AMP Class of 2014.
What: Thanks for generously contributing to this book.
Where: New York, Los Angeles, Barcelona.
When: Yesterday, today and tomorrow.
Why: To prove that reports of our death are greatly exaggerated.
How: That depends on you!

Preface

Chances are, we only need to say, "The dress: white and gold or blue and black?" and you will instantly know what we're talking about. For a few days in February 2015, the Great Dress Debate was the reigning topic of conversation on the planet, dividing public opinion and leading some to experience "a brief existential crisis over the meaning of color and life and a bout of embarrassing squealing before some powerful newsroom bosses," as Terrence McCoy confessed in *The Washington Post* [1]. The fact that millions of people could look at the exact same image and see entirely different realities confounded and alarmed people in equal measure.

As part of a recent Advanced Management Program (AMP) in Media & Entertainment held at IESE Business School, we conducted a similar experiment. We presented a picture to a group of participants and asked them to describe what they saw. One saw a Hindu god. Another an African mask. Another insisted it was a Mexican mask. Everyone saw something completely different.

We gave them an "answer" for what the picture actually was, but that wasn't really the point—just as when scientists finally weighed in on the Great Dress Debate, explaining how our eyes and brains process light and color differently, and proclaiming that the dress was indeed blue and black, the issue remained far from settled. More than two-thirds of an online poll insisted it was white and gold. It seemed people preferred the magic of their original perceptions.

What if the person who originally posted the picture of the dress online had simply said, "Look at this blue and black dress"? Having been told the color of the dress—having been given the "answer"—most of us would probably never have given the matter a second thought. Similarly, our participants would probably not have seen the god or the masks or whatever other image sprang to mind, because we would have conditioned their ability to see what it was that we wanted them to see.

"Conditioned" is the key word here. We are all conditioned to see the world through our own particular lens, which is influenced by our backgrounds, characters, cultures and experiences (and as we now know, by how our eyes and brains play tricks on us under certain light conditions). Is it any wonder, then, that in our particular picture puzzle, a participant of Indian heritage saw the Hindu god, the African participants saw the African mask and the Mexican participants saw it as Mexican, though they were in disagreement as to whether it was Aztec or Mayan? We all have certain mental models, or frames, as well as preferred modes of behavior, that have a strong bearing on how we interpret reality and how we act based on those interpretations.

Why does this matter? Think about this in terms of your business, where the picture you are asked to look at on a daily basis is rather more serious than a trivial dress. Maybe it's looking at your publishing business and asking, "What future do I see in newspapers, magazines or books?" Maybe it's looking at your digital venture and asking, "How do I monetize this?" Or maybe it's looking at both print and digital, and asking, "How do I make these two platforms work together?"

Your answers to the questions that vex your media or entertainment business will depend on your frame—a frame that needs to be broken if you are to survive in times of such rapid change.

Frank Bennack, the veteran chief executive of the Hearst media empire, knows this to be true. As he told us during a "fireside chat" in our New York center, 90 percent of his business today bears no resemblance to what it was when he started as CEO in 1979. You need to be like a pilot, he said, who is mentally running through the flight long before stepping into the cockpit. Proficient pilots visualize the path they want the airplane to take. They don't wait until they're at the desired altitude and then suddenly bank right. They're constantly looking ahead, thinking about where they need to go, compensating for whatever might break the pattern—and in this way, they arrive at their destination.

To not do so is to end up like the music industry, which thought that being like a pilot simply meant that you winged it. When digital arrived, the industry stuck to its traditional frame—the sale of CDs and total control of the value chain—and it did all it could to oppose anything that challenged its way of seeing the world.

A decade later, listen to what Warner Music Group executive Michael Nash had to say to those who are overly attached to their frames: "Get over it. Move on. Understand where the world is going. Understand the core strength of your company, and figure out how to harness that core strength in a new context" [2].

This book is precisely about that: Understanding where the world is going, understanding the core strength of your company and figuring out how to harness that core strength in a new context.

This book is based on IESE's AMP in Media & Entertainment, which IESE Business School has been running in New York and Los Angeles since 2011. The program combines contributions from leading professors and practitioners, as well as real-life case studies, to establish a base upon which you can start to build the set of managerial tools that you will need to manage fast-changing media and entertainment businesses.

Mirroring that program, this book tells a story and takes the reader on a journey of self-knowledge and self-discovery. There are numerous plot twists and constant guessing games, as befits an industry going through unprecedented disruption. But by the end we hope that you will have learned some important new lessons and gained deeper insights into how to apply general management principles to the particular challenges you face.

The Editors

References

1. T. McCoy (February 27, 2015), "The Inside Story of the 'White Dress, Blue Dress' Drama that Divided a Planet," *The Washington Post*, https://www.washingtonpost.com/news/morning-mix/wp/2015/02/27/the-inside-story-of-the-white-dress-blue-dress-drama-that-divided-a-nation/
2. L. Cabral (2011), "Interview with Michael Nash, Warner Music Group," *IESE Insight* magazine, Second Quarter, Issue 9.

Contents

List of Contributors

Miguel A. Ariño is Professor of Managerial Decision Sciences at IESE Business School.

Adrian Caldart is Senior Lecturer of Strategic Management at IESE Business School and Professor of Business Policy at AESE Business School (Lisbon and Porto).

Rafael de Santiago is Professor of Managerial Decision Sciences at IESE Business School.

Iris Firstenberg is Adjunct Associate Professor of Management and Organizations at the UCLA Anderson School of Management.

Hillel M. Maximon is Senior Lecturer of Accounting and Control and Financial Management at IESE Business School.

Philip Moscoso is Professor of Production, Technology and Operations Management and holds the Eurest Chair of Excellence in Services at IESE Business School.

Ahmad Rahnema Alavi is Professor of Financial Management and holds the Fuel Freedom Chair for Energy and Social Development at IESE Business School.

Mike Rosenberg is Assistant Professor of Strategic Management and Academic Director for the Advanced Management Program in Media and Entertainment at IESE Business School.

Philip H. Seager is Senior Editor of *IESE Insight*, the quarterly management review of IESE Business School.

Sandra Sieber is Professor of Information Systems at IESE Business School.

Jan Simon is Visiting Professor of Financial Management at IESE Business School.

Julian Villanueva is Professor of Marketing at IESE Business School where he also participates in the Center for Innovation Marketing and Strategy (CIMS) and the Institute for Media and Entertainment (IME).

List of Figures

List of Tables

1

The Big Picture: Four Trends That Change Everything

Mike Rosenberg and Philip H. Seager

The year 2016 saw independent-minded forces in Britain make a "decisive move" to set themselves on "a clear and secure future path." No, we are not talking about the dramatic Brexit vote on June 23, 2016, in which the UK decided by referendum to opt out of membership of the European Union—though that was certainly a game changer in its own way. We are talking about the announcement by *The Independent* national newspaper to cease publication after 30 years and go completely digital. This is either good news or bad news, depending on how you choose to interpret it. *The Independent*'s owners presented it as a daring, innovative move to meet the real needs of modern readers and "ensure a sustainable and profitable future" [1]. The headlines elsewhere were less enthusiastic in their interpretations, seeing it as definitive proof that the end of print media was not just nigh but well and truly here and predicting more bruising rounds of layoffs during the inexorable march of traditional media toward the ash heap of history. In a way, both views are right. The writing is on the wall for much of the media and entertainment industry as it currently stands—unless they decide to do something about it. This chapter highlights some of the big-picture trends

M. Rosenberg (✉)
Strategic Management Department, IESE Business School, Barcelona, Spain
e-mail: MRosenberg@iese.edu

P.H. Seager
Research Content Unit, IESE Business School, Barcelona, Spain
e-mail: pseager@iese.edu

© The Author(s) 2017
M. Rosenberg, P.H. Seager (eds.), *Managing Media Businesses*,
DOI 10.1007/978-3-319-52021-6_1

gathering momentum so that with these predictions in mind, media and enter-tainment executives and managers can plan some decisive moves of their own.

Granted, trying to predict the future of anything is "absurdly ambitious," as Daniel Franklin, Executive Editor of *The Economist*, frequently reminds us when he comes to IESE Business School at the beginning of every year to serve up his prognostications as editor of "The World in" series [2]. There is always the very real risk that anything stated on these pages today will be yesterday's news by the time you read this.

Be that as it may, we believe there are four overall trends that will remain relevant to media and entertainment professionals operating in this world of rapid change. The rest of the book has specific chapters, each going deep on a general management topic, to help you deal with each challenge.

The Global Economy in Perspective

Depending on where in the world you are reading this, the global economic outlook may be looking better or worse for your particular business, but one thing is certain across the board: uncertainty. The legacy of the global financial crisis has left its mark in several ways—with austerity, low interest rates, slow growth, scaled-back expectations and an aversion to embarking on ambitious debt-financed adventures being "the new normal." The only thing that seems to be growing significantly is inequality, both within and between countries.

The roots of this inequality are complex, as IESE Economics Professor Xavier Vives explains. You can say this situation is being aggravated by the ten-dency of developed economies to offshore much of their productive capacity to emerging economies, which dims the middle-class prospects of low-skilled workers in developed nations, even as it fuels the rise of the middle class in emerging ones. You can also say that globalization and digital technologies are playing a role: "Globalization and digital technology expand the market for talent, giving rise to the 'superstar' phenomenon. Indeed, the value of a top soccer player is much greater today, thanks to digital global media, than in a world dominated by national TV or, going further back in time, a world with no TV," states Vives [3].

Admittedly such inequality has always existed in the media and entertain-ment business, but today we see the effects being amplified and exaggerated in ways that are giving rise to unsustainable extremes. An American Society of News Editors survey is but one example, revealing in 2015 the biggest sin-gle-year drop in full-time editorial professionals since the economic crises of 2007 and 2008, meaning that US newsrooms are now staffed by almost half of what they were at their peak in 1990 [4]. (The 2016 data were not available at the time of writing, but by all accounts, the cuts were going to be even worse.) That double-digit drop in employment happened at a time when the US economy was supposedly doing its best in a decade. This bleeding of lower-paid staff from local newsrooms is counterweighted by the rise of even bigger media conglomerates with rapidly expanding global digital footprints. The small is being replaced by the big; the middle goes to the extremes.

When that happens, to quote Yeats, "Things fall apart; the center cannot hold; mere anarchy is loosed upon the world; the blood-dimmed tide is loosed, and everywhere the ceremony of innocence is drowned; the best lack all conviction, while the worst are full of passionate intensity" [5].

Evidence of this "passionate intensity" is all around. It dominates our headlines and feeds our news cycles. Witness the World Economic Forum's annual report on global risks. In its 2015 report, marking 25 years since the reunification of Germany after the fall of the Berlin Wall, "interstate conflict with regional consequences" topped the list and in 2016 remained among the Top 5 most likely risks ahead. When measured by their interconnectedness, the two most interconnected risks were "profound social instability" and "structural unemployment or underemployment" [6].

Europe has given us a taste of these risks already with the Brexit. Suddenly, the issue of Scottish independence, which many thought had been settled by their referendum in 2014, is again up for discussion. Across the European Continent, yearnings for independence are rearing their heads like a game of whack-a-mole. And other nationalist movements—extending to Asia, the Middle East and North Africa—are being reinvigorated.

The more things change, the more people seek comfort and insulation among old, familiar tribes and traditions. Leaders need to be mindful of these tendencies and manage them in several important ways:

Be relevant. "How can we be relevant for our customers, for our audiences?" This is the key question that Steve Capus, the executive editor of CBS News and one-time Executive-in-Residence at IESE, insists on asking over and over again. "If we have any hopes of growing our businesses, we have to stay relevant," he told our Media AMP group in New York.

As audiences become more splintered and local in their interests and concerns, media managers have to work much harder at "making sure we are relevant in people's lives, in the editorial decisions we make, with the decisions about where we send our people to cover the news, the decisions about what kind of coverage we're going to do, and yes, the way people consume it."

"If you don't have people who are dedicated to delivering smart, quality content that is relevant to people's lives, then you have to ask yourself: why have you cut those areas? You may not have the same size newsroom as before, but as you constantly rethink how you staff every operation of your business, you have to make sure you are investing in the right areas," Capus urged. "The quest for relevance is critical."

To deliver on local relevance, Sir Martin Sorrell, CEO of WPP, told an IESE gathering in London how he organizes his British multinational group of advertising and public relations companies: "How can I, sitting in London, know what goes on in 111 countries? Our answer is to have global account directors and, at a local level, country managers who have no authority but they have the responsibility to find the best people, the best acquisitions and the best local companies that we should be working with. So, a more agile, technologically adept global center, and being heavily focused locally. Regional management is being taken out. This is a big change" [7].

Rethink what qualifies as "emerging." The slowdown in emerging economies after a decade of continuous growth is causing consternation. The end of super-fast growth, particularly in China and Latin America, has created headwinds for the global economy. While the market prospects for Africa don't appear so bleak, multinational media and entertainment companies doing business across borders are certainly susceptible to volatility in exchange rates and capital flows and greater exposure if they hold a lot of unhedged dollar-denominated debt.

At such times, it's worth remembering "the moral of the story," as IESE Economics Professor Pedro Videla puts it. "To set the foundations of solid growth, one should always try to compensate for a region's structural weaknesses. That means focusing on institutional development, education, equality of opportunity and the business climate" [8].

For too long, "emerging markets" were shorthand for "the BRICS," and companies simply poured investment there because those countries presented the hottest bets. But investors forgot that the adjective "emerging" was there for a reason: it meant that some of the basic institutional frameworks and mechanisms required for a market to function properly were either absent or still evolving.

Harvard Business School's Tarun Khanna and Krishna Palepu described it this way in *IESE Insight* magazine: "Suppose you take down the fence around a large, open field. What have you created? A golf course? Not exactly. For it to be one, you would need flags and holes, closely trimmed greens, meticulously planned fairways and a clubhouse that creates and enforces a world-class golfing culture. By the same token, pure deregulation—simply lowering the barriers to entry and creating an open market space for business—doesn't, in and of itself, create a developed market. What you have, certainly, is a large, open field. But it takes more than that to have a healthy functioning market" [9].

This is not to say that market opportunities no longer exist in what have been traditionally referred to as "emerging markets" now that those economies have faltered: they certainly do. However, the slowdown has hopefully taught managers to be more sophisticated and nuanced in their notion of what constitutes an "emerging market." So instead of asking, "What's my BRIC strategy?" companies should be asking themselves, "In which ways is this particular market emerging?" As Khanna and Palepu explain, by understanding which institutional structures are missing—whether in terms of labor skills or third-party service providers or regulatory standards—companies can potentially position themselves to offer the solution for filling that void. By learning to view market opportunities by their gaps, even the USA and Europe might become regarded as "emerging markets." (See Chap. 2 on Strategy.)

The legendary Hollywood studio executive Peter Bart made this point to us in Los Angeles: "The fascinating anomaly is that the studios have totally focused on the overseas youth demo. Russia, Brazil, China: those are the audiences that Hollywood really wants to capture. Meanwhile, we older people in the United States constitute 35-40 percent of the market, and nobody gives a damn about us. The interesting thing is that the older sector is the only loyal sector of the audience out there. Yet pictures open overseas first." In other words, might the overlooked older audience qualify as an "emerging market"?

It's time to think beyond the BRICS: what might your real "emerging market" be? (See Chap. 10 on Corporate and Entrepreneurial Finance.)

Seek multilateral cooperation. In an interview with IESE Professor Pedro Videla, Jaime Caruana, the general manager of the Bank for International Settlements (BIS)—what is essentially the bank of central banks—warned executives of the serious dangers of "inward-looking tendencies" and "zero-sum games."

"After a crisis, there is always a tendency to become more inward-looking," Caruana said. "But this can only be negative for the economy as a whole. In this globalized world we live in, where everything is interlinked, cooperation becomes vital. It would be devastating for the global economy if countries failed to work together.

"Ultimately, in a global economy, the decisions you make will come back to you, so it's in everyone's best interest to think about the repercussions of what you do. It is simply not enough anymore to keep your own house in order; you have to help keep the neighborhood in order, too. If your neighborhood is not totally in order, you cannot claim to be in order yourself, because you will always be affected by the neighborhood.

"The first step is to better internalize the effects that your decisions will have on the rest of the world. We need to internalize the potential spillovers and spillbacks that may come from our own actions. We have to accept that the world is a mass of complex and difficult-to-understand systems. There will always be shocks with subsequent dynamics that we cannot fully predict. We need to be prepared, ex ante, and build room to maneuver. It's essential to take a long-term view and have a global perspective" [10].

(See Chap. 3 on Accounting for help in considering the wider ramifications of the financial decisions you make, to see how all the parts fit together to tell the whole financial story of your company.)

Demographics and Employment

In 2016 China officially scrapped its one-child policy, allowing couples to have two children. According to the Xinhua news agency, "The change of policy is intended to balance population development and address the challenge of an ageing population" [11]. For the Communist Party to end more than 35 years of state-imposed population control signals that demographic imbalances must be reaching crisis proportions.

Indeed they have, not just in China but in many Western industrialized nations. Lower fertility rates combined with longer life expectancy are creating precarious societies stacked with fewer young people and higher proportions of older people. This has major implications for the workplace—especially in the media and entertainment sector, where, as Martin Sorrell noted, "Talent is everything."

"If we think there is a talent war to date, stand by," he said. "If you look at all the demographics—even for the 'young' countries like Pakistan and Mexico—in the next five, 10, 15 years, you see a decline in the birthrate and a prolonging of life expectancy, and the supply of talent is going to be constricted even further. This is going to be a big problem for all companies. The supply of talented people is going to be under pressure, and the demand will intensify" [7].

There simply aren't enough young trained leaders coming through to replace the sheer number of Baby Boomers retiring. And those that do exist "are more attracted to smaller, more networked, more entrepreneurial, less bureaucratic companies," said Sorrell.

Most people running traditional media companies today are in their mid-to-late 50s, whose career horizons resemble the political lifespan of a president or prime minister of a country: five to six years for CEOs; three to four years for CFOs; two to three years for CMOs. But when you reach the C-suite of a media or entertainment business, you have to speed things up, not ride it out to retirement, said Sorrell. Companies urgently need to invest in young high-potentials before they find themselves struggling with succession planning. The more young managers in place who already think in digital terms, the faster traditional media companies will be able to make the switch to "lower cost digital business models evaluated on different criteria," said Sorrell.

"Even digital businesses have to go faster," he added. "Even Eric Schmidt (Google Alphabet Chairman) when you ask him, 'What is the thing you worry about?' he's worried about the two young people in a startup in Bangalore or Beijing who may disintermediate his business. So you have to have continuous paranoia."

If you do succeed in attracting young creative talent, you have to be prepared to adjust your management and organizational environment to account for their different needs and expectations. (See Chap. 9 on Managing Creative People.) Speaking to our Media AMP group in Los Angeles, the marketing strategist Jamie Gutfreund highlighted how those workers weaned on the Internet and social media technologies may behave differently from what older generations of managers are used to.

On the one hand, she said, they can be resourceful problem-solvers: "Rather than hide from problems, they want to understand and confront them. If you tap their inquisitive natures and give them a voice to actively contribute their own ideas and opinions, they can customize solutions or take existing ones and repurpose them in new and creative directions." In addition, given their affinity for online group sharing, they are generally quite good at building social capital.

On the other hand, they have also grown up during the Great Recession. They have witnessed firsthand its devastating effects on family members and friends, or they have experienced unemployment themselves; they may even still be living at home with their parents for pragmatic reasons. This early loss of innocence may make them cautious, wary and security-minded.

And as with increasing numbers of us who have come to rely on technology, new hires may seem a bit more disorganized and impatient, due to constant information overload and instant gratification. Already psychologists have given names to new anxiety disorders—FOMO (fear of missing out), FOMA (fear of missing anything) and Nomophobia (no-mobile-phone phobia)—which may paralyze people when it comes to making decisions as they will always be thinking of what the next search result might turn up or how tomorrow's analytics might change everything. (See Chaps. 5 and 6 on Decisive Leadership and Decision Analysis.)

The expectation that every new hire comes as tech savvy has a further impact. Not only is the talent pool shrinking, but those most in demand will be expected to bring not just content knowledge but a wide array of technical competencies as a given. This has given rise to a new specialism known as Data Journalism, whereby reporters use the competencies of computer programmers to tell stories using data and infographics. In some cases, it may even involve automating certain parts of the job, getting computers to do things that humans can't do or that it would take humans an awful lot longer to do. (See Chap. 7 on Operations Management.) The Associated Press is one of a growing number of media outlets using the services of Automated Insights to generate quarterly earnings reports for its business wire without any humans involved. As an AP business editor told The Verge, the goal is not to replace reporters with computers but to free up writers "to write smarter pieces and more interesting stories" and "not have to focus on the initial numbers," which a computer can do faster and more accurately [12].

Martin Sorrell was unsure of the true impact of all this artificial intelligence and automation. "Does 'Internet everywhere' actually add to employment or destroy employment? We're going to see employment increasingly a major issue. I see what's happening and I'm not convinced that the employment that is removed by these very sophisticated processes will be replaced by what comes as a result of Internet penetration or changes in those techniques. That is a key issue."

Digital Debates

The year 2015 was when audiences crossed over to "mobile first," when for first time more content was consumed on a mobile or tablet device than on traditional media. That affects everyone and ought to signal big strategic shifts, as it did for Martin Breidsprecher, COO of the Hispanic broadcaster Azteca America, who told us: "What I see, first of all, is people are not watching live television as they used to, except for sports. People are either TiVo-ing or DVR-ing their shows, and you come home and watch whenever you want. My kids, for instance, watch TV on their tablets: they go to the specific website or to Netflix, they click the program they want to see, they see it when they want to see it, how they want to see it.

"So, even if broadcast television today allows you to record programs, you don't need the broadcast to deliver the programs to your home anymore. That is changing the whole way we receive content. I'm not saying that the TV per se—the set, the big screen—is going to disappear. You are still going to have it, because you still want to watch your sports or other programs together. But I think the way that you deliver the content is changing dramatically.

"You are seeing it a lot already. Netflix is doing it, Apple TV, Samsung, Google—everybody is trying to tap into it, because they see it's very important to get that content. Content is still going to be king, but how you deliver that content to the end user is going to be very different." Or as Martin Sorrell put it, content is going to be "kinger."

Breidsprecher continues: "Cable and direct broadcast satellite (DBS) penetration in the United States is already around 80 percent. Emerging markets are fast adopting these technologies and catching up. Soon, you are going to be able to see your content on any tablet, any phone, any type of device. For that reason, I believe that broadcast TV is eventually going to disappear."

His prediction is not far-fetched. As the tech guru Greg Harper told us in New York, "We are in a pivotal moment for television. I'm a former television producer. I've lived it. I've been through it. But we're going to see more changes in television in the next five years than we have seen since its creation." (See Chap. 8 on the Digital Economy.)

The rise of "over the top" players—those new media services, like Netflix or Skype, that ride over top of people's existing broadband connections—has become a hotly contested issue. Telecom companies and cable providers complain that those others are free-riding, and they have been trying to force the issue through the courts. They have proposed a two-speed Internet, suggesting that those who consume more bandwidth and who benefit from their investment in infrastructure should be required to pay more. Every country is adopting different stances on this issue. In an important 2015 ruling, the USA came down decisively in favor of "net neutrality," effectively classifying broadband as a public good akin to a utility to which everyone deserves equal access. The European Union, on the other hand, has left the possibility open for local players to get preferential positioning if they pay more. Other countries have yet to weigh in [13].

This shifting regulatory landscape makes it all the more important that media and entertainment managers engage in the public policy debates that will affect them both now and in the future. For example, every country has communications regulators. In the USA, broadcast is regulated by the Federal Communications Commission (FCC). One issue up for grabs in recent years was whether TV programming rebroadcast on the Internet had to meet the same legal requirement of being closed captioned for the hearing impaired. Should the rules of television apply to video programming on the Internet? If so, how? Under what circumstances? By when? As Breidsprecher told us, "There is always some underserved population, and the FCC will want to make sure that you are really providing local programming, programming in people's own language, and closed captioning. The FCC will make sure that everybody is complying." It's already happening. The FCC has introduced a whole series of captioning rules for Internet video programming, with various deadlines for compliance. Most have come into effect within the past year or two, covering full-length programming as well as clips, pre-recorded as well as live or near-live content (shown online within 24 hours of being shown on TV). By 2017, even multiple straight-lift video clips (montages) as well as live news and sporting events will have to be closed captioned on the Internet if shown on TV in the USA first [14]. "This means that when you formulate your business strategy, you have to consider what the FCC and all the other different regulatory bodies might do and how they interact, and the impact of that on your strategy and on how you will deliver your content," says Breidsprecher.

"Another debate is whether cable industries should be able to charge a fixed fee for all the channels. In the United States, you pay $70, $80, $100 for hundreds of channels of which you may only watch 10 at most. Should I really have to pay $100 for five channels? Or can I have the ability to pick and choose? So, I'm going to have CNN, ESPN, ABC and Azteca America, and for that, I want to pay $20. Can I do that? This is the debate that government regulators are having. How are we going to do this? How are we going to implement this? If you're a cable operator, this is going to have a huge impact on your industry. You have to anticipate these debates." (See Chap. 11 on Scenario Planning.)

Reputation: What Do You Stand For?

Remember the Ice Bucket Challenge? For several weeks in 2014, every man, woman and child seemed to be uploading videos of themselves dumping a bucket of ice water over their heads to raise money to cure ALS, aka Lou Gehrig's disease (yes, IESE participated) [15]. Looking back on it now, we ask: what was that all about?

The media and entertainment world is famous for making memes. But is that all the Ice Bucket Challenge was: a passing fad that burned bright and faded fast? Or did it signal something else: a trend worthy of deeper reflection and managerial attention?

The ALS Association says it raised $115 million from the 2014 Ice Bucket Challenge in eight weeks—five times what the charity typically received in an entire year [16]. One can argue whether any of this one-off activism provides a sound basis for sustainable philanthropic giving. But what's really worth analyzing is the peer-to-peer aspect to the activism, which is what should interest media managers. Particularly among the next generation of media consumers, they look for things that start with their peer group, have a social or experiential element, are instantly shareable and, best of all, include some pro-social end to help make the world a better place or one's life easier.

As the executive-in-residence at Georgia Tech's Institute for Leadership and Entrepreneurship John Bare told CNN, "The critical innovation of the Ice Bucket Challenge is not the funny visual." Rather, it's the powerful demonstration of "peer-to-peer connections (that) honor informal influence over traditional authority … moving from relying on an expert critic to relying on a peer" [17]. We see this same dynamic being replicated in untold business models, from Uber to Airbnb to Zopa. (See Chaps. 4, 7 and 8 on Marketing, Operations Management and the Digital Economy.)

Guy Kawasaki was the Chief Evangelist at Apple before he became a venture capital investor in numerous new media startups. Speaking at IESE, he told us that, to his mind, this social dynamic "is the best thing that ever happened. It's fast, it's free and it's ubiquitous. Some day we won't even distinguish between social media and marketing. We'll just say 'marketing' and it includes mostly social media and this little thing called 'advertising' in there." Although critics of new media still demand proof of the ROI of social media advertising versus traditional print advertising, Kawasaki thought that mentality was woefully misguided because it failed to fully appreciate the way that the relationship between the media and the public was being radically redrawn. To demand such a thing was to act "as if traditional advertising is somehow building relationships with people. I don't see that at all," he said. "In print advertising, do you think people take their magazine and hug it because there's an ad for Cadbury chocolate?" he remarked sarcastically. "At least with social media, I see the potential for that (kind of powerful emotional connection and relationship-building) to happen" [18].

Even wearables represent more than the latest fashion statement. "Intelligent devices will provide the (Silicon) Valley with a new-found seriousness," stated *The Economist*. "Social-media companies essentially dealt with virtual candy-floss: nice to have but, for the most part, hardly essential. The new generation of entrepreneurs will deal in devices that can save lives. Truly, all that is airy will become solid" [19].

In short, the new media landscape pushes us to ponder once again the existential question of why we do what we do. And whether it is leveraging the peer-to-peer dynamics that make our media stickier, tapping into the human experience that makes our marketing effective, or being sensitive to the competitive dynamics that can arise in creative teams, in the end it is all about making a deep, positive, lasting impact on people and society through management that prioritizes more than just hitting the bottom line. As the Ice Bucket Challenge demonstrated, it is about using your power for good, maybe even to help save lives.

Steve Capus summed it up best: "I'm really interested in watching the companies that can grow by positioning in a smart way. Everything they do—their editorial sensibility, the people they hire, the way they market themselves, how they reinforce those messages—is about *enhancement*. Those are the companies that I think are going to stand out—because they *stand for something*."

So the big question to keep in the back of your mind as you read through this book is: what do *you* stand for? And how will you take the management principles described in these pages and use them to make a deep, positive, lasting impact in the media and entertainment world?

References

1. *The Independent* (February 12, 2016), "The Independent Becomes the First National Newspaper to Embrace a Global, Digital-Only Future," Independent. co.uk/news/media/press, http://www.independent.co.uk/news/media/press/the-independent-becomes-the-first-national-newspaper-to-embrace-a-global-digital-only-future-a6869736.html
2. IESE News (February 11, 2016), "The World in 2016: *The Economist*'s Daniel Franklin Shares 12 News Headlines for the Next 12 Months," IESE Business School Website, http://www.iese.edu/en/about-iese/news-media/news/2016/february/the-world-in-2016/
3. X. Vives (July 2015), "Inequality," *International Economic Overview*, Year 28, No. 10.
4. K. Doctor (July 28, 2015), "Newsonomics: The Halving of America's Daily Newsrooms," NiemanLab, http://www.niemanlab.org/2015/07/newsonomics-the-halving-of-americas-daily-newsrooms/
5. W.B. Yeats (1919), "The Second Coming."
6. World Economic Forum (2016), *The Global Risks Report 2016, 11th Edition*, http://reports.weforum.org/global-risks-2016/
7. M. Sorrell (2015), "Martin Sorrell, CEO WPP: Trends to Shape the Future," IESE Insight Business Knowledge Portal, http://www.ieseinsight.com/fichaMaterial.aspx?pk=123675&idi=2&origen=1&ar=20&
8. P. Videla (May 2015), "Latin America: The Manna Has Run Out," *International Economic Overview*, Year 28, No. 8.
9. T. Khanna and K. Palepu (2013), "Emerging Markets: Look Before You Leap," *IESE Insight* magazine, Second Quarter, Issue 17, p. 46.

10. P. Videla (2015), "Jaime Caruana: 'It Would Be Devastating for the Global Economy if Countries Failed to Work Together'," *IESE Insight* magazine, Fourth Quarter, Issue 27.

11. Xinhua (October 29, 2015), "China to Allow Two Children for All Couples," Xinhuanet, http://news.xinhuanet.com/english/2015-10/29/c_134763645.htm

12. R. Miller (January 29, 2015), "AP's 'Robot Journalists' Are Writing Their Own Stories Now," *The Verge*, http://www.theverge.com/2015/1/29/7939067/ap-journalism-automation-robots-financial-reporting

13. IESE News (March 19, 2015), "Net Neutrality Agreed, But What's Next for Media Sector?" IESE Business School Website, http://www.iese.edu/en/about-iese/news-media/news/2015/march/net-neutrality-agreed-but-whats-next-for-media-sector/. Also, IESE Insight (March 20, 2015), "The New Challenges of the Media Industry," IESE Insight Business Knowledge Portal, http://ieseinsight.com/fichaMaterial.aspx?pk=121881&idi=2&origen=1&ar=5&

14. Federal Communications Commission (June 9, 2016), "Closed Captioning of Internet Video Programming," FCC Website, https://www.fcc.gov/consumers/guides/captioning-internet-video-programming

15. IESE Business School (2014), "IESE Business School: ALS Ice Bucket Challenge," https://www.youtube.com/watch?v=6_ZIMXw0fCE

16. The ALS Association (2014), "Impact of ALS Ice Bucket Challenge," ALS Association Website, http://www.alsa.org/fight-als/edau/ibc-progress-infographic.html

17. J. Bare (August 26, 2014), "Ice Bucket Challenge Is Not a Gimmick," CNN, http://edition.cnn.com/2014/08/23/opinion/bare-ice-bucket-challenge/index.html?hpt=hp_mid

18. IESE Insight (2015), "The Medium Is the Message," *IESE Insight* magazine, Second Quarter, Issue 25, and also the video "Starting a Business: The Entrepreneur Without a Business Plan," IESE Insight Business Knowledge Portal, http://www.ieseinsight.com/fichaMaterial.aspx?pk=118574&idi=2&origen=1&ar=19&&idioma=2

19. A. Wooldridge (2014), "United States: Going Physical," *The Economist: The World in 2015* print edition.

2

Strategy: The Soul of Your Business

Mike Rosenberg, Adrian Caldart, with Philip H. Seager

Hearst Corporation has come a long way from its start as a single newspaper, *The San Francisco Examiner*, launched by William Randolph Hearst in 1887. Indeed, by the time Frank A. Bennack, Jr., became CEO of Hearst in 1979, the company had added book and magazine publishing to its multitude of newspaper holdings and was pursuing radio and television acquisitions. When Bennack stepped down in 2013, 90 percent of the businesses Hearst was in did not even exist or were not part of the company in 1979, as he explained to us during a Media AMP Leadership Forum in New York City.

Today Hearst is one of the world's largest diversified media companies, with some 200 businesses in more than 150 countries, ranging from cable networks (A&E, History, Lifetime, ESPN); significant holdings in automotive, electronic and medical/pharmaceutical information businesses; a 50 percent stake in the global ratings agency Fitch Group; Internet and marketing

M. Rosenberg (✉)
Strategic Management Department, IESE Business School, Barcelona, Spain
e-mail: MRosenberg@iese.edu

A. Caldart
Strategic Management Department, IESE Business School, Barcelona, Spain
e-mail: ACaldart@iese.edu

P.H. Seager
IESE Business School, Barcelona, Spain
e-mail: PSeager@iese.edu

© The Author(s) 2017
M. Rosenberg, P.H. Seager (eds.), *Managing Media Businesses*,
DOI 10.1007/978-3-319-52021-6_2

services; television production; newspaper features distribution; real estate; not to mention its flagship magazines ("There's a Mongolian edition of *Cosmopolitan*," Bennack has quipped, "Need I say more?").

"One of the things you have to realize and recognize," he said, "apart from the fact that the business has changed and is continuing to change dramatically, is that this change is accelerating. Neither radio nor television has effected change as rapidly as what we have seen in the last decade. When somebody says to you, 'That's going to take years,' not today, because the pace of change is so rapid. So what does this mean from a strategic point of view? What does this mean for what you have to do as someone employed to change the strategy of your company?"

This chapter deals with strategy. We will consider the frameworks most commonly used today. By the end, managers should be in a position to discuss their own organization's strategy and then make decisions regarding the strategic directions of their companies or business units, taking into account how the frameworks play out in the realm of media and entertainment.

What Is Strategy?

"Strategy" refers to the set of activities that managers engage in to boost the performance of their enterprises relative to their rivals. To paraphrase Sun Tzu, the ancient Chinese military leader whose *Art of War* is considered the earliest treatise on the subject, "Strategy is important to a company. It is a matter of life and death. It is the way to survival or to destruction. So study it."

The goal of business strategy is to achieve two things: (1) superior performance, measured not just in terms of net profitability but profitable growth sustained over years (or in Hearst's case, over centuries); and (2) competitive advantage, which means doing the previous things better than rival companies vying for the same customers.

Harvard Business School professor Michael E. Porter, a leading scholar on competitive strategy, has noted that competitive advantage derives partly from operational effectiveness in the way that you choose to create, produce, sell and deliver your product or service. However, because the best practices of operational effectiveness are susceptible to being copied by others, the more important factor for competitive advantage is your strategic positioning—that is, defining what is different about your product or service that distinguishes it from rivals, in order to deliver what Porter refers to as "a unique mix of value" that is hard, if not impossible, for others to replicate [1].

Frank Bennack described this "unique value" in terms of "the soul of the company." In other words, Hearst has not enjoyed strategic leadership over 125-plus years simply by maintaining operational effectiveness in the way it creates, produces, sells and delivers printed publications.

Rather, "every magazine has a core and a soul and a feeling," he explained. "*O, The Oprah Magazine* is the easiest one to talk about. You can't just put Oprah Winfrey's name and picture on a magazine and stick a few recipes in there. It's got to incorporate what she's about: positive, motivational, reaching for your dreams and making choices that will lead to a happier, more fulfilling life. The editors have to capture that. Clearly the biggest example of what I'm talking about is Helen Gurley Brown and what she accomplished with *Cosmopolitan*. She had a message: that's the soul."

Even though these magazines have had to change with the times as they move with their audiences online, they have to remain faithful to the soul of the brand as they reinterpret their strategies for how these products will be delivered digitally. Otherwise, they will lose their unique positioning and consequently their competitive advantage.

Before getting into the details of formulating business strategies at the industrial, global and corporate levels, it is necessary to grasp this fundamental distinction about competitive advantage. It is not about your core competence per se (though, granted, knowing what you do best is a vital first step in planning your strategy if you are to capitalize on your strengths and identify which opportunities and investments are worth pursuing). But far more important than *knowing* your core competence is being able to *leverage it better than anyone else*.

So Hearst has a core competence—to publish magazines, or to put it in the broader terms of its mission statement, "to inform, entertain and inspire" through its various media channels. But as Bennack stressed when talking about *O* and *Cosmopolitan*, Hearst has also found a way to execute on this core competence *better than anyone else*. This is its competitive advantage vis-à-vis other media companies.

Such an understanding must lie at the heart of whatever particular configuration of business activities you assemble to guide your pursuit of net profitability and profitable growth over time; in short, what will ultimately constitute your business model.

Pause for Thought

What is your core competence?
What is your competitive advantage?

In terms of how you create, produce, sell and deliver your product or service:
Are these activities different from how your competitors perform them?
If similar, how might these activities be configured in different ways?
In terms of your customers:
Are they different from those whom your competitors are trying to reach?
If similar, how might they be served in different ways?

Thinking Beyond Low Cost

Business strategy experts, like Porter, have put forward a multitude of theories on how best to position a firm to gain competitive advantage over rivals. Although every decade brings distinct challenges, and every industry, whether media or otherwise, develops novel means to deal with those challenges, experts agree that differentiation is one of the keys to competitive advantage. The other key is cost.

By cost, we don't just mean lower cost—though being able to achieve cost savings does contribute to competitive advantage. There are any number of ways that companies can lower their overall cost structures in how they create, produce, sell and deliver their products or services, such as introducing self-service or no-frills features, leveraging economies of scale, outsourcing certain business processes or going for standardized components.

Media companies will be well aware of the savings afforded by technology, particularly digitization, which is revolutionizing business strategies at the breakneck speed that Bennack talked about earlier. Many people may not realize it, he said, but producing editorial content for a newspaper or magazine really only costs between 12 and 20 percent of revenue. The major costs are related to manufacturing, delivery, sales and so forth. So if most newspapers and magazines can be consumed on electronic devices, as Bennack believed would happen eventually, then being able to deliver a product without the cost of ink on paper and all those other traditional publication costs, combined with large enough scale, can amount to great savings for a company like Hearst.

However, cost must be understood as more than being the lowest cost provider. First, basing your strategy solely on cost can lead to a race to the bottom, with rivals seeking to outdo each other on lower and lower costs and cutthroat pricing. This is unsustainable, leading to diminishing returns that will hamper a company's ability to invest in the future.

Moreover, the cost savings as just described by Bennack are not unique to Hearst but hold true for any newspaper and magazine publisher. This shows that cost, in and of itself, does not necessarily lead to competitive advantage. Greater operational efficiency, yes; but, we reiterate, this is not the same as competitive advantage.

Consider another key concept concerning cost: willingness to pay. As represented by Fig. 2.1, companies have to set prices for their products or services that are above cost but below the limits of what consumers are willing to pay so that both perceive some value in return: profit for the firm and utility for the consumer. Obviously, the more that companies can cut their own costs, the more profit they can extract by keeping prices the same. In a competitive marketplace, a firm's ability to set prices will be conditioned by the prices of its rivals, as will its ability to reduce costs if competing for shared suppliers, distribution networks and so on.

For media and entertainment businesses, the Digital Revolution is adding pressure to this basic profitability paradigm.

For one thing, wholly digital market entrants have much lower or none of the same legacy costs of a traditional media enterprise, meaning they can set the same or lower prices and reap greater profits.

On the other hand, digital players are encountering challenges at the top end of the equation, as a colleague of ours in the Strategic Management Department at IESE, Govert Vroom, highlights in his case study on the streaming music service Spotify [2].

While digitization affords the possibility of zero transaction costs, Spotify's 50 million users appear unwilling to pay for the service. This is the dilemma facing not just Spotify but many other vendors of digital content operating "freemium" business models: how to convert the "free riders" into paying customers. Until these businesses resolve this issue, they are stuck paying out more money and getting less revenue per user. And while they figure it out, more competitors are piling in to the same space.

All this is why, as Porter and other business strategy experts insist, lowering costs has to go hand in hand with the differentiation we talked about earlier. There has to be a strategic "fit" between all of the activities you engage in, namely:

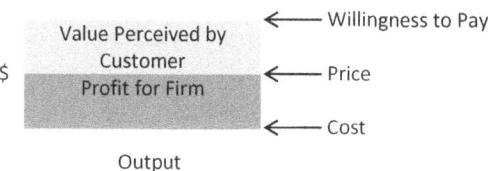

Fig. 2.1 Willingness to Pay

- What you sell: preferably differentiated product or service offerings.
- To whom you sell it: preferably differentiated customer segments.
- How and where you sell it: resources configured in ways that reinforce the above.

More than lowering costs, differentiation addresses the top half of the equation, helping consumers perceive more utility and thus value of a company's products or services. This, in turn, elevates consumers' willingness to pay, permitting more pricing options and, consequently, raising profitability and fueling business growth for the future.

Take note: strategic positioning or "fit" is as much about what you choose *not* to do as it is about what you determine to do. According to Porter, central to the strategy-making process is the constant need to make trade-offs. Without trade-offs, he has argued, there will never be any sustainable competitive advantage [1].

A good question to ask yourself as you consider your own strategic positioning is: what trade-offs have you made? Which products, activities or customers have you deliberately chosen *not* to pursue so that you can concentrate on your differentials?

Think about it: with differentiation, competitive advantage can be achieved without always having to go head to head with another firm, because you have chosen not to compete in the same space. This means you aren't playing zero-sum games: you can find advantages that don't depend on putting someone else at a disadvantage. This also reduces competitive price wars: your cost advantages won't be at the expense of another. As such, high profitability can be earned without vicious rivalry or mutually assured destruction.

Analyzing Your Industry: May the Force Be with You

Until now we have been discussing the principles that should underlie strategic thinking and guide managers as they consider how they organize their operations and position themselves in the marketplace at the functional or business level. Yet firms don't operate in a vacuum but in competitive industry environments.

To assess their environment, many firms start with a SWOT analysis, weighing their internal Strengths and Weaknesses against external Opportunities and Threats. There are two problems with SWOT. One is that people can use the framework in a superficial way, stating the obvious and not really digging deeply enough into the issues in order to develop sound strategic thinking.

This is SWOT as "Strategy With Out Thinking." The second, more serious problem is that it can ignore the duality that exists in real life. In other words, every strength can become a weakness, every opportunity a threat, and vice versa. Take classified advertising: what was once a newspaper's core strength became its biggest weakness as soon as Internet advertising entered the scene. As we will see in Chap. 8 on the Digital Economy, the digitization of content and distribution channels is both a threat and an opportunity, and the important thing is how a company chooses to deal with it. So rather than compartmentalize the issues by arbitrarily labeling them as either Strengths or Weaknesses, Opportunities or Threats, it may be more useful to look at all the different issues together and then discuss in what way each affects the business in both positive and negative directions.

The analysis of the *microenvironment* of your own particular business operations has to be extended to include the *macroenvironment* of all the other companies competing to fulfill the same customer needs (your industry) as well as the ecosystem of related industries on which your firm depends (your sector).

Michael Porter's "Five Forces" framework has become the widely accepted model for carrying out this level of analysis. As depicted in Fig. 2.2, Porter postulated there are other competitive forces that will have a strong bearing

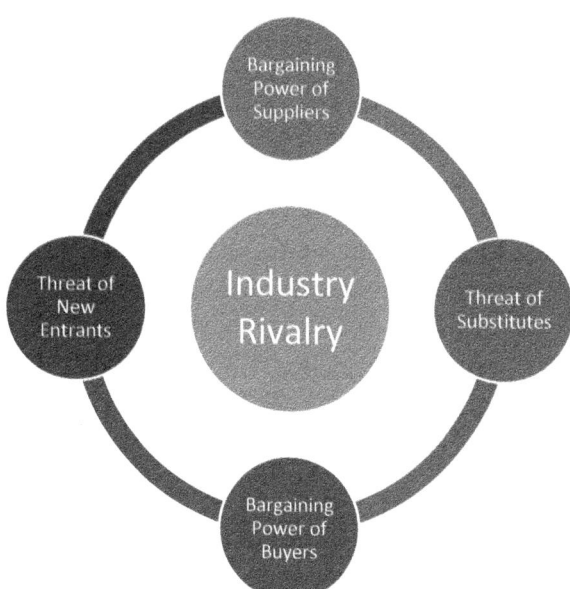

Fig. 2.2 Michael Porter's "Five Forces" Framework (Porter [3])

on a firm's business strategy apart from the rivalry that exists among current competitors (the middle circle) [4]. Here we highlight the other forces at play that will condition the intensity of industry competition and profitability, and we suggest some of the strategic actions that a firm may take to deal with these forces.

Threat of New Entrants

The more companies that can enter your same arena, the harder it is to protect your market share. Conversely, the fewer companies, the more scope to raise prices and generate higher profits. The key, then, if you are an established player, is to try to build barriers to entry, whereas new entrants will want to find ways around the barriers.

Typical barriers are economies of scale, brand loyalty and customer-switching costs. Hearst's Frank Bennack spoke to us about the power that a hugely successful brand has on strengthening one's competitive position: "One of the strange things about the world we live in is that, despite the global economy being relatively weak, luxury is where business is still being conducted, especially in places like China. All of the prestige brands are trying to establish market share there. Obviously *Elle* is a great vehicle for that, because the magazine carries a huge amount of branded advertising. *Elle* is very much a luxury title and a powerful brand for us. Clearly any woman would want to buy fashion goods from *Elle*. In fact, *Elle* is so successful in China that we have had to go to two editions a month, because the monthly magazine was getting so big it needed a wheelbarrow and a small boy to carry it away."

Anyone who uses Microsoft's Windows versus Apple will understand switching costs as a barrier to entry. Making it hard for customers to switch to a competitor, because they are effectively "locked in" to your ecosystem of products, is an effective strategy to fend off the threat of new entrants or industry competitors stealing your market share.

Allied to this idea of lock-in are so-called network effects: the bigger you get, the more people go with you; the more people go with you, the bigger you become, and the greater the value everyone derives, in a self-reinforcing positive feedback loop, until the winner takes all. Think of Facebook and Google as prime examples of this force in action.

Bargaining Power of Buyers

This force refers to powerful companies in an industry that can use their stronger position to bargain down prices—when they purchase in bulk, for example—or raise the costs to others that are in a weaker bargaining position, squeezing the others' profits. To deal with this force, weaker companies may have to lower their own product or service quality in order to offset the higher costs they face—yet this could also become a source of opportunity and strength, if aiming at discount or low-cost customers.

Bargaining Power of Suppliers
With this force, it is powerful suppliers who may pose threats, especially if they control vital inputs—whether materials or labor—that an industry needs. Intel is an example of a supplier that enjoys competitive advantage in the PC industry.

Another example is the open-source movement. For all the advantages that external innovators afford to media and entertainment companies to provide new value through creative inputs at little or no cost, managers need to be mindful of the implications of this force on their industry position. In some cases, such as software development, innovation communities actually own the product and its creative process, which could be a force that works against you.

During a Continuous Education session at IESE Business School in Barcelona, Harvard Business School's Michael Tushman highlighted the potential threat of open innovation or crowdsourced suppliers—a growing trend especially for media and entertainment companies, given the defining role that digitization and the sharing economy are playing in this industry and sector. "How do you externalize innovation necessary for your survival without undermining your own core competency?" he asked. "Even if it makes economic sense to externalize innovation, how can you manage something outside of your firm that you don't own or control, and keep it aligned with your firm-specific strategy? While you can't deny the reality of open innovation, you still need to exercise some control. But how much is too much? When should you look to open innovation and when is it better to consider strategic partners, multi-firm collaborations or intra-firm problem solving?" [5]

This requires a special skill—what he termed managerial or organizational ambidexterity—to make strategic choices regarding how and when to reduce the threats of powerful suppliers on your industry position.

Threat of Substitutes
Who can forget the classic scene from the 1983 film *Risky Business*, when, after a high-speed car chase, Tom Cruise pulls up to the curb, turns to his passengers and coolly pronounces, "Porsche, there is no substitute." This catchphrase succinctly captures the final force—the threat of competitors satisfying the same customer needs with substitute products or services. If "there is no

substitute," then companies can charge higher prices and earn more profit. If, on the other hand, your product can be replaced, such as what happened in the music industry when digital replaced CDs, then you may be in trouble, and your best defense may be to launch a good offense. Trend analysis is an important tool in this regard, because it enables you to anticipate the coming threat and build it into your strategy as a future business reality. In hindsight, music industry incumbents would have been better off doing this rather than resisting the inevitable march toward digital substitutes.

Complementers

Although Porter's original "Five Forces" framework does not treat "comple-menters" as a separate force, others have insisted there is a sixth force that is just as significant and needs to be considered on its own terms when analyz-ing your industry environment. "Complementers" are governments, regula-tors, public policymakers—basically any complementary actor that shapes or impacts demand in your particular industry [6] (Porter believes these external influencers would turn up as features of all five forces) [3]. At any rate, it is important to think systematically and explicitly about the power of "comple-menters" to affect the competitive landscape of your industry and, like with all the forces, assess the possible strengths, weaknesses, opportunities and threats they pose to your business.

Pause for Thought

Which forces pose the biggest threat to your business?
What steps should you be taking now to reconfigure your business to deal with these threats?

Bridging Two Views of Value Creation

Increasing the perceived utility, or value, of your products or services for the market is seen to arise in one of two ways: through processes and through resources.

In the process-based view, companies engage in a chain of activities that takes inputs and transforms them into some output that is highly valued by the market. Figure 2.3 illustrates a typical "value chain." At every stage of the chain, critical decisions are made regarding process simplification, the lowering of costs and differentiation, so that as the product or service passes through each step, it gains some additional value, with the end result being that the whole process adds more value than any one part.

In the resource-based view, value depends on firm-specific resources such as company infrastructure, information systems, management and human resources. Unlike purely process-based value creation, resources like management skills, capabilities and competencies are what distinguish one firm from another and are much harder to imitate or substitute, leading to competitive advantage that truly is unique.

Of course, value creation is not a consequence of either processes or resources but of both. Arnoldo C. Hax of Massachusetts Institute of Technology and Dean L. Wilde have proposed a third view—the Delta Model, so-named for its Greek reference to transformation and change—which encompasses aspects of both views, while also adding what they considered to be the missing link: the customer, who is exerting an ever greater influence on value creation in light of the pervasive role of the Internet and new technology on all business today (particularly media and entertainment businesses) [7] (Fig. 2.4).

The Delta Model consists of building a technology-enabled ecosystem based on three points: having the best product, offering a total customer solution (where products may not be the best individually but are the best collectively) and achieving a lock-in effect. Crucially, it shifts the strategic aim from using firm-centric processes or resources to come up with the best product or service as the means of value creation and instead considers the extent to which each point of the triangle bonds customers together as the formula for success.

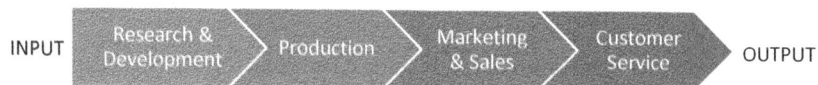

Fig. 2.3 A Typical "Value Chain"

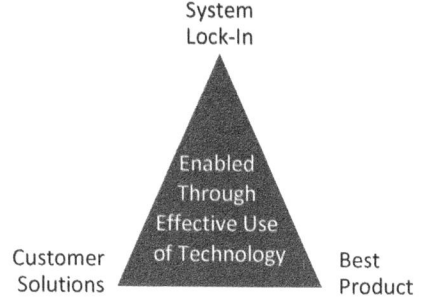

Fig. 2.4 The Delta Model (Hax and Wilde [7])

So while having the "Best Product" is important, only ever pursuing this strategy may lead to standardization and commoditization unless it forms part of "Customer Solutions" that bond customers and industry "complementers" together in a cooperative relationship. As the authors explained in their paper on the subject: "The relevant overall measure of performance becomes the total customer share, whose needs we are attempting to satisfy in as comprehensive a way as possible. It is not our supply chain that is relevant; it is the combined chain that includes us, the customer and our key suppliers. It is not our internal product development capabilities that exclusively carry our innovation initiatives; rather it is the joint development efforts, particularly with our customers, that are central to our success. What guides us is not exclusively our product economics, but it is the customer economics, since we are trying to help the customer in enhancing his or her financial performance" [7].

At the top is the ultimate objective, "System Lock-in," the hardest to achieve but certainly the best means of achieving closer linkages and generating the network effects and virtuous circles mentioned in the previous discussion of Porter's "Five Forces."

Instead of focusing on the myriad competitive forces "out there," the Delta Model provides an alternative framework for focusing executives' minds, so they can decide at which point of the triangle they need to target their strategic actions in order to achieve the greatest possible bonding with their customers.

Diving into Blue Ocean Strategy

Another pair of strategy theorists, W. Chan Kim and Renee Mauborgne, have proposed shifting the focus away from the idea of competition altogether and carving out new markets where no competition exists. Their argument is that no matter how many trade-offs or industry forces you try to consider in your business strategy, you're still operating within the confines of existing competitive structures—what they call "red oceans," in reference to a school of sharks turning the water bloody. A far better strategy, they say, is to seek "blue oceans," wide-open, uncontested spaces where there are no markets or industries established yet [8].

Cirque du Soleil serves as the classic illustration. The Canadian troupe didn't just try to be a better circus; it eliminated all the standard industry definitions of what constituted a circus and instead went for something more akin to a high-end theatrical experience, blending street acrobatics with operatic music and storylines. This boosted customers' willingness to pay while simultaneously lowering company costs by eschewing expensive stars and high-maintenance animals. Cirque du Soleil is the uncontested global leader of an entirely new genre of its own making [9].

During IESE's Media AMP, a general manager of an African Radio Group started to think how his peak drive-time slots of 6 to 10 a.m. and 4 to 7 p.m. represented "red oceans" because everyone was competing in that space for the same advertising dollars. He shifted his focus to what might be his "blue oceans." What could he be doing during the daytime dead zone, when people were at work, to change the rules of the game? How might he convert those peak times into "blue oceans," perhaps by putting a camera in the studio, and live streaming and syndicating that content to television, at no extra cost?

As "blue ocean" proponents say, it is important to first understand the traditional rules of the game, but then, like this manager, challenge those rules and change them by looking for "blue oceans" where you create the demand and render the competition irrelevant.

Pause for Thought

Are there elements to your business that people no longer value but you keep doing them for the sake of doing them because it's what your industry has always done?

Map out the key set of attributes on which you compete to compare where you have advantages/disadvantages.

Are there costs you can reduce or eliminate?

How can you maximize value or push up willingness to pay?

Which attributes can you increase or create new ones entirely?

Global Strategy: Distance Matters

The search for "blue oceans" may take you not just outside the competitive dynamics of your traditional business, industry or sector but abroad. Why might you choose to expand your operations beyond your home market to compete on a global playing field?

The primary reason is for ADDING value, according to IESE professor Pankaj Ghemawat, who has produced several leading theories on global business strategy. ADDING is an acronym for Adding volume, Decreasing costs (such as through outsourcing), Differentiating, Improving industry attractiveness, Normalizing risks (to spread risk across more markets to be less susceptible to local ups and downs) and Generating knowledge (to learn something from new markets that can be deployed elsewhere) [10].

For the past 50 years, globalization—the greater ease, faster movement and intensification of social and economic transactions across national borders—has opened up vast opportunities for corporations to rethink how they operate. Companies have usually regarded globalization as a lowering of the drawbridge to additional markets, either to expand their sales or to generate scale for existing product portfolios.

In his 2007 book, *Redefining Global Strategy*, Ghemawat identified three ways for companies to create value across borders, and he recommended that companies seek to beat their competitors on at least one A or combinations of the following A's [10]:

- **Adaptation:** adjusting to cross-country differences in order to be locally responsive. This is indispensable for participating in emerging markets, where differences loom large.
- **Aggregation:** overcoming cross-country differences to achieve scale/scope economies that extend across national borders.
- **Arbitrage:** exploiting differences, typically by buying something low in one country and selling it higher in another place where it's worth more.

During the Media AMP, the COO of Azteca America recognized the arbitrage strategy at work when the Hispanic broadcaster established a subsidiary in Los Angeles to serve the growing Spanish-speaking market north of the border with content generated in lower-cost Mexico.

Organizing different parts of your value chain across different geographies, using offshoring and outsourcing strategies, is certainly one way of achieving competitive advantage and profitability. But Ghemawat has argued that this strategy needs to be taken further than "buy low/sell high" and include arbitraging business model ideas between one region and another. Our colleagues in the Strategic Management Department at IESE, Fabrizio Ferraro and Bruno Cassiman, believe this tactic—of arbitraging business opportunities from one region and adapting them to the specificities of another—is one of the most important skills that corporate leaders need to develop as they think afresh about how they create, capture and sustain value in light of the globalization trends of the twenty-first century [11].

Besides arbitrage, media companies need to pay special attention to adaptation. Globalization may give the impression that "the world is flat" and if "it plays in Peoria" (Illinois) then it'll play equally well in Pretoria (South Africa). While this strategy largely seems to work for Hollywood blockbusters, such "flat world" thinking proved disastrous for Star TV.

In the early 1990s, the media mogul Rupert Murdoch thought he had it all figured out. He would leverage his Twentieth Century Fox film library and beam a steady supply of programming via satellite to media-starved homes throughout all of Asia, using an aggregation strategy that would stretch from India to China.

What seemed a good idea on paper turned out to be a heavy loss maker, mainly because Murdoch failed to grasp a central truth about global strategy: distance matters.

Although geography is one factor to account for why some countries interact more than others, Ghemawat cites research showing that, other things being equal, two countries trade 42 percent more if they share a common language, 47 percent more if they are part of a common trading bloc, 114 percent more if they share a common currency and 188 percent more if one of them had colonized the other. As such, he recommends managers use his CAGE distance framework—which assesses Cultural, Administrative and Economic criteria alongside Geographic factors—to judge the ease or difficulty of doing business across borders [12].

Consider an example of German exports. Ghemawat has devised an online tool that distorts maps to depict graphically the relative size and weight of business interactions between countries. (The website www.ghemawat.com contains the CAGE Comparator tool, enabling you to generate custom maps as well as see hundreds of others.) By mapping cross-border activity, Ghemawat finds instances when most German merchandise exports go to neighboring countries. This is partly due to the *cultural* dimension, as Germany shares a language with Austria and Switzerland. It is also down to *administrative* reasons: the EU trading bloc and shared euro currency favor Germany trading with other European member states. *Geographically*, Germany is in Europe. And *economically*, countries within Europe are more or less on the same level. Mapping German food exports reveals that German food doesn't travel very far. This can be explained by *cultural* differences in tastes, *administrative* differences associated with agricultural regulations and different government dietary requirements, and the problem of perishability associated with *geographic* distance. German cars, on the other hand, are much less distance-sensitive than food. That's because cars—as with many products in the luxury or prestige category—are relatively insensitive to cultural and language differences [13].

It pays to think creatively about which CAGE factors are relevant to your industry and how sensitive the types of international business you want to conduct are to each factor.

In Murdoch's case, he seemingly failed to adequately consider which audiences would be most receptive to predominately Anglo-American, English-language programming, with the result being that Star eventually scaled back its Chinese arm and focused on the Indian Subcontinent. A look at Star today reveals an adaptation strategy—a shift from offering the same content everywhere to delivering highly localized content via dozens of different channels and languages.

Pause for Thought

Does globalization of the media business apply to content?

When can globalized content work and when won't content travel?

Map your business using the CAGE factors:

Which dimensions count for more or less in creating, capturing and sustaining value?

How should your global strategy be adjusted to take account of distance factors?

Corporate Strategy: Time to Branch Out?

At the beginning of this chapter, Frank Bennack remarked that 90 percent of the businesses Hearst is in today were not part of the company when he became CEO in 1979 and that those businesses go well beyond Hearst's original core competence—print media—to include cable networks, television production, medical information and real estate. Why would a company venture outside its original industry, diversifying into related and sometimes unrelated business activities? This is the final piece that managers need to be familiar with: corporate strategy.

Take ESPN, the American sports channel, which is jointly owned by Hearst and the Disney-ABC Television Group, which is itself an M&A between The Walt Disney Company and the ABC American television network. For any of these companies, they have confronted two strategic choices in the lives of their businesses:

1. **Horizontal Integration.** This involves sticking to the industry and markets you know best, aligning all your resources and processes toward a single goal. For example, Hearst acquiring other competing newspapers across the USA enables it to merge assets, sharing articles and advertising across titles. As Bennack explained, this corporate strategy has enabled Hearst to "consolidate sizeable business interests, eliminate a lot of overheads and strengthen our company, putting us on the ground in a bigger way in markets as far as the eye can see."

2. **Vertical Integration.** This involves venturing into new industries and markets that are meant to support the core business model and add value. The logic is that, instead of relying on another business or competitor for resources or processes on which your performance, profitability and competitive advantage depend, you can acquire those other businesses, either backward to upstream suppliers or forward to downstream retailers. Disney is the supreme example, not just excelling on its core creative content but owning the studios and all the means that go into producing that content, as well as the stores and outlets where content-related merchandise can be sold.

In theory, Disney's acquisition of ABC, and together ESPN, could be seen as furthering this vertical integration, giving Disney yet another channel for supporting or adding value to its core. Yet strategy research finds that vertical integration on average underperforms. This is because there need to be compelling conditions to make such corporate strategies work.

Corporate Synergies
When two or more entities merge, there have to be synergies in three important areas: complementary resources and capabilities; a common market focus; and the combination of resource/capability synergies and market-focus synergies can be leveraged and shared across categories, opening up new markets. This is what creates competitive advantage.

Unique Features That Are Hard to Replicate
As stated at the beginning of this chapter, the key to competitive advantage is to uphold Porter's "unique mix of value" or Bennack's "soul of the company" that is hard, if not impossible, for others to replicate. If there is some specialized asset on which your business depends, there comes a stage when you will have to weigh whether it is better to contract that input from an external supplier or acquire that vital input for yourself.

Controllable
Vertical integration is often pursued so as not to be held hostage to independent suppliers, who may drive up your own costs if they have to make too many investments to deliver a highly specialized input, or worse, they could turn around and sell that same input to other trading partners, thereby eroding your competitive advantage. Vertical integration is a means of exercising a greater degree of control to ensure consistency and predictability of quality, scheduling, delivery and cost structure.

Value Can Be Appropriated

This condition is especially relevant when diversifying. There has to be some value that can be transferred between businesses because of some related value-chain functions, such as sharing one marketing and sales department between two different business units. It may also be that certain competencies developed in one business unit may be the missing key that unlocks another unit's competitive advantage.

Judging Disney's acquisition of ABC against the above criteria raises questions over whether Disney may be drifting from its strategy and diversifying too far away from its core. Does Disney meet the necessary conditions or is it moving into areas that many others can do?

Disney's vertical integration of Pixar appears more justifiable. Disney started by contracting 3-D animation to Pixar at a time when it wasn't clear whether there was much a future for 3-D movies. Outsourcing like this is a safer bet, because Disney did not have to make its own costly investments in 3-D capabilities when the market was still uncertain. However, as demand for Pixar movies took off, contracting put Disney in a position of dependency. At that point Disney had a compelling reason to want to own Pixar's capabilities, as those become central to Disney maintaining its own competitive advantage.

Having said all this, it is possible to maintain a diversified portfolio of unrelated businesses without all of the compelling conditions being met. The celebrated corporate investor Warren Buffett is a case in point. His company, Berkshire Hathaway, has holdings in everything from insurance, utilities, clothing, building products, flight services, retail, media and financial services, with seemingly little rhyme or reason linking them together.

However, maintaining a portfolio as diverse as this requires a special set of conditions and a leader as special as Warren Buffett. He sticks to what he knows, he's prepared to walk away and never overpay for a deal, and he's in it for the long haul, not the dictates of short-term business cycles. Most important, he does business with people whom he knows, so the whole thing is predicated on high levels of trust and personal relationships, where he always has the final say.

While we are tempted to say, "Don't try this at home unless you are in as privileged a position as Warren Buffett," unrelated diversification, though unusual, does seem to work in emerging markets, for many of the same reasons that it works for Buffett.

For one thing, the State tends to be a much bigger player in those markets, making personal and political ties count for more than what the business plan says on paper. The synergies you seek may have less to do with shared resources and capabilities and more to do with some opportunistic alignment that gives you access to businesses and markets that you would otherwise not be able to reach, either because they are heterogeneous or at the base of pyramid.

Also, given the general lack of capital, unstable political environments, economic volatility, changeable regulatory frameworks and underdeveloped infrastructure, the usual market logics often don't apply, so a company can afford to be undercapitalized and inefficient, for example, and not be punished by the market. Conglomerates in emerging markets essentially internalize and assume many of the institutional shortfalls, which is why unorthodox corporate strategies can work there—for a time. Ironically, as the overall country context starts to improve and these conglomerates face external competition, they start to perform less well, at which point they begin to de-diversify and move toward a more traditional or dominant strategic logic.

In recent research on Disney's corporate strategy in Latin America, we discovered some of the adaptation strategies that Walt Disney International experimented with across different regions, managing all business lines—movies, videos, products, trips—through a single channel out of Buenos Aires instead of through separate business units as happened elsewhere in the world. This required strong local leadership with full political support from CEO Robert Iger. In the end, this novel corporate strategy proved so successful that it was adopted for the Indian and Chinese markets. Today the regional head of Latin America heads the Europe, Middle East and Africa (EMEA) region, where he is implementing a similar strategy there. This shows that sometimes you may have to break from your dominant corporate logic to deal with local (especially emerging) market realities [14].

Experiment, Place Bets, Take Risks—and Fail Fast!

The previous discussion should underscore the need to include some space in your corporate strategy for experimentation. As well as asking how you can leverage your existing competencies in existing industries, or how to recombine and redeploy them in new industries, you need to be taking a few risks and seeking new competencies in new industries to ensure your future survival.

As Michael Tushman writes in *IESE Insight* magazine, "Aligning people, processes and structures is an important ingredient for success. A strong corporate culture gives balance, fit, flow and consistency to management decision-making. When alignment is doing its job, the system gets tighter and tighter, and execution runs smoothly. However, when there is tremendous alignment within a company, people risk becoming inward-looking, generating inertia. And in today's fast-moving business environment, inertia is suicide. While you are busy ensuring that your corporate machinery is perfectly oiled and all the systems, procedures and controls are working in sync, the world shifts and you disappear" [15].

The strategy scholar Henry Mintzberg believes that some of the greatest strategies come not from some fancy business plan but from a process of "try it and see," and the thinking comes later [16].

For Frank Bennack, the corporate strategy to invest in ESPN represented a big bet. Sometimes you have place bets like this, he said, likening the process to being a pilot—constantly looking ahead, visualizing the path you want to take and compensating for whatever might break the pattern. In this way, you are far more likely to survive whatever changes the world throws at you.

"While none of us can see around corners," Bennack said, "you do the best you can and access the best information you can to try to predict what's going to happen in the world of media. How do you do that? Obviously you've got to seek advice. But in the last analysis, you have to be courageous enough to take some really big risks along the line. Not risks that could put you out of business but that are just short of being so important that they could change the world.

"One of the problems that I find managers have is that they're afraid of making mistakes. We had to change our culture because ours was an old company, very proud of its history as a newspaper company and a little bit unready to put out a magazine and then have to say six months later, 'This magazine doesn't work, so we're going to kill it and launch another magazine instead.'

"We have a saying in our company which is, 'Fail fast.' Try a new thing but decide early if it's working or it isn't, and if it isn't, get away from it and do the next thing. You must do that because there's nothing worse than a business that doesn't succeed but languishes some place in the middle. We learn that failing fast is very important.

"One of my least favorite statements is, 'If you want to be in this business, this is what you have to do.' Well, I didn't say I wanted to be in *that* business. I said I wanted to be in media businesses which are profitable and which are growing and which you need—which the public needs. And if those things are not present, get out and go do something else." Well said.

References

1. M.E. Porter (1996), "What Is Strategy?" *Harvard Business Review*, November–December Issue.
2. G. Vroom and I. Sastre (2014), *Spotify: Face the Music* (IESE Publishing).
3. M.E. Porter (2008), "The Five Competitive Forces That Shape Strategy," *Harvard Business Review*, January Issue.
4. M.E. Porter (1979), "How Competitive Forces Shape Strategy," *Harvard Business Review*, March–April Issue.
5. M. Tushman (2014), "Leadership Tips for Today to Stay in the Game Tomorrow," *IESE Insight* magazine, Fourth Quarter, Issue 23, p. 38.
6. A.M. Brandenburger and B.J. Nalebuff (1996), *Co-opetition* (Currency Doubleday).
7. A.C. Hax and D.L. Wilde (2003), "The Delta Model: Toward a Unified Framework of Strategy," *Journal of Strategic Management Education*, Vol. 1, Issue 1.
8. W.C. Kim and R. Mauborgne (2005), *Blue Ocean Strategy: How to Create Uncontested Market Space and Make the Competition Irrelevant* (Harvard Business School Publishing).
9. W.C. Kim, R. Mauborgne, B. Bensaou and M. Williamson (2002), "The Evolution of the Circus Industry (A)" and "Even a Clown Can Do It: Cirque du Soleil Re-creates Live Entertainment (B)," INSEAD.
10. P. Ghemawat (2007), *Redefining Global Strategy: Crossing Borders in a World Where Differences Still Matter* (Harvard Business School Press).
11. F. Ferraro and B. Cassiman (2014), "Three Trends That Will Change How You Manage," *IESE Insight* magazine, Fourth Quarter, Issue 23, p. 26.
12. P. Ghemawat (2011), *World 3.0: Global Prosperity and How to Achieve It* (Harvard Business Review Press).
13. P. Ghemawat (2013), "Globalization and Global Problem Solving," Global Solutions Network.
14. A. Caldart, R.S. Vassolo and L. Silvestri (2014), "Induced Variation in Administrative Systems: Experimenting with Contexts for Innovation," *Management Research: The Journal of the Iberoamerican Academy of Management*, Vol. 12, Issue 2, 123–51.
15. M. Tushman (2014), "Leadership Tips for Today to Stay in the Game Tomorrow," *IESE Insight* magazine, Fourth Quarter, Issue 23, p. 33.
16. H. Mintzberg (2014), "Think Less, Learn More," *IESE Insight* magazine, Fourth Quarter, Issue 23, p. 6.

3

"Show Me the Money!" Getting Inside the Bottom Line

Philip H. Seager as told by Hillel M. Maximon

Remember the 1996 hit movie *Jerry Maguire*? In it, Tom Cruise plays a sports agent who becomes disillusioned with his profession: "Who had I become? Just another shark in a suit? With so many clients, we had forgotten what was important."

Following a dark night of the soul, he pounds out a manifesto, delivering a stark indictment of a profession that had lost its way by prioritizing earning a fast buck over doing what was in the best long-term interests of the client. The answer, he believes, is "fewer clients. Less money. More attention. Caring for them, caring for ourselves."

He prints off his diatribe and shares it with everyone in his office. The title is, "The Things We Think and Do Not Say." And for good reason, because by thinking out loud, he loses his job.

He ends up with the loyalty of only two people: the staff accountant (played by Renée Zellweger), who becomes his wife, and one offbeat client (played by Cuba Gooding Jr.), who tests the courage of Tom's conviction by making him shout at the top of his lungs the line that becomes the movie's catchphrase: "Show me the money!"

A lot has changed in the world since that movie came out. For one thing, the first time you saw it, you may have rented it on VHS video (remember

P.H. Seager (✉) • H.M. Maximon (✉)
IESE Business School, Barcelona, Spain
e-mail: PSeager@iese.edu; HMaximon@iese.edu

© The Author(s) 2017
M. Rosenberg, P.H. Seager (eds.), *Managing Media Businesses*,
DOI 10.1007/978-3-319-52021-6_3

that?) from your local Blockbuster store (remember them?), whereas now you can just stream it on Netflix.

But what interests me most are the movie's themes viewed from this side of the 2008 global financial crisis. Might we courageously rephrase the catch-phrase "Show me the money!" to "Tell me the story—and I'll show you the money" as the cri de coeur for less obfuscation in our business dealings today? And is it really only trite Hollywood fiction to believe that redemption can come in the form of a humble accountant, even one who looks nothing like Renée Zellweger?

I am reminded of this as I teach basic accounting principles to media executives. With few exceptions, these are not CFOs—yet even they could stand a refresher in realizing the limits of what they do, before committing their firms to bold courses of action based on what the balance sheet is telling them. Presumably CFOs were involved in scrutinizing the financial statements prior to the AOL-Time Warner merger, and that turned out to be what some have called "one of the biggest mistakes in corporate history" [1].

I suspect that many media executives are like the CEO of a radio and television station who told me that, when it comes to financial matters, he generally leaves it to other people. But he wonders: "If they don't tell me the whole story, would I know enough about the financial performance of the company?"

In this brief chapter, I can't tell you all there is to know about financial accounting—which is the subject of a whole book I have written with George H. Sorter and Monroe J. Ingberman [2]. But I aim to share enough so that hopefully you will have the wherewithal to shout, "Tell me the story—and I'll show you the money!"

"What Is Accounting?"

I always start by asking media executives this question: "What is accounting?" Predictably their answers go something along the lines of "a way of showing the financial health of a company." To which I say, "We're accountants, not doctors, so don't talk to me about health." Or it's "a way of showing you are doing the right things in the right way." To which I say, "I wish."

In a similar vein, I ask, "What is the purpose of business?" Again, media executives bandy about terms like, "to create value" or "to create worth." To which I counter, "What is value? What is worth?"

Here's a revealing story about value: A man buys a new car but refuses to drive it out of the dealership because he has been told that a car loses a third of its value as soon as it leaves the lot. Is that so? Well, if the man's plan is to turn around and resell the car to someone else, then yes, by driving the car home, he will have sacrificed some of the car's resale value. But if by value we mean the utility of the car for the man to get to work and to take his children to school, then it is equally true to say that the car has no value until he drives it out of the lot.

Do you see what I'm getting at? Value is subjective and personal: It depends. The same goes for "worth" and "health" and moralistic concepts like "doing the right thing." Accounting is concerned with utility, not with questions of "right or wrong" or "revealed truth."

Don't get me wrong: I am in no way saying that accountants condone false or misleading statements, or that accounting reports should be consciously untruthful.

What I am saying is that we need to define our terms carefully and make sure we are using precise language, especially when non-accountants are attempting to engage with the numbers or have a meaningful dialogue with their CFO. When we don't speak the same language, we go astray. Accounting is already the subject of enough misunderstanding without us adding to it.

Here are my definitions, which make some critical distinctions:

Accounting is a system for assembling and communicating information that is useful to users—like you—in reaching rational *economic decisions*.

Economic Resources fall into three general categories:

- Products or goods
- Services (especially relevant to the media and entertainment industry)
- Money (especially cash but also checks, deposits, etc.)

A Business is an entity whose objective is to increase economic resources with the expectation of returning to its owners economic resources greater than they invested or contributed.

Under these definitions, accounting statements become useful for business insofar as they *report accounting activities that help in making decisions aimed at increasing returns*; in other words, insofar as they *tell you the story that will show you the money.*

To Record or Not to Record?

Let's drill down into the definitions, using another illustration. Let's say you decide to hire Mark Zuckerberg to create a new social media platform for your company. Or maybe you decide to hire Steven Spielberg to direct your next movie. Take your pick. In either case, you agree to pay him $100 million for his services, and he will start next month. However, in order to do the job, Mark (or Steven) requests some paper clips, which you duly go out and buy for $2.99.

Now, which of these two activities—the planned payment of $100 million or the purchase of the $2.99 paper clips—will be recorded by the accountant?

Notice I didn't ask which event is more important for your company's future, or which event is more interesting for you to know about as a shareholder. The answer, under generally accepted accounting principles, or GAAP, is to record the paper clips but not the agreed payment of $100 million to Mark Zuckerberg or Steven Spielberg.

Yes, you read that correctly. And there is a reason for it. It is because there are many economic activities, but not everything qualifies as an *accounting* activity. To qualify as an accounting activity, it must meet the following two conditions:

- It must be measurable in terms of currency amount (how much).
- There must have been performance.

The reason you record the purchase of paper clips is that there has been performance—you received the paper clips—whereas Mark and Steven are still biding their time at their current digs in California until they start their new jobs with you next month. Not a cent of that agreed $100 million contract is recorded until either they start working (performance) or they have been paid—even though the contract is quantifiable, in terms of currency amount.

If this seems slightly perverse and counterintuitive—that an entity requiring *information useful for reaching rational economic decisions so that it can increase its economic resources* would not be able to tell from reading the financial statements of said entity that Mark Zuckerberg or Steven Spielberg was associated with the business—then you are starting to see the world through the eyes of our friend Jerry Maguire: "Tell me the story—and I'll show you the money!"

The Balance Sheet: What's the Story?

The key point for a non-accountant to grasp is that financial statements are historical records, not a magical revelation of everything you need to know about a firm. They do not reveal the current financial state of a firm, nor do they provide hot-off-the-press news about a firm's assets and liabilities because they appear weeks, sometimes months, after the activities they describe. Accountants are not wizards with crystal balls offering you a glimpse into some distant future so you can speculate about impending fortunes; rather, accountants are historians, reporting only on certain past activities and their effects. In this regard, they are somewhat like your old-school newshound who reports "just the facts, ma'am."

When an event occurs, journalists have to sift through lots of information and filter it through the Five Ws (who, what, where, when and why). Their stories follow the inverted pyramid structure, with the broadest, most essential elements reported at the beginning, and the finer points or extraneous details reported in descending order of importance until the end.

Accountants, too, have their own unique way of recording activities. At some point in history, they arbitrarily determined that all accounting activities will be reported in terms of the impact on assets and/or equities—and that the monetary quantification of all assets must equal the monetary quantification of all equities. As such, the process of recording accounting activities must always maintain equilibrium between assets (A) and equities (E), as expressed below:

$$A \uparrow = E \uparrow$$
$$A \uparrow = A \downarrow$$
$$E \downarrow = A \downarrow$$
$$E \downarrow = E \uparrow$$

As before, it is important that we define our terms, as assets are not what the last group of media executives defined as "tangible resources that a company owns that have value" or "something of value the company owns"; and liabilities are not necessarily "debts that a company has to pay back" or "something bad that the company has to pay back."

Here are my definitions, which again make some critical distinctions:

Asset: the right to utilize (or receive) an economic resource with the expectation of receiving (greater) future (cash) benefits.

Equity: a responsibility to distribute an economic resource.

Equity takes two forms:

- **Liability:** an *explicit* responsibility to distribute an economic resource, where the amount and timing are known and estimable.
- **Owners' Equity:** an *implicit* responsibility to distribute an economic resource, where the amount and timing are indeterminable.

Notice these distinctions: A leased factory can be a vital asset to a manufacturer, just as an owned machine that breaks down, becomes obsolete and cannot be sold is not. And even though paying dividends to its shareholders is something that a publicly traded company endeavors to do, if it is unable to do so, does a debt collector come around and confiscate all of its worldly goods until it pays up? If that were the case, there would be a lot of companies in receivership right now. This is why the definitions given by the media executives—that an asset is something you own and a liability is something you have to pay back—are inadequate.

Another way of thinking of assets and equities is in terms of rights and responsibilities: the right to utilize an economic resource, and the responsibility to distribute an economic resource.

The accountant records the purchase of paper clips, for example, as one number having two effects. Since the accountant considers the world solely in terms of assets and equities, as we saw in the previous chart, each accounting activity produces either two effects on assets (A), two effects on equities (E) or one effect on an asset (A) and the other on an equity (E). In addition, each accounting activity will result in a benefit and a sacrifice. This means that there are only four possible combinations as summarized in the table below:

Benefit	Sacrifice
A ↑ results from a right increasing	= E ↑ results from a responsibility increasing
A ↑ results from a right increasing	= A ↓ results from a right decreasing
E ↓ results from a responsibility decreasing	= A ↓ results from a right decreasing
E ↓ results from a responsibility decreasing	= E ↑ results from a responsibility increasing

Let's consider this framework using the purchase of the paper clips as an example. Your media company buys paper clips for $2.99. The first question to ask is: Does this qualify as an accounting activity? As explained earlier, it does, as this was not an exchange of promises to buy paper clips for a future payment next month when Mark or Steven starts work, but there has been actual performance.

Now suppose you bought those paper clips on your credit card. Which type of accounting activity is that? You have acquired an asset, so your benefit of (or right to) that economic resource increases. But accountants require equilibrium. Buying those paper clips on credit means that your responsibility to pay also increases, which means that your responsibility to distribute economic resources also increases.

Here are the consequences of recording the purchase of paper clips on credit on the balance sheet:

Assets	Beg. balance		End balance	
Merchandise inventory	$	0	$	2.99
Total assets	$	0	$	2.99
Liabilities and owners' equities				
Accounts payable merchandise	$	0	$	2.99
Total liabilities and owners' equities	$	0	$	2.99

Easy, right? Now, here's a question for you: If you only looked at this balance sheet, without knowing anything about the previous back story, what would you really know? You would merely know that a media company bought some merchandise, and they still had $2.99 of it on hand. What merchandise? How many items? For what purpose? More to the point, what in this particular balance sheet tells you that this economic resource was acquired because it is going to be utilized by Mark Zuckerberg or Steven Spielberg when either starts working on a mega project for this media company next month?

The answer, of course, is nothing. Hopefully, you should be starting to see that the unique way in which accountants report activities—just as journalists or movie directors have their own particular reasons for framing their stories the way they do—leaves out a lot of information, some of which may very well be *information useful for reaching rational economic decisions so that economic resources increase.*

In sum, don't hang your hat on the balance sheet. It doesn't tell the whole story or anywhere near as much of the story as you might like to think. One CFO of a major American cable and satellite news television channel found this exercise to be a real eye-opener: "I realized the limits of what a balance sheet can and cannot do. What it doesn't say or reveal is as important as what it does in order to make informed decisions." I think what this CFO really wants to say is, "I need to know the story so that I can tell you where the money is."

The Story Behind the Story

In October 2011 the British *Telegraph* newspaper reported the following story:

> Rob Sloan claimed third place in the Kielder Marathon after completing the 26.2 mile course in an impressive time of 2:51:00. But suspicions were raised by fellow runners bemused that they had not seen Sloan pass them during Sunday's race. After initially denying any wrongdoing, Sloan admitted to hopping onto a bus at the 20 mile mark because he was feeling tired. He then re-emerged from a wooded area of the course and picked up the bronze medal. Witnesses reported seeing him hide behind a tree until the first and second placed runners went past, then rejoining the race behind them. The 31-year-old now faces dismissal from his club, Sunderland Harriers, and could be banned from taking part in future marathons [3].

There are two stories here. One is about a man who started a race at Point A and finished it at Point B. The second story is about a man who between

Points A and B left the course, hopped a bus, hid in the woods and then rejoined the race, having skipped the final 6.2 miles. In both stories, the outcome is the same: The man placed third and won a bronze medal. But if you were a fellow competitor in the Kielder Marathon, which story would you rather know? Aren't they different stories?

This is a useful analogy for considering accounting statements. The balance sheet is like the first story: It tells you the beginning balance and the end balance, but nothing in between. As a business competitor or investor, isn't there more to the story that you would be interested in knowing? As the disgraced runner Rob Sloan can attest, the journey matters as much as the destination (if not more). And the balance sheet reveals very little about that journey.

To help us understand the journey, we need the information that is provided in the Income Statement and the Statement of Cash Flows. Think of these statements as the story behind the story—the telling details in between the start and the finish lines that give you vital information about how the race was run.

The Balance Sheet

There are those who believe that the balance sheet got its name because it lists all of the balances in an entity's assets, liabilities and owners' equities—at an exact point in time. There are others who believe that it was so named because the sum of all of the assets equals the sum of all of the liabilities and owners' equities—at an exact point in time. Hence, the assets are said to be "in balance" with the equities.

While it is true that the statement does list all of the balances in the account, and that the assets are "in balance" with the sum of the liabilities and owners' equities, a more descriptive and practical interpretation is that the balance sheet is a statement of incomplete accounting cycles. For example, merchandise inventory that was purchased and not yet sold to a customer results in an asset, and services that were utilized and not yet paid for results in a liability.

Figure 3.1 presents the basic elements of the balance sheet, depicted to show the equilibrium between assets and equities; rights and responsibilities; and benefits and sacrifices, as explained earlier.

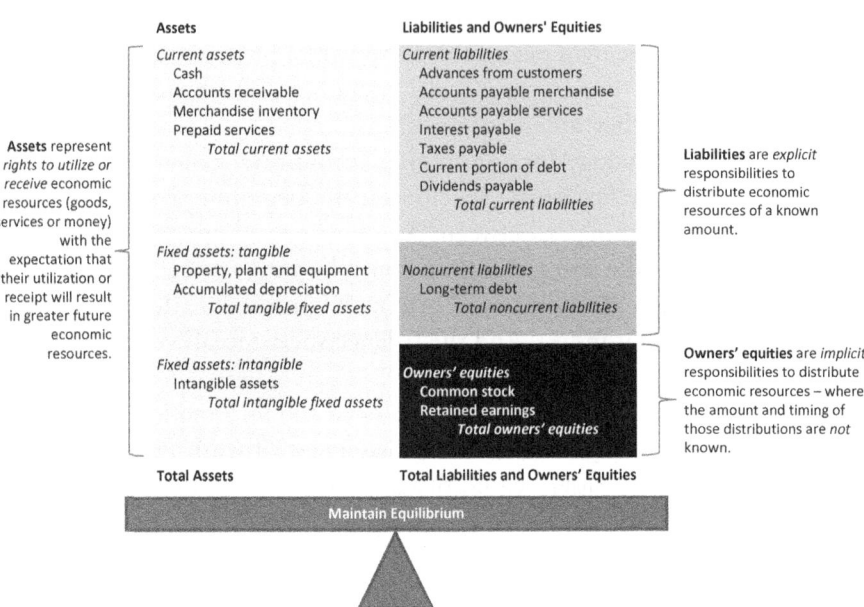

The Balance Sheet

Assets

Assets represent rights to utilize or receive economic resources (goods, services or money) with the expectation that their utilization or receipt will result in greater future economic resources.

Current assets
  Cash
  Accounts receivable
  Merchandise inventory
  Prepaid services
    Total current assets

Fixed assets: tangible
  Property, plant and equipment
  Accumulated depreciation
    Total tangible fixed assets

Fixed assets: intangible
  Intangible assets
    Total intangible fixed assets

Total Assets

Liabilities and Owners' Equities

Current liabilities
  Advances from customers
  Accounts payable merchandise
  Accounts payable services
  Interest payable
  Taxes payable
  Current portion of debt
  Dividends payable
    Total current liabilities

Noncurrent liabilities
  Long-term debt
    Total noncurrent liabilities

Owners' equities
  Common stock
  Retained earnings
    Total owners' equities

Total Liabilities and Owners' Equities

Liabilities are *explicit* responsibilities to distribute economic resources of a known amount.

Owners' equities are *implicit* responsibilities to distribute economic resources – where the amount and timing of those distributions are *not* known.

Maintain Equilibrium

Fig. 3.1 This figure depicts the equilibrium between assets and equities; rights and responsibilities; and benefits and sacrifices reported in the Balance Sheet

The Income Statement

The Income Statement, sometimes called the Profit and Loss (P&L) Statement, is an activity statement. What the statement reports can be seen from a number of different perspectives. At its simplest, it reports the increases and decreases to retained earnings (excluding the activity known as the declaration of dividends). The increases are called revenues and gains, and the decreases are called expenses and losses. I will simplify the discussion by focusing only on revenues and expenses.

> **Revenues** result from providing economic resources with the expectation of receiving greater future (cash) benefits.

> **Expenses** result from the final utilization of economic resources.

Revenues result from selling goods or providing services to customers, or they are earned from investments in stocks, bonds and bank deposits.

Expenses result from:

- The delivery of goods to customers (cost of goods sold)
- The utilization of services such as rented space, insurance and utilities (operating expenses)
- The utilization of depreciable assets (depreciation expense)
- The utilization of intangible assets (amortization expense)
- The utilization of other people's money (interest expense)
- The utilization of government services (income tax expense), to name a few

The difference between total revenues and total expenses is called net income. Therefore, an Income Statement can also be seen as an activity report of revenues, expenses and net income.

> **Net Assets** represent the difference between the total assets and total liabilities.

Yet another perspective of the Income Statement is that it is an activity report of the increases and decreases to net assets (excluding any activities that impact the common stock accounts).

All three perspectives discussed above have the following in common: They report the degree to which a business is potentially meeting its expectation of returning to its owners more than they invested.

The Statement of Cash Flows

Like the Income Statement, the Statement of Cash Flows depicts the journey, but as its name suggests, it reports an entity's cash flows in terms of significant operating, investing and financing activities.

Examples of *significant operating activities* reported in the Statement of Cash Flows include collections from customers, payments to suppliers of merchandise, payments to suppliers of services, payment of interest and payment of income taxes.

Examples of *significant investing activities* include the purchase and sale of property, plant and equipment for cash, and the purchase and sale of intangible assets for cash.

Examples of *significant financing activities* include borrowing cash from the bank and its subsequent repayment, the issue and repurchase of shares of common stock for cash, and the payment of dividends.

How These Statements Relate to Each Other

Figure 3.2 depicts the relationship between the Balance Sheet, the Income Statement and the Statement of Cash Flows.

Every activity reported in the Income Statement either increases retained earnings (revenues) or decreases retained earnings (expenses) and impacts another balance sheet account—but never cash. (The one exception to this is the accounting activity known as cash sales. For the sake of this discussion, I will treat cash sales as an instantaneous credit sale.)

For example, credit sales increase retained earnings (revenue) and increase accounts receivable. The utilization of borrowed money decreases retained earnings (expenses) and increases interest payable.

Similarly, every activity reported in the Statement of Cash Flows either increases cash (cash inflow or cash receipt) or decreases cash (cash outflow or cash expenditure) and impacts another balance sheet account—but never retained earnings.

For example, collections from credit customers result in an increase in cash (operating cash inflow) and a decrease in accounts receivable (an asset). Borrowing from the bank results in an increase in cash (financing cash inflow) and an increase in long-term debt (a liability). The purchase of property, plant and equipment for cash results in a decrease in cash (investing cash outflow) and an increase in property, plant and equipment (an asset).

In other words, those activities reported in the Income Statement do not impact cash, except for the one case previously noted; and those activities reported in the Statement of Cash Flows do not impact retained earnings.

When I gave this presentation to a group of media executives, three journalists from major broadcasters in Denmark, Kenya and the United States all said this had awakened an interest in them to start critically questioning their financial statements, now that they realized there was a much bigger story behind the story—perhaps a sneaky runner hidden among those dense clusters of numbers. So, in honor of those journalists and anyone else who at this point would like to join me in saying, "Show me the money," I list some key points that any user of financial statements should know enough to find out for themselves in order to make a rational economic decision.

The Missing Links: Where to Probe Further

With reference to the Balance Sheet, the **balance in cash** represents the excess of the total cash receipts over the total cash expenditures, since the inception of the firm. **What it does NOT describe**, necessarily, is the amount that you can spend because there might be deposits and withdrawals that are still pending.

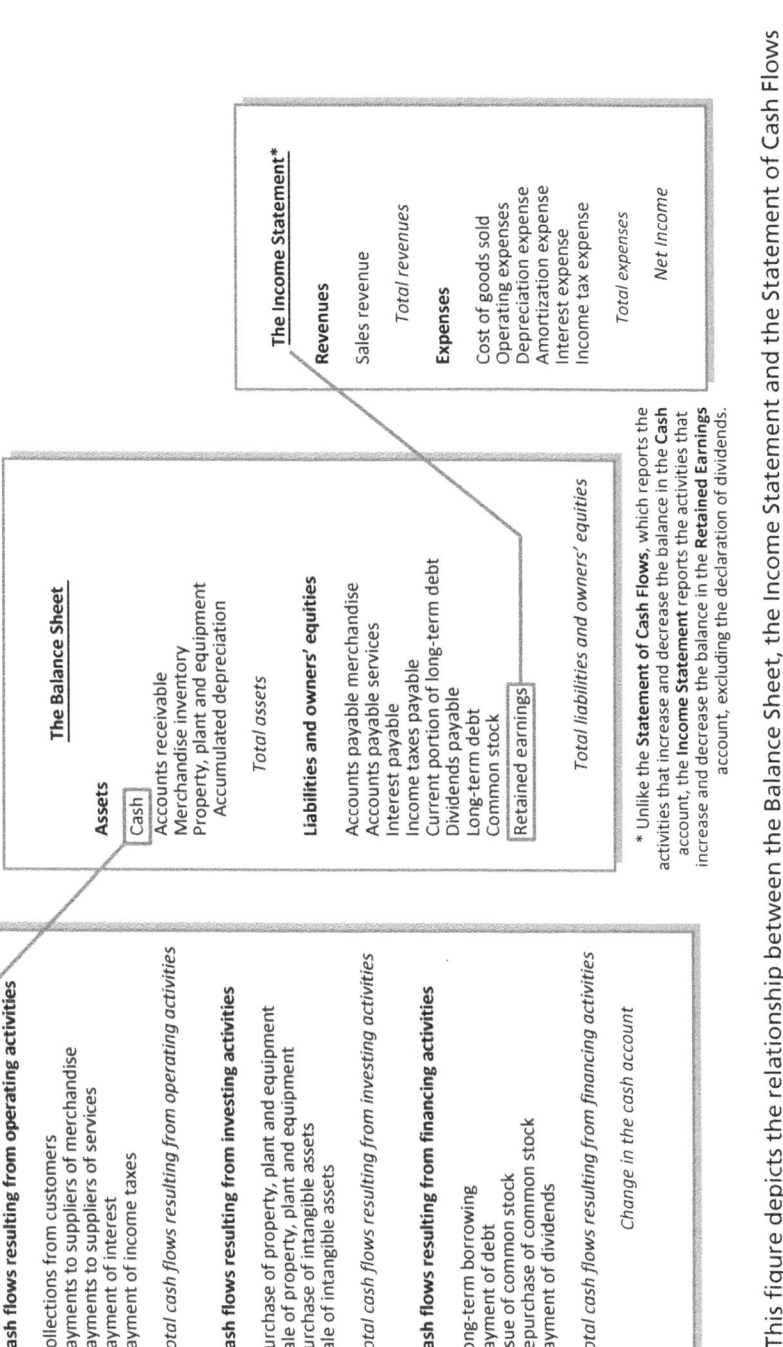

The Statement of Cash Flows

Cash flows resulting from operating activities

Collections from customers
Payments to suppliers of merchandise
Payments to suppliers of services
Payment of interest
Payment of income taxes

Total cash flows resulting from operating activities

Cash flows resulting from investing activities

Purchase of property, plant and equipment
Sale of property, plant and equipment
Purchase of intangible assets
Sale of intangible assets

Total cash flows resulting from investing activities

Cash flows resulting from financing activities

Long-term borrowing
Payment of debt
Issue of common stock
Repurchase of common stock
Payment of dividends

Total cash flows resulting from financing activities

Change in the cash account

The Balance Sheet

Assets

Cash
Accounts receivable
Merchandise inventory
Property, plant and equipment
Accumulated depreciation

Total assets

Liabilities and owners' equities

Accounts payable merchandise
Accounts payable services
Interest payable
Income taxes payable
Current portion of long-term debt
Dividends payable
Long-term debt
Common stock
Retained earnings

Total liabilities and owners' equities

The Income Statement*

Revenues

Sales revenue

Total revenues

Expenses

Cost of goods sold
Operating expenses
Depreciation expense
Amortization expense
Interest expense
Income tax expense

Total expenses

Net Income

* Unlike the **Statement of Cash Flows**, which reports the activities that increase and decrease the balance in the **Cash** account, the **Income Statement** reports the activities that increase and decrease the balance in the **Retained Earnings** account, excluding the declaration of dividends.

Fig. 3.2 This figure depicts the relationship between the Balance Sheet, the Income Statement and the Statement of Cash Flows

The balance in accounts receivable represents the total amount of expected future collections from credit customers. **What it does NOT describe is:**

- the number of customers who owe for goods and/or services provided
- how long the customers have owed for the goods and/or services provided
- how likely it is that what is owed will be collected
- the time elapsed between the provision and the collection

The balance in the merchandise inventory account represents the currency amount of goods purchased that have not been sold. **What it does NOT describe is:**

- when the merchandise was purchased
- how many units are available for sale
- the condition of the units
- the potential for selling the merchandise
- when they might be sold
- the expected sales price
- the time between purchase and sale

The balance in the property, plant and equipment account represents the currency amount spent to acquire the right to utilize property, plant and equipment. **What it does NOT describe is:**

- the location of the property, plant and equipment
- when the property, plant and equipment was acquired
- the remaining utility of the property, plant and equipment
- the marketability of the property, plant and equipment
- the current market value of the property, plant and equipment

The balance in the accumulated depreciation account represents the accumulated depreciation since the acquisition of the associated property, plant and equipment.
What it does NOT describe is:

- the number of years over which the assets have been depreciated
- the remaining utility of the depreciable assets

The balance in the intangible assets account represents the remaining right to utilize intangible assets. **What it does NOT describe is:**

- when the intangible asset was acquired
- the remaining utility of the intangible asset
- the marketability of the intangible asset
- the benefit of the intangible asset

The balance in accounts payable merchandise represents the amounts to be paid for goods purchased in the past. **The balance in accounts payable services** represents the amounts to be paid for utilizing services in the past. **What they do NOT describe is:**

- how many suppliers are owed
- for how long they have been owed
- when they will be paid
- the time between purchase or acquisition and payment

The balance in the interest payable account represents the amounts still owed for utilizing borrowed money. **What it does NOT describe is:**

- the interest rate
- the date(s) of the required periodic payment(s)

The balance in the income tax payable account represents the amounts still owed for utilizing government services. **What it does NOT describe is:**

- the tax rate
- the date(s) of the required payment(s)

The balance in the current portion of long-term debt account represents the indebtedness incurred in the past that is payable in the current accounting period. **What it does NOT describe is:**

- what is owed long-term
- when the obligation is due
- the cost of borrowing (interest rate)

The balance in the dividends payable account represents the amount to be disbursed to shareholders as of a certain date in the future. **What it does NOT describe is:**

- when the payment will be made

The balance in the long-term debt account represents the indebtedness incurred in the past that is payable in future periods. **What it does NOT describe is:**

- when the obligation is due
- the cost of borrowing (interest rate)
- the annual payment

The balance in the common stock account represents the excess of the total currency amount received from shares issued and outstanding. **What it does NOT describe is:**

- the date at which the shares of stock were issued or repurchased
- the market price of the shares at the time they were issued
- the market price of the shares at the balance sheet date
- the marketability of the shares
- the obligation that the firm has to its shareholders
- how many shareholders there are
- the amount or timing of distributions to shareholders

The balance in the retained earnings account represents the excess of revenues and gains over expenses and losses, less dividends declared, since the inception of the firm. **What it does NOT describe is:**

- what the objectives of the firm are
- when and how the firm will be able to meet its objectives

Don't Let the Smoke Get in Your Eyes

For media and entertainment executives, I would urge you to give careful consideration to the notion of assets. I can think of few other sectors where people play as central a role, and yet how are they accounted for on the balance sheet? Think of your many ideas, airtime, the Internet, trademarks, logos, and why they are not expressed in financial terms in financial statements.

If nothing else, I hope this chapter has shown you that numbers are smoke, and that it is your job to look for the fires. "If they do not tell me the whole story, would I know enough about the financial performance of the company?" asked the radio and television CEO. He said he was going to insist on a proper engagement with his CFO from now on.

Is it time for you, too, to ask your CFO to "Tell me the story—and I'll show you the money"?

References

1. E. Barnett and A. Andrews (September 28, 2010), "AOL Merger Was 'The Biggest Mistake in Corporate History', Believes Time Warner Chief Jeff Bewkes," *The Daily Telegraph*, http://www.telegraph.co.uk/finance/newsbysector/mediatechnologyandtelecoms/media/8031227/AOL-merger-was-the-biggest-mistake-in-corporate-history-believes-Time-Warner-chief-Jeff-Bewkes.html
2. G.H. Sorter, M.J. Ingberman and H.M. Maximon (1990), *Financial Accounting: An Events and Cash Flow Approach* (McGraw-Hill).
3. A. Singh (October 12, 2011), "Marathon Runner Caught Bus to the Finish Line," *The Telegraph*, http://www.telegraph.co.uk/news/newstopics/howaboutthat/8820301/Marathon-runner-caught-bus-to-the-finish-line.html

4

Marketing in a New Media World

Julian Villanueva with Philip H. Seager

Is marketing to blame for ruining the media and entertainment industry? Peter Bart seems to think so. During a week spent in Los Angeles as part of IESE's Media AMP, our group was regaled with stories from the good old days by the veteran journalist-cum-studio executive who helped bring such classics as *The Godfather* to the big screen before he became editor of the showbiz bible, *Variety,* for which he still writes.

"When I left *The New York Times* to become vice president for production at Paramount Pictures, it was pre-corporate Hollywood. So if you fell in love with a film project, you could simply go out and do something about it. You didn't have a marketing committee, and you didn't have to consult about the international rights or about the video rights. The green light process today is extraordinarily complex."

He recalls how he and his Paramount boss, Robert Evans, agreed to do *The Godfather* during a car ride together in which Bart said he had optioned an interesting book and Evans agreed it was a darn good story and within 20 minutes they had decided to proceed with it. Now, he laments, "the marketing concept is what's controlling things."

The entertainment business these days is based on tent-pole pictures—those bombastic blockbusters that exploit audience awareness of the source material

J. Villanueva (✉)
Marketing Department, IESE Business School, Barcelona, Spain
e-mail: JVillanueva@iese.edu

P.H. Seager
IESE Business School, Barcelona, Spain
e-mail: PSeager@iese.edu

© The Author(s) 2017
M. Rosenberg, P.H. Seager (eds.), *Managing Media Businesses*,
DOI 10.1007/978-3-319-52021-6_4

long before the movie opens and are buttressed by tie-in merchandise. "These are the pictures that support the studio structure, and that's why the big hero of the moment is, of all things, Marvel Comics. An interesting trick is that most of the superhero pictures open overseas first. Why? Number one, that's the market: the overseas market represents about three-quarters of the overall business. Number two, it's a safety valve," meaning the studio is able to recoup its costs overseas before the movie is killed off by negative reviews at home.

"Frankly, I'm concerned that the art-house picture could become a thing of the past. It's a bit on life support at the moment. You look at the multiplexes: it's almost impossible to find a picture that any adult would want to see. You really are at the mercy of the superheroes. I don't know about you guys, but I find it tough going. I don't like all my protagonists to wear spandex," he deadpans.

And for Bart it's not just Hollywood that has been destroyed by the marketing guys in suits. He has equally scathing things to say about the media industry, especially those news networks that seem more interested in incorporating market-driven entertainment into their news cycles. "News has to stay about news," he insists. "There's already a great world out there for prepackaged, predictable opinion, but there's very little that you can find in the way of straight news anymore. A company like CNN has to, in my opinion, focus on the fact that news is their franchise, and they're not going to succeed through quasi-entertainment."

Is Bart's assessment as bleak as he makes it out to be? Should the ills of the media and entertainment industry be laid at the door of marketing?

To explore this question, we need to make sure we have a proper understanding of what marketing is, and its role in addressing business needs, including strategy development.

In this chapter, I will introduce several key marketing concepts and show how media and entertainment executives might use them to refine their analysis of business problems, enrich their debates and improve their decision-making. Hopefully even the most hard-bitten reader might come to see—as Bart himself admitted by the end of his talk—that in spite of all the ills, "there's extraordinary opportunity around the world in new media; we're in a great moment in terms of the way the world is acknowledging content." And in this regard, I believe good marketing can help.

What Is Marketing?

It's an oft-repeated gripe: marketing is about getting people to buy stuff they don't need. But that's not true. Marketing is about identifying and satisfying a customer need and, in doing so, creating value that can be captured and sustained.

Ted Levitt, considered one of the founding fathers of modern marketing, was adamant on this point. He famously challenged executives to ask themselves, "What business am I in?" How you answer that question, he said, would reveal your true orientation [1]. If, for example, you say, "I produce superhero blockbusters," then you will probably be in the camp that Bart decries. You will have fallen into the product-focused trap, in which marketing is, indeed, used as a crude lever to get people to buy more of your stuff.

What Levitt wanted was for executives to reconceptualize their business in terms of "providing customer-creating value satisfactions" [2]. On this basis, marketing becomes the means of better understanding consumers and, with that understanding, capturing their attention and their business.

No matter whether you've heard this before, it's worth going back and asking yourself, "What business am I in?" And make sure your answer is framed in terms of what superior value you are creating for your customers, not what kind of products you sell.

As a refresher, Fig. 4.1 presents a well-known marketing framework, which will probably be familiar to many readers in the media industry [3].

Every marketing analysis begins with this textbook analysis of the 5 Cs:

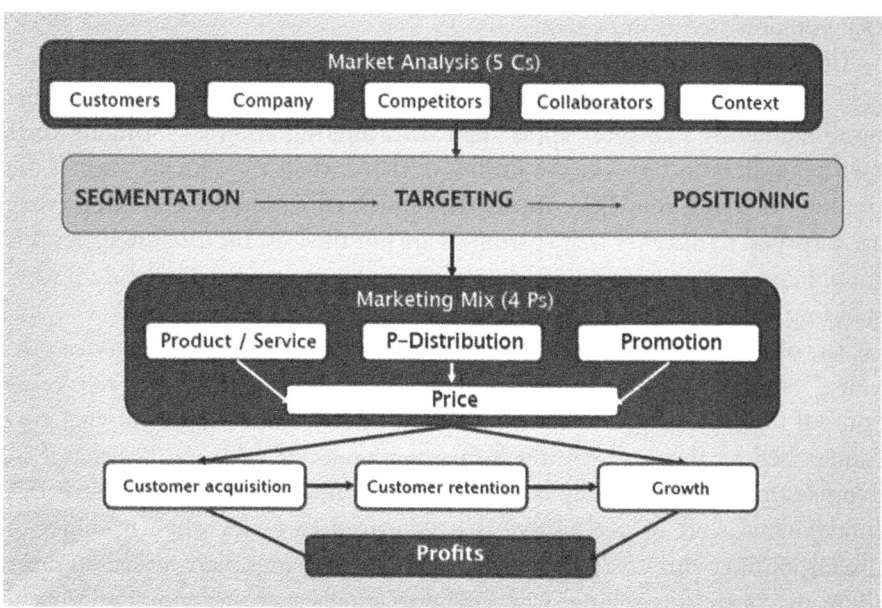

Fig. 4.1 Well-known Marketing Framework
Source: Note on Marketing Strategy, Prof. Robert J. Dolan, Harvard Business School, https://cb.hbsp.harvard.edu/cbmp/product/598061-PDF-ENG

- **Customers:** what customer needs am I attempting to satisfy?
- **Company:** what special skills does my company have to satisfy those needs?
- **Competitors:** who's my competition?
- **Collaborators:** whom can I enlist to help me reach my customers?
- **Context:** which external factors will condition my effort?

As this framework shows, the proper formulation of a marketing strategy always begins with an orientation on the customer.

Question: How do you know <u>your</u> customers?

That's easy, you say. We do a survey. The problem with market research surveys is that they tend to be self-reinforcing, telling you things you already know—or think you know. To borrow an old phrase, customer surveys get used like drunks use lampposts—for support rather than for illumination.

This is especially true if you have a product orientation. Say you do a customer survey and it returns high demand or satisfaction for a particular product but rates soft or intangible factors lower. A product-focused manager will take this as a sign of approval and proceed in his or her desired direction. Meanwhile, the customer may, in fact, be more interested in the very things that you don't see as important.

This problem is compounded by the wealth of customer data being generated by today's digital tools. The more big data there is to sift though, the more marketing managers apply their own filtering criteria—bringing their own prejudices to bear on the findings. Then, when they finally launch the product in which they have invested so much time, money and effort, they are surprised to discover that customers are not the least bit interested. Yet this should come as no surprise, if they never really spent any time truly understanding their customers.

Part of the problem is contained in the very term "product or service provider." Stop thinking of yourself as the *provider* of anything, as it reinforces yourself as *the great giver* when you should be *the great perceiver* of what customers believe they are getting from their point of view. As Levitt put it, people don't buy drills, they buy the ability to make holes [4]. And it is this fundamental shift of perspective that you need to make when it comes to understanding your customers and your role in serving their needs. So don't think of yourself as selling a magazine so much as "entertainment"; not a newspaper but "knowledge"; not a movie but "an experience."

Bart tells the following story that perfectly illustrates this point: "The first hit picture that Bob Evans and I put together was a really ridiculous movie called *Love Story* with Ali MacGraw and Ryan O'Neal. The script wasn't good, the cast was undistinguished, but when I saw the preview, there was something that went right. It was a real tearjerker. Everybody in the audience cried. Within a week, there were lines around the block to see this picture, for two reasons. First was the shared emotional experience of everyone crying together. Second, because of this experience, it was the most popular date movie of all time. It was a gigantic hit for us."

In other words, their success was owed not so much to the quality of the product but to the experience that those customers were having. As such, don't fall in love with your own product, as it can blind you from knowing your customer.

Take even the most disruptive innovations of recent times: the electric car, online shopping for home delivery, video-on-demand and e-book readers. All great products, as companies will tell you. Eco-friendly! Convenient! Great selection! Portable and space-saving for travel! But ask customers and you may get an entirely different story: poor performance, boring image, no spontaneity, spoiled for choice, irritating for those who like to flip back and forth or take notes. Such feedback might come to you through surveys, but the question is, are you paying attention?

The best way to know what you don't know is to put yourself in the shoes of the customer, even one who may be very different from you. You have to go spend time with your customers: understand what delights them. And this has to involve those outside the marketing department. You will gain far richer insights by involving diverse groups of people that traverse various functions.

In Chap. 7 on Operations Management, we will see that when operational mistakes occur, they are usually because managers failed to devote sufficient attention to the decisive gaps among expectations, perceptions and reality. The same holds true for Marketing. According to the marketing scholar A. Parasuraman, clumsy marketing efforts arise as a consequence of not minding the following five gaps [5]:

- between marketer perceptions and consumer expectations;
- between marketer perceptions and the actual specifications established for a service;
- between the service specifications and the actual service delivery;
- between service delivery and external communications to consumers;
- between consumer expectations and consumer perceptions.

It is in these gaps where value creation frequently lies. Your marketing, as well as your operations, pricing strategies and business models, will be improved by adjusting your expectations and perceptions in light of your customers'.

One caveat concerns how to interpret unarticulated customer needs, either because, like having a clean bathroom, they go without saying, or because they are features that customers didn't even know they wanted until they had them. This is an issue addressed by the Japanese professor Noriaki Kano, who developed the Kano Model to help get at this level of analysis. As he highlighted, what delights a customer today will eventually be old-hat tomorrow, so if you just keep giving customers more of what they have come to expect from you, it won't boost their perceptions of you any—but if you stop delivering as expected, it will certainly lower them [6]. As such, you must constantly be reassessing your customer needs as they evolve over time.

Segmentation, Targeting and Positioning

Once you have analyzed your customers, the next step is to segment them so you can target and position your marketing messages effectively. Again, as with operations, critical to delivering breakthrough service is being clear about who your target markets are (or aren't); otherwise your marketing efforts will amount to shots in the dark.

How should you segment consumers? Traditionally, this is done by grouping people according to age, income, gender and other demographic variables. Speaking to our Media AMP group, the marketing strategist Jamie Gutfreund shared a commonly used segmentation approach based on:

- those born post–World War II (Baby Boomers);
- those born between the early 1960s and the early 1980s (Generation X);
- those born between the early 1980s and the early 2000s (Generation Y, often referred to as Millennials);
- those born since the early 2000s (Generation Z, though marketers frequently refer to this cohort as the Internet Generation or Digital Natives, reflecting the all-pervasive influence of technology on their lives).

Gutfreund is particularly interested in the Millennials, whom she said impacted everything today—from how you set marketing goals to how you recruit. With an estimated two billion people in the Millennial age bracket globally, their purchasing power is going to be in the trillions, she said.

My colleague in the Marketing Department at IESE, Jose L. Nueno, agrees. He supervised a consumer research project on teens and their shopping patterns in eight countries and found that 12–19 year olds already represent a sizeable global market valued at $1 trillion annually. If that's today, imagine their purchasing power in 2020 [7].

However, he makes an important distinction between the young people of mature economies (France, Japan, Spain, the UK and the USA in the study) and those of emerging economies (Brazil, China and Mexico). With nine times the number of children and teens in emerging markets as there are in developed ones, as well as higher ratios of working adults to senior citizens, the center of gravity is going to shift to emerging markets to serve the needs of their aspirational middle classes. This is something that marketers—especially those in the media and entertainment industry—need to be preparing for now, given the unique way that young people consume content (more on this later).

It should be noted that these generational categorizations are largely pegged to North American phenomena—namely, the end of World War II, then various social revolutions, followed by a backlash and moral panic as those previous generations had children. So when a marketer says, "People in their 30s (Gen X) tend to be cynical, whereas people in their 20s (Gen Y) care more about the community," it needs to be contextualized to your own sociocultural reality. There are studies showing that in Europe, for example, the same behavioral and attitudinal tendencies are exhibited at least a decade later than in the United States, with one British study finding so-called Millennials to be more cynical and less civic-minded and that the characteristics typically associated with Gen Y may, in fact, turn up more with Gen Z [8]. Indeed, as a Brazilian Media AMP executive pointed out, many of these generational characteristics are shaped by country-specific socioeconomic factors, so you have to be sure to consider disposable income and purchasing power before hastily defining a segment according to US-inspired realities.

Apart from demographic and geographic characteristics, you can also segment according to lifestyle habits, which is very relevant for the fast-changing media landscape. One thing on which everyone concurs is that today's consumers defy easy categorization or description. With the plethora of social media tools available today, it has never been easier to reach an audience— nor harder to engage them. They are fickle media multitaskers, surfing the Internet, chatting online, using their cell phones and watching TV, all at the same time. This has an advantage: namely, that they are more receptive to a wide variety of messages via any channel. But there is also a drawback:

their dwindling attention spans. In spite of, or perhaps because of, so much constant stimuli, they are binge watchers, viewing several episodes of a series back-to-back in one sitting—but it has to be a show worth them investing their time and attention. Their ideas about gender roles, categories and depictions are also less fixed, with three-quarters of women watching programs intended for men, said Gutfreund.

With consumers behaving so differently within each segment, and moving so much between segments, managers really need to question the assumptions upon which they do their market segmentation. Are age, income, gender and geography the correct bases? Is there even such a thing as the "average" customer that is homogeneous in his or her behavior and thinking?

It is important to give this careful consideration, because your subsequent marketing strategy will be positioned according to the behavioral rules of the segment you wish to target. In positioning yourself, you are essentially asking: Who am I? Who are my competitors? What do I offer? What is the reason for them to believe me (the why)?

Many pundits believe it was the failure to adequately address these fundamental questions that kept TiVo, the original digital video recorder, from ever taking off. Despite having a genuinely disruptive product on its hands, the benefits weren't obvious to the consumer. Was it just a souped-up VCR? Yet another set-top box to buy? And the price point was too high for the average consumer to justify the expense, especially if they didn't grasp the benefits. By the time consumers woke up to the joys of skipping commercials and watching programs whenever they wanted—in other words, the instant streaming, on-demand reality that we take for granted today—the market conditions had shifted, and there were other, cheaper services widely available. TiVo is a cautionary tale of how, even with a superior, game-changing product on your hands, it counts for little if you aren't able to position it properly, with observable benefits aimed at the right target.

Allied to this, you need to anticipate what you will do if certain scenarios come to pass, such as how the competition may react. If you have got the segmentation wrong from the start, you will take aim at the wrong target, and your positioning scenarios will be woefully misguided.

A more useful approach may be to segment consumers according to social moods and value shifts—what the historians William Strauss and Neil Howe refer to as "turnings," when people change how they feel about themselves, the culture, the nation and the future [9]. This may yield better market groupings that resonate beyond facile descriptors like age, income, gender and geography.

Gutfreund used the example of Gen Y and Gen Z. The cutoff ages between the two can be blurry. One way of distinguishing the split, she said, is according to their defining moments. For some, it's pre–9/11 and post–9/11, between the idealists and those who see the world as a much darker place. For others, it's Edward Snowden the hero versus Edward Snowden the traitor, when the actions of the whistleblower divided people into camps over the acceptable limits of information privacy.

Apart from coming up with some key differentials like these, so that your market segments are clearly distinguishable from each other, an effective segmentation must be measureable, substantial, accessible and actionable. Each segment requires a distinct marketing offer, so you don't want your segments to be too small or narrow, as gathering the variables on them will get costly and you could end up targeting outliers, which won't be profitable.

Pause for Thought

Is my market segmentation right? What other variables should I be looking at?

What are the behavioral rules of my target?

What are the possible positioning concepts for each target segment?

How should I adjust my current positioning?

How am I setting the terms of the competitive game?

What steps can I take now in anticipation of how my competitor might react, which would put them on the back foot?

Going to Market: Designing and Managing Channels of Distribution

Now you are ready to develop a marketing plan, which consists of 4 Ps:

- **Product:** what is your brand's identity and what associations do you want it to have in the customer's mind?
- **Price:** Chap. 2 on Strategy has a full discussion on price-setting strategies but suffice to say here that your price will be set somewhere between the cost to the firm and the willingness of the customer to pay, and how much leeway you have there depends on how well you have differentiated yourself in the customer's mind so they are willing to pay more for your brand.
- **Place:** otherwise known as your distribution channels.
- **Promotion:** this is your actual marketing communication—what you say, how you say it, to whom you say it and how you will evaluate its success.

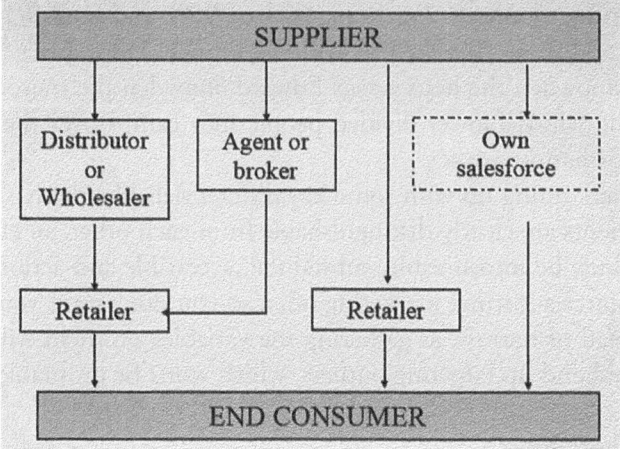

Fig. 4.2   Going to Market: The Traditional Way

Rather than dwell on these basics, in this section I want to focus on the distribution strategy. The media industry is facing the most profound transformation in this regard. New technology and consumer trends are creating new channels of distribution that threaten the very existence of many incumbent players. This requires new strategies to go to market.

Traditionally, the distribution process to get your product/service to market looked something like the figure below. Firms had to go through the usual intermediaries or perform the intermediary functions themselves. Where they could cut out the middlemen, they would, as naturally you want the shortest channel possible between you and your customer (Fig. 4.2).

Think of the newspaper business: it used to need delivery vans, kiosks, home deliverers and so on just to get its core product into the hands of the reader in time for breakfast. Now, the Internet has eliminated the need for all those intermediaries, which, on the face of it, should mean a shorter channel, making it cheaper for the newspaper to reach readers and put more control back in the hands of the business.

In reality, it is not working out that way. The balance of power has indeed shifted away from those old intermediaries, but instead of going back to the business, it has gone toward a new set of intermediaries—to the digital platform providers.

Zinio is a good example. This online kiosk converts magazines to digital formats so they can be read on multiple devices. If you are a magazine, you pay to be distributed there and take a small percentage of any sales. The concern is, there is little selectivity and Zinio cross-sells your product with other

Fig. 4.3 Going to Market: The New Ecosystem

titles—and you are just one of thousands of other titles. In some ways, your magazine might be better positioned in your old physical corner kiosk. In theory, an online channel partner like Zinio should give you more scale to off-set your loss of power, but the results so far are mixed. What you end up with is a new ecosystem model of distribution with some advantages but complex new challenges (Fig. 4.3).

Movie distribution is another example, as a guest speaker who works for an international movie distribution company made clear during the Media AMP. The new digital ecosystem has made her job easier, she said: "On the plus side, it has become much cheaper, as we just beam a signal via satellite." She showed how she could just punch up a video on her iPad and send the file to the theater via a content delivery network (CDN). She is able to release the content simultaneously in theaters and through video-on-demand (VOD) systems. The latter is especially important in countries like Spain, where VOD surpasses DVDs. "We are going straight for VOD the way you used to release straight to DVD. This means no more DVD packaging costs," she says. "And we are able to reach audiences the way they want to consume."

But it is not all good news. First, the initial conversion costs to go from manual to digital distribution and exhibition have had to be absorbed by the traditional players. Taking a short-term hit may be tenable if you are able to renegotiate a better position for yourself in the new ecosystem.

Which brings us to the second, more critical issue going forward: in a world where content producers can reach their audiences directly, what exactly is the role of the distributor anymore? As with the music industry, when physical assets become instantly shareable virtually, the distributor has to find another way to add value, or its place in the ecosystem will be made redundant. Is it about becoming a better rights manager for the plethora of platforms that are emerging on which to distribute content? Is it about offering better marketing promotion and pricing of content targeted at specific segments in the "long tail" of media assets?

What we see increasingly are companies going for vertical integration—content producers like Disney owning the theaters in which its musicals are performed, or new media providers like Netflix now producing their own content. This is genuinely disruptive. Netflix has already signaled the shift by dropping major distribution deals—first with Starz in 2012 and then with Epix in 2015—in favor of positioning itself as the self-styled provider of more original, exclusive content. This leaves the distributers of Hollywood block-buster fare having to negotiate new deals with other VOD services. They want to get their content out there, but the more platforms they do distribution deals with, the more that intermediaries like Netflix react to differentiate themselves.

But even owning a large part of the distribution network is no guarantee of controlling the marketing channel, as is illustrated by a case I have done on the Shubert Organization. This company owns and operates 17 Broadway theaters, as well as Shubert Ticketing and Telecharge.com to provide box-office sales, telephone sales, Internet sales, season and subscription sales, group sales and more. You would think they would have their marketing needs locked up. But the new digital ecosystem is making their job even harder. Search for "Broadway musicals" online and the top search result in Google is Broadway.com, an independent broker that sells tickets above list price. Prospective theatergoers will unknowingly pay the higher price, or they will angrily not pay for such an expensive ticket at all. Either way, Shubert loses out.

What can you do if you find yourself losing through the crowded online channel where a multitude of other ticket brokers and resellers vie for consumer attention? The high-earning, 55-to-65-year-old woman who may still buy a ticket by turning up at the box office is a dying breed. Shubert knows it has to attract more families, ethnic groups who don't have the habit of going to the theater, and youth—none of whom has the disposable income to fork over $100-plus a ticket for a couple hours' worth of entertainment.

The Hollywood marketing channels need to change, too, as Peter Bart explained: "The fascinating anomaly is that the studios have totally focused on the youth demo. Yet surveys indicate that the average frequent moviegoer in his early 20s owns at least four devices, multiple devices. That's obviously competing for their attention. That's what they want to do. My youngest daughter, for example, watches movies on her handheld and she hasn't been to the movies in a long time."

The only way to deal with such a proliferation of customer needs and to make yourself stand out in an ever more crowded media marketplace is through multichannel marketing.

Customers today are more knowledgeable: they do their market research online but make their purchase offline, or conversely, they use the physical outlet to do their market research but then make their purchase online. Mobility is huge, especially for group-oriented Millennials, said Jamie Gutfreund: "Seventy-five percent look at online reviews written by other fans, and 84 percent of their purchasing decisions are based on the opinions of friends and family. Ninety percent sleep with their phones within arm's length. Half of consumers aged 12-17 have access to the Web only via mobile." With at least a third of e-commerce clicks coming from a mobile device and rising, what does that tell you? The average person looks at his or her phone 150 times a day—you have to be top of mind in one of those 150 opportunities. Yet I continue to be amazed by how many websites are not mobile friendly.

Writing in *IESE Insight* magazine, Nueno states: "Companies have to make the most of all opportunities to interact with and relate to their customers at every stage of the marketing process. Social networks have become much more than platforms for self-promotion. A few years ago, brands were content to create Facebook fan pages, Twitter accounts, YouTube channels and blogs for sharing information of interest, with the aim of attracting followers and eventually converting them into customers. Today, they can sell directly through these channels. Sites such as Pinterest, where communities form according to interest, have seen spectacular growth and are turning into huge product recommendation platforms. Companies should not let channel proliferation or the rise of new media overwhelm them. To persuade the new consumer, they must arm themselves with a marketing strategy that integrates the various channels and uses each channel in the most appropriate way for each type of customer" [10].

That said, it is worth bearing in mind the observation of another Media AMP executive who said: "In a multichannel media environment, it seems rational to think that a traditional distribution channel should be out of business, and yet who knows? It only seems rational based on today's information. And if there's one thing I've learned in this new media landscape, it's that nothing stays constant. There are always new disruptors, so by tomorrow the terms of the competitive game may have changed yet again, and the interme-diary that seemed redundant by today's standards may well be in a new posi-tion of strength." As we live in this in-between state of affairs, we have to stay open-minded and ready for anything.

Media executives need to strike a tricky balance. If you divest your-self too much or too quickly of traditional channels in order to embrace the new, you may end up hurting yourself. Multichannel marketing is not about ditching the traditional channels, which may still serve some role; rather, it is about understanding how all the various channels must work together.

In order to navigate a multichannel environment, managers need to become equally multichannel in their thinking, developing what the Harvard Business School professor Michael Tushman calls "ambidexterity" [11]. Just like being able to use both hands equally well, media managers need to build marketing strategies that can attend to disparate logics at the same time.

Take the example of a traditional approach: an advertising agency pro-duces a slick TV commercial costing millions of dollars. Then along comes a start-up that produces a low-budget commercial through crowdsourcing—perhaps not as slick but just as effective in terms of brand-building and reaching the target audience, at a fraction of the cost. If you are the tra-ditional agency, how do you regard the start-up: as competency destroy-ing or as competency enhancing? Actually, it's both, and an "ambidextrous" response would be to do what Havas Media Group did when faced with precisely this scenario in 2012: it went and acquired a majority stake in Victors & Spoils.

As Tushman explained in research he shared at IESE: "This move dem-onstrates that Havas was at least prepared to embrace new technology and a very different business model from its own. Perhaps for Havas the move was nothing more than a preemptive strike against a competitive threat that it regarded as competency destroying. But maybe Havas real-ized something else, too: that open, distributed, peer-to-peer, community innovation is here to stay. As such, bringing game-changers like Victors & Spoils into the fold guarantees Havas' own future—it is competency enhancing—as the company manages the tension between the 'old world' of innovation (one that depends on all creativity coming from inside the organization) and 'the new.' Solution-seeking organizations need to be on the lookout for this, learning how to adapt and benefit from these disruptions" [12].

Digital Marketing: A New Marketing Paradigm

There has been perhaps no greater change affecting marketing in recent years than the rise of social media. Marketers have always had to allocate budgets, opting either to "push" marketing messages on consumers or to be "pulled" by consumers who dictated the terms of the marketing effort. Social media have not only tipped the balance in favor of the latter approach, but in many cases consumers can cut out the marketers altogether and do their own marketing by talking among themselves. Today it is the consumers who control brand. This makes the job of marketing more challenging—but also more exciting and potentially more rewarding.

Take a quick straw poll among the people in your office to see how many of them use the following social media—Facebook, Twitter, LinkedIn, Pinterest, Instagram, Foursquare—or how many of them blog. By "user" I mean an active, daily user, and not a work account but for personal, non-work use. What surprises you most about your findings? How are they using these media? The important thing to realize about social media is that it is no longer a question of whether you should be present there or not; the fact is, you (and they) are there already, whether you consciously want to be or not.

One journalist commented that the rules of her profession dictated that she had to maintain a semblance of objectivity and neutrality at all times. "You're not allowed to take sides," she said. "Sometimes the best thing is to stay quiet and not engage in these media."

That's debatable. It is true that journalists don't think like marketers, and marketers don't think like journalists. But increasingly they need to start working together. Marketers can learn from journalists how to construct compelling storylines that connect with audiences, while journalists can learn from marketers how to make sure their stories are delivered through the best channels so they can generate conversations around an event or a cause.

Marketers sometimes fall down when it comes to content, bombing unsubtle promotional messages at consumers, which is not what they want. "Millennials don't want pre-packaged, off-the-shelf brands," said Gutfreund. "They want to be part of the story and its trajectory, knowing that they influenced the direction in some way. They want to be involved in the process. They're not just 'consumers,' they're 'investors.' As such, they don't mind ads so long as they are relevant to their needs and interests, and engage them in some meaningful way—making them feel part of something larger, with some community or emotional aspect."

And it is not just Millennials who are like this. It may have started with them, but more and more people think this way, said Gutfreund. "We want the context for the news: how does this affect me, what's the backstory, how can I get involved? We look for the infographics, to see this story's place in history." Is it any wonder that one of the most talked-about media launches of 2014 was Vox.com whose motto is "Explain the news"? Its clickable headlines are all variations of "X Explained," "Why X Matters," "Here's What X Means" and "X in Maps and Charts."

No matter your personal level of engagement with social media, everyone needs to capitalize on this trend to a degree: some might be in social media only as observers, monitoring what is being said but not being proactively involved. That is a basic step, to at least be exposed to the tide of opinion out there, and to catch any dirty laundry being aired about your brand, which will show up online, so it is best to be prepared. The point is, you have to "be there" in some way, shape or form.

Think about it: for the first time you are able to be in direct contact and communication with people who "like" you, on a scale unheard of before. One journalist uses her Facebook page to take the pulse of readers. Another uses Facebook to connect in real time with listeners to her radio show, where they upload photos and share feedback. The goodwill and audience insights gained from such interactions can be priceless.

Facebook knows this, which is why it invests so heavily in wooing businesses to pay for advertising to reach desired segments. However, as great of an advertising platform as Facebook is, you don't always have to pay a social media provider what you used to pay a newspaper to advertise. You can save money by running your own social media campaigns—especially if the aim is chiefly to build awareness, positive associations and engagement. Ad spots used to do that, but increasingly today's social media conversations can do that for free. That is their beauty.

Again, it is not about ditching one for the other but of understanding how social media marketing fits as part of the whole marketing mix and being ambidextrous in managing them together. Traditional media, like television, still enjoy the greatest reach, and big established brands will continue to favor TV advertising—for now. But as the Internet increasingly replaces television as the main channel of leisure, you have to be positioned to make the switch, going from using social media as a complement to television, to the other way around as market needs demand.

Whichever medium, you need to be clear about the marketing objectives for each. Is it to attract new customers? Hear what people are saying about you? Get mentions? Become an opinion leader? Promote something? Is it for information or for entertainment?

It goes without saying that you need to have content. But what social media underscore is that, beyond having content, it needs to be *relevant* content. As the saying goes, content is king, but context is queen. What is the genuine conversation around your brand? Too many brands fall down on this point, thinking, like Kevin Costner's character in *Field of Dreams*, "If we build it, they will come." In social media terms, they won't—not without a compelling reason that connects with them personally and that they care about passionately. As the Ogilvy & Mather advertising veteran Shelly Lazarus quipped, "Advertisers just have to understand that when we go to Facebook, it's not to have a relationship with Wish-Bone Salad Dressing. Forget it. Give it up. It's not working for us." But if companies learn to get it right, social media platforms have the potential to institutionalize word of mouth. "And there's nothing as powerful in advertising and marketing as word of mouth. For your friend to tell you, 'I tried this, and it's amazing,' that's almost a sure sale," said Lazarus [13].

Movies are one of the best illustrations of how word of mouth, or WOM, affects sales, given the decisive role that personal recommendations play in getting potential spectators to actually go to the theater. Even the Oscars are essentially a sort of movie industry WOM. Simply being nominated for an Oscar (never mind actually winning it) generates more audience and more revenue. Social media networks have this same kind of signaling effect in the way they reinforce and amplify messages.

Guillermo Armelini, Jorge Gonzalez and I once carried out a study of movie releases to measure the impact—and interrelationships—of three key variables on movie success: paid-for advertising, publicity (i.e. media presence that hadn't been paid for) and the conversations generated among potential and actual spectators. One of our conclusions was that WOM about a movie in social networks always had a positive impact on box-office revenue, independent of any prior advertising investment [14].

Given findings such as this, it is vital to understand how social media work, as electronic word of mouth (e-WOM) obeys very different rules from traditional advertising. By distinguishing between the two, it helps to see when one or the other might be more appropriate.

	Traditional advertising	Social media e-WOM
Reach	Mass market	Targeted communities
Credibility	Limited	High
Control	Full control over message, medium and frequency	Stimulated, but not controlled
Interactivity	Less scope for reaction or subsequent adjustment	Highly interactive and immediate
Intrusiveness	Message may be annoying, in content or frequency	Voluntary and consensual
Cost	High, among the most expensive	Low, though some hidden costs
Brand	Plays a decisive role in awareness and recognition, increasing brand value	Enhances brand value when positive, but no guarantee that comments will be favorable, and negative e-WOM can do serious brand damage
Sales	Stimulates interest and short-term sales elasticity, but better for "push" than "pull"	Correlation between conversations and behavior (sales), with strong "pull" effect
Products/ Services	Useful for informing the consumer of existence of products/services	Less useful for informing consumer of existence, better for encouraging consumption of products/services
Context	Generally works in all cultures	Frequency and intensity seem greater in more collective societies

As with any marketing plan, you need to consider the best means of communicating with your intended audience. If you cannot act transparently, if your product/service is not the kind that generates conversations, or if there are reputational risks, such as the very real possibility of generating hostile conversations, then perhaps you should hold back from, or keep a low profile on, social media. Decide exactly on which platforms you want to be, as well as the type of content (knowledge, promotions, applications, games), the user participation model (comments, surveys) and the balance between content and selling (with the rule of thumb being firstly inform, secondly entertain, thirdly interact and lastly sell). Finally, be sure to establish metrics to assess whether you have met your goals. Is it the number of registrations, ideas or conversations? Number of followers, recommendations or mentions? Always make sure the results are proportional to the investment.

Question: Looking at the previous table, if you worked in the movie business, how would you choose to market a blockbuster (with high production costs, requiring a big-bang hit) versus a sleeper (with lower costs, whose success builds on a slow boil)?

Admittedly, deciding what strategy to pursue is not easy. As many companies are unsure of the effectiveness of social media, they just continue to spend where they know it still works (traditional advertising). That may work for the time being, but ask yourself: when do you need to start caring or worrying? Even though you may be doing quite well without social media marketing today, you don't want to end up like the proverbial boiled frog that didn't jump out of hot water until it was too late. Though the evolving digital realm can be confusing, with no tried-and-tested formulas or recipes, you have to do some experiments and start placing some bets today. If it feels to you like playing a (more or less educated) guessing game, take comfort from the fact that everyone else feels the same, and the ones who are making advances in digital marketing are those who have tried and failed more times. One Media AMP executive recommended allocating, say, 10 percent of your marketing budget to experimental campaigns, which may even be considered a write-off. The point is, you need to be doing something.

Creating Customer Value: The Marketing of Experiences

Most readers will be familiar with the marketing funnel, which depicts the stages of a customer journey leading to acquisition and retention. Historically, this was treated as a linear process, with the marketing effort designed to intervene at key moments to influence the consumer in funneling down their choice-sets until they eventually "buy" and afterwards tell all their friends (Fig. 4.4).

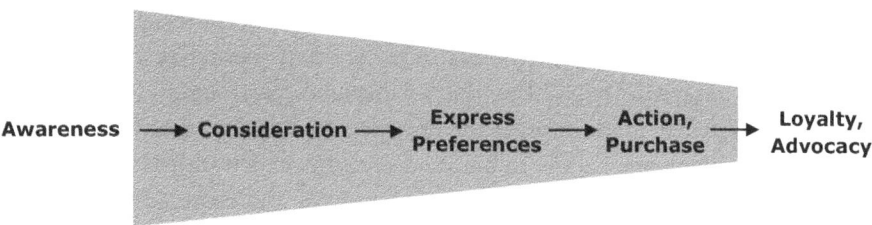

Fig. 4.4   The Marketing Funnel

However, given the new digital paradigm, this journey is no longer linear or sequential. In fact, many brands don't consider "awareness," "consideration" and "expressing preferences" as intermediary steps to the end goal but as strategic opportunities to extend reach, create fans, strengthen engagement and even take action or buy in parallel. Moreover, all these "touchpoints" occur simultaneously and immediately in time and space, and the best lever to optimize them is by offering your customers *experiences*.

Jamie Gutfreund expanded on this idea: "The majority of Millennials say that, rather than buying a cool product, they would much prefer buying a cool experience, which they can share on social media and earn social capital for themselves. In this day and age when you can know everything beforehand—for example, when you can pirate the movie before it is released—the 'extra' you pay for by actually going to the theater is to have a shared experience." (She gave the example of Secret Cinema, which is analyzed in Chap. 7 on Operations Management.)

This goes back to Peter Bart's *Love Story* movie anecdote. Even though digital is changing the marketing approach, he says, "I'm retro enough to believe firmly that the experience of seeing a movie in a theater will forever be important. There's simply no substitute for sharing, say, a comedy. Experience is the key now and always will be."

Growing numbers of companies are on-board. D-Box, for instance, integrates motion systems into seats at movie theaters, museums and planetariums to create immersive experiences that synchronize velocity, engine vibrations and vehicle dynamics to the on-screen action. Several filmmakers have been experimenting with breaking the fourth wall by getting moviegoers to download apps before the movie begins. At certain points in the movie, audience members receive messages in real time. In one movie, the actors on screen call audience members for help, and depending on the answers given, the story unfolds in different directions, meaning that it is the audience that controls the story arc, and the same movie can have entirely different endings.

Jose L. Nueno stresses that this need for experiences is not just limited to domains that have always been associated with providing escapist entertainment; even traditional media like newspapers need to appreciate this shift. The big challenge facing print media today is often framed as an economic one: how to monetize news? But that's a mistake, says Nueno. News never made money: what made money for newspapers was always advertising. As such, the real challenge is how to boost ad revenue, which ultimately depends on reader engagement. The more readers you have, the more advertisers you attract, and the more you can charge to reach them. And how do you attract and engage the attention of more readers? By offering them experiences. This doesn't mean you have to drop all news stories that fail to entertain. It means understanding your readers' habits and adopting a multichannel approach, as mentioned earlier. Maybe it is ramping up a different mix of content during the weekend when newspaper readership tends to drop off. Maybe it is adopting a hybrid model, one that blends offline and online worlds—turning newspapers into radio or TV by offering more audiovisual or multimedia content, or blending radio with imagery.

A useful exercise is to take each of your key customer segments and plot their touchpoints according to the actual channels they use. As shown by Table 4.1, one segment might become aware of your brand via friends on Facebook; do their research online; get advice in mobile chat forums; go to the store, kiosk, theater, and so on, to purchase; and then spread the word by posting comments or returning feedback online. Another might go to the store, kiosk, theater, and so on, to find out about your brand; do their research in mobile chat forums; express "likes" on Facebook and post photos on Instagram; purchase online; and then give feedback by posting a YouTube video review. By depicting the funnel this way, you can take targeted marketing actions aimed at heightening the experience at just the right moment, in the appropriate channel.

Try mapping the consumer journey for your own business, looking for those key moments when you can intrigue and surprise the consumer, respecting the human psychological need for adventure, transcendence, awe, wonder and delight. Don't just think of one marketing idea and run with that one. You have to take a multidisciplinary approach, prototyping various ideas, and discarding those that don't work, before you arrive at the marketing plan that works. As one Media AMP executive rightly observed, this requires striking a careful balance between pragmatism (making a profit) and passion (doing it just for fun). Though paradoxical, in modern media marketing you cannot have just one or the other—you have to have both. The management of creative marketing is not a momentary brainstorm but demands a serious dedication of time.

Table 4.1   Plot your customer touchpoints by the different channels they use

Channel	Awareness	Consideration	Preferences	Action/Purchase	Loyalty/Advocacy
Website					
Social Media					
Mobile					
Real World					

Question: How much time are you dedicating toward reconceiving your marketing funnel and intentionally thinking of new ways to heighten consumer engagement through experiences?

Outside-in: A Change of Mindset

Reconceiving your value chain is the most useful but also the most painful thing you can do. Useful, in that the information on consumers available today is rich and plentiful, enabling you to identify and address blind spots like never before, in real time. Painful, in that because there is so much information, it takes that much more work. There are companies available to do the work for you (Conzoom.com springs to mind) but you do not have to pay for everything. There are free tools available. However, you do need to have a team dedicated to systematically collecting data on your marketing funnel.

In addition, this team needs people with the right sensitivity, as Nueno explains: "Market research used to be about knowing what question to ask, and framing the question to get an answer. Today, it's a case of having lots of answers, and then knowing what to ask yourself to understand the answers in front of you. It is a completely different mindset. Instead of interrupting and asking, it is about listening and observing, and learning how to interpret the answers."

Do you have this sensibility in your organization? "You need to have a healthy workplace culture where this is encouraged in a deliberate, conscious way," said Gutfreund. "To know your audience, to speak their language, you have to understand their world. Outside-in thinking is your secret weapon. Get out of your bubble to connect with the market 'out there.' Get some fresh input and inspiration from unlikely quarters, maybe even from other industries, to unleash those serendipitous 'aha' moments." (Chap. 5 on Decisive Leadership makes a similar point, recommending that you "visit your future," looking at how others tackle related problems to yield surprising solutions for your own situation.)

During a visit to IESE's New York Center, Nancy Dubuc, president and CEO of A&E Networks and the History channel, shared a story of how she literally brought consumer-led creativity into her organization.

"We had an incident where we got a call from a studio, upset because they saw a promotional trailer online for *Bates Motel* that we hadn't shared with them, since we usually would share the marketing with them. The producers of the show also saw it and said, 'It's great, but how could you not run it by us?' I had no idea what they were talking about. So I immediately went on

YouTube and found a *Bates Motel* promo, complete with our logo. We traced it back to a 21-year-old fan in Ohio who had produced it himself. He got very scared that he was getting a phone call from the legal department at A&E."

Did they sue? "He was then promptly hired," said Dubuc. "I hope that's a small example of where we can see this going. Technology is getting smaller and more user-friendly. Our online editors in the marketing groups are all doing their own editing on desktop now. That's been happening for years, and hopefully that will continue to get more and more sophisticated. But what I'm the most concerned about is: where are the true creators? Where are the people (like this 21-year-old) who are making and writing and doing this stuff? As the market continues to fragment, and the point of entry keeps getting lower and lower, the biggest challenge with YouTube and all the digital platforms is how do you break through, how do you get noticed? There's such a sea of material out there that it's very hard to find what's good. If you can hold on to your brand as a curator, then you have a winning advantage as relates to your two-way conversation with the consumer. You have to learn to become a curator of great things."

The way Dubuc reacted to this consumer-led initiative suggests a radically different, outside-in mindset, which is how marketing needs to be managed today. Doesn't this also echo Havas' acquisition of Victors & Spoils mentioned earlier?

To become that "curator of great things," able to spot and leverage the myriad opportunities out there, media managers must learn to do marketing in a "mindful" rather than mindless way. The Harvard psychology professor Ellen Langer talks a lot about training your brain to behave in a "mindful" way, derived from decades of research she has done on the topic. When we do things on autopilot—either out of habit or because we have enjoyed some past success by doing it that way before—we unwittingly set traps for ourselves and miss out on vital opportunities for learning, discovery and growth. This is dangerous, says Langer, especially when situations and circumstances change, because we lose the mental agility to process new inputs and fail to act in novel ways appropriate to the new context [15].

Georgetown University Professor Luc Wathieu and I once collaborated on a case study on El Bulli, the world-famous restaurant of chef Ferran Adria. Inspired by Adria and the work of Langer, we developed a conceptual model to understand the impediments to innovation. We grouped them according to two big concepts: walls and frontiers. As you manage marketing in the new media context, you will invariably run up against barriers. In some cases, these can be physical obstacles or constraints that others put before you, such as work silos, lack of time, no resources, short-term targets set by your boss, your board or another management body. We call these "walls," and it is the CEO and board's responsibility to remove some of them.

But there other kinds of barriers, called "frontiers." These exist in the mind. We become trapped by categories and stereotypes; fall back on automatic behavior; act from a single perspective. This is the mindlessness that Langer refers to, and which she says can be overcome through reframing techniques. (Remember the discussion on "breaking the frame" from the opening of this book?) This requires a conscious, daily effort on your part to train your mind to keep your thought patterns in check every time you are tempted to surrender to old habits or fatalistic thinking. The good news is, as conveyed by the word "frontiers," these borders can be crossed; "frontiers" implies a degree of porousness or plasticity that "walls" does not.

Try This Exercise for Yourself and Within Your Teams: *In your company: What are the walls? What are the frontiers?*

In pondering these questions for himself, one Media AMP executive noted that "the broadcasting guys get successful but then don't think they can learn from anyone else. Someone in radio doesn't think across categories and disciplines or beyond current revenue streams. There's a lot of arrogance that comes with success. But many times 'success' for them means they've just perfected the art of doing the same thing hundreds of times over."

Another executive added: "The journalist's mind is conditioned to deliver to an agreed story format. There's an automatic way you approach a story. The perception of what 'success' means is defined by a predefined set of news values that the industry rewards as successful."

Other executives suggested that ethical or legal compliance issues could be walls or frontiers, alternatively putting constraints on or releasing creative freedom, depending on the circumstances and how you approached them.

Being able to conceive of your media challenges in this way is the first step in being able to solve them. But it takes humility to learn from others—and that is a quality in short supply in the media and entertainment industry.

So as Peter Bart alleged, is marketing to blame for ruining the media and entertainment industry? It depends on whether you perceive marketing as a wall or frontier. The Hollywood studio structure, with its huge overheads, certainly throws up plenty of walls for delivering big-screen entertainment. But there are plenty of new frontiers, particularly when it comes to your channel. Bart quotes studio exec Jeffrey Katzenberg, who predicted that before long movies will be released ubiquitously in a variety of formats to suit customers' viewing preferences, with prices set according to screen size. Instead of competing with the small screen, Hollywood can embrace it as a new outlet to market its content [16].

Bart also likes Katzenberg's advice to the next generation who will need to manage these challenges: "People used to tell young people, 'Follow your dream.' That's bull. Follow your skill. If you're good at something, pursue that, because it's a lot better bet than trying to figure out what your dreams are."

To put it another way, even in an industry whose lifeblood is artistic creativity, you need to be properly skilled in business basics like marketing. Then you have a shot at building and sustaining a dream brand.

References

1. J. Villanueva (2015), "What Business Are You in Again?" *IESE Insight* magazine, Second Quarter, Issue 25.
2. T. Levitt (1960), "Marketing Myopia," *Harvard Business Review*, July–August Issue.
3. R.J. Dolan (1997, Revised 2000), "Note on Marketing Strategy," Harvard Business School Background Note.
4. T. Levitt (1983), *The Marketing Imagination* (The Free Press/Simon & Schuster).
5. A. Parasuraman, V.A. Zeithaml and L.L. Berry (1985), "A Conceptual Model of Service Quality and Its Implications for Future Research," *Journal of Marketing*, Vol. 49, Issue 4, 41–50.
6. N. Kano, N. Seraku, F. Takahashi and S. Tsuji (1984), "Attractive Quality and Must-Be Quality," *Journal of the Japanese Society for Quality Control*, Vol. 14, Issue 2, 39–48.
7. J.L. Nueno (2011), "Teens Today, Young Adults in 2020," *IESE Insight* magazine, First Quarter, Issue 8.
8. N. Howe and W. Strauss (2000), *Millennials Rising: The Next Great Generation* (Vintage).
9. W. Strauss and N. Howe (1997), *The Fourth Turning* (Broadway Books).
10. J.L. Nueno (2013), "The Decline of Main Street, the Rise of Multichannel Retail," *IESE Insight* magazine, Fourth Quarter, Issue 19, p. 53.
11. M. Tushman (2014), "Leadership Tips for Today to Stay in the Game Tomorrow," *IESE Insight* magazine, Fourth Quarter, Issue 23.
12. M. Tushman (2014), "Leadership Tips for Today to Stay in the Game Tomorrow," *IESE Insight* magazine, Fourth Quarter, Issue 23, p. 35–36.
13. S. Lazarus (2012), "Shelly Lazarus: Social Media Platforms Still Have a Way to Go," IESE Insight Business Knowledge Portal, http://www.ieseinsight.com/fichaMaterial.aspx?pk=94641&idi=2&origen=1&ar=5&
14. G. Armelini and J. Villanueva (2011), "Adding Social Media to the Marketing Mix," *IESE Insight* magazine, Second Quarter, Issue 9.
15. E. Langer (1989, 2014), *Mindfulness* (A Merloyd Lawrence Book/Da Capo Press).
16. BBC News' Technology section (April 30, 2014), "Film Download Prices 'To Be Determined by Screen Size'," http://www.bbc.com/news/technology-27223622

5

Decisive Leadership: Leaders That Create Extraordinary Outcomes

Mike Rosenberg, Iris Firstenberg, with Philip H. Seager

People are complex beings, yet most educational systems reduce us to one of two kinds, asking us to choose at an early age whether to pursue Science/Math or Liberal Arts/Letters. Chances are, if you work in the media or entertainment industry, you are a creative type who gravitated toward the latter. You tend to see the world in terms of ideas, emotions and feelings rather than numbers. You have a strong capacity for abstract thinking, for assimilating opposites, for interpreting facts and for setting them within a larger context. You like adventure and enjoy unplanned surprises. You are more likely to rely on flashes of insight or intuition to decide what to do in a given situation instead of just crunching the numbers.

For someone living in this new millennium, this is not a bad type to be. In the past, people's access to information was limited. A seventeenth-century English gentleman, for example, was likely exposed to less information in

M. Rosenberg (✉)
Strategic Management Department, IESE Business School, Barcelona, Spain
e-mail: MRosenberg@iese.edu

I. Firstenberg
UCLA Anderson School of Management, Los Angeles, CA, USA
e-mail: ifirsten@gmail.com

P.H. Seager
IESE Business School, Barcelona, Spain
e-mail: PSeager@iese.edu

© The Author(s) 2017
M. Rosenberg, P.H. Seager (eds.), *Managing Media Businesses*,
DOI 10.1007/978-3-319-52021-6_5

his entire lifetime than there is today in a single edition of a daily newspaper. When confronting new situations, he had little choice but to rely on tried-and-tested categories and labels in order to make a rational decision based on the information available to him at the time.

Today, however, we have access to a wealth of information. The new age before us demands that we form new categories and labels and look for differences, not just similarities, between past and present experiences in order to take action based on evolving interpretations of fast-incoming information. Change is rapid, and we must learn not only to accept chaos and uncertainty as everyday realities, but also to embrace them as opportunities. Creative people generally have high tolerance levels for this.

Omar Essack is one such case. A man of Letters, he pursued an Arts degree with majors in Literature and Drama and earned a postgraduate diploma in Education. He started his career as a teacher while freelancing as a radio presenter during an unpopular Sunday evening shift at a local radio station. Over time he began doing more radio and less teaching—until one day, at the age of 31, he found himself as the Managing Director of East Coast Radio in South Africa.

"I was young," he recalls. "I had no management training. I was surrounded by people who had been in the business for longer and were expecting to be appointed to the position. On my first day, I brought the entire team into the boardroom to present my vision for the station. Our world was changing quickly but the station was caught in a time warp, staffed by talent who had spent their lives working in a context and an environment that were no longer relevant. We needed to change and reposition ourselves. There were very few people in that meeting who owed me any loyalty or respect. A title meant nothing and I knew it was up to me to win their support. That respect would only come if I was able to bring them along with me. Looking back now, I can see I was driven more by my conscience and intuition than by any great strategic smarts."

Essack, like many others with similar backgrounds, found himself as a manager with a business problem unlike any he had faced before. This wasn't a structured problem, like flipping a switch to go to a commercial break, but an unstructured problem for which there was no single, clear-cut solution; indeed, there were an untold number of ways he could play that meeting and an equally unpredictable variety of outcomes.

This is what distinguishes a manager from a technician. Good technicians solve problems by following certain approved steps or protocols that have been proven to work in defined situations; they may even have to work in cooperation with other technicians to get the job done. Managers, on the other hand, may be master technicians, but they do something more. Yes, they have to get results and achieve desired goals, but they do it not just by enlisting the help of other people, but by working through and for other people as well. This entails certain qualities of charisma, emotional intelligence and moral authority, so that people learn and grow through the management process, and everyone emerges with a stronger sense of purpose and identification with the larger business project. It is to achieve something almost transcendental, where people are not just a means to an end, but the connection they share becomes an end in itself.

This chapter details a six-step process for resolving unstructured problems like the one Essack faced. It also reveals some key leadership principles that will help people use all facets of their complex natures—the rational and the intuitive—to match the highly complex situations being thrust upon them as managers in creative fields.

Pause for Thought

How has my background influenced who I am and where I find myself today?
What can I draw on to face the professional challenges before me?
What am I missing?

Making a Decision in Six Steps

IESE Business School works with a six-step process for dealing with unstructured problems—that is, problems that require a combination of fact-based data analysis and highly subjective, even intuitive judgments about aspects of the problem (Fig. 5.1).

1. **Define the Problem.** In our results-driven world, when confronted with a problem, our first impulse is to do something about it: we want solutions and we want them fast.

Say you have two containers, one with 1000 red marbles and the other with a 1000 blue ones. You are about to deliver them to a client when someone tells

Fig. 5.1 A six-step process for dealing with unstructured problems

you that six blue marbles have somehow gotten mixed up in the red container. You only have a minute to fix it. The client is waiting. What would you do?

Maybe you dump them out and start sorting. Maybe you develop a mathematical model to calculate how to move the blue marbles back to the blue container using the fewest moves in the least amount of time. On the rare occasion someone might ask, "Does it matter?" Good question. Does the client actually care about the mix-up? Do the colors have to be separated or does the client only want two containers of 1000 marbles? In which case, just take any six marbles out of the red container and move them over to the blue one. Problem solved.

This illustrates a key lesson: before thinking about solutions, make sure you understand the exact nature of the problem.

For one thing, you want to make sure you are treating the root causes and not just the symptoms. A separate issue has to do with scope. You need to define the problem in such a way that it is within your authority and ability to solve.

Going back to Omar Essack, he had a formidable problem on his hands: how to convince the entire radio station staff as well as the listening public that East Coast Radio was no longer a station for white listeners only, but that it would become a station that truly reflected and united black, white, Indian and every other people of color as part of the new Rainbow Nation envisaged by the newly democratic and free South Africa of the time.

"Worse than nobody believing in my vision," recalls Essack, "the one person to challenge me in front of everyone was the station's star anchor, the voice and face of the radio station for 13 years, who commanded the respect of everyone in the room. The last thing I needed in my first days was a confrontation with the station's most valuable asset. The boardroom fell silent when the anchor said, 'Some of the smartest people in the country have tried to do what you're saying we should do, and they have failed miserably. Why should we believe that you can do it?' It was a direct challenge to my authority. The entire team was watching. It was my first day at work."

Some might say the problem is too big and do nothing. Others might say the problem is the anchor's antagonism or Essack's lack of experience. The key is to define the right problem. Is it really about changing the minds of an entire nation—or is it about earning credibility in the eyes of the staff? Formulate the problem in a way that is manageable. Rather than, "How can I convince every single person in this room of the brilliance of my vision," perhaps the real question is "How can I win over this anchor," or "What else can I do to win support from the staff in the absence of the support of this anchor?" Instead of changing the direction of the radio station overnight,

"How can I introduce changes to the playlist? During which slots? For which audiences?" These are bite-size problems that you can do something about.

2. **Select the Criteria.** Once you have defined the right problem to tackle, you next need to consider all the issues surrounding the problem and select the ones that are most critical to you being able to make a decision. The word "select" is key, because you have to be selective. The issues will be endless, as any problem will invariably involve customers, employees, suppliers and various other stakeholders with vested interests in the outcome. Your job is to distinguish between the interests and then select which criteria you will use to go about solving the problem.

To some degree, this step is closely allied with the definition of the problem. If, for example, your problem is "lack of job safety," you need to select some criteria by which you will measure the problem. Number of workers injured? The cost to the company in lost production? Public perception of your company? Each of these measures defines the problem differently and will influence the type of solutions considered.

In general, your criteria will include a tangible aspect related to the problem you want to fix, a measure of risk and something that takes account of the human element involved in making the decision. For Essack, he decided to hone in on the playlist. "I wanted to start by fixing the product. I was warned that I was trying to be all things to all people. So my first area of focus became the playlist, and I held back on marketing initiatives for the time being."

In introducing a new playlist to become a more inclusive radio station, Essack knew that this would imply changes to the presenters in terms of their training as well as recruiting new profiles to ensure adoption of the new direction.

3. **Develop Alternatives.** Alternatives are the different ways that you can go about solving the problem. The fact that unstructured problems have an infinite number of alternatives is why going through the previous steps is so essential.

Take a simple example: when moving to a new city, your problem might be, "Where should I live?" The alternatives would be all the different neighborhoods. Then you have the question of which real-estate transaction to make. If you have framed the problem as, "Where can I afford to live with the amount of money I have," then the alternatives might be buying a large house in a cheap neighborhood or a small house in a wealthy neighborhood.

But if one criterion was to be close to work so as not to have a long commute, then your alternatives might be between buying an apartment downtown or renting one. Your definition of the problem and the criteria you select to solve it will condition the set of alternatives available to you, so be sure to invest time in these steps.

4. **Do an Analysis.** Armed with this information, you are ready to analyze the various alternatives against the criteria you have selected. It helps to plot these on a grid. The analysis should be both numerical and subjective.

	Alternative 1	Alternative 2	Alternative 3
Criterion 1: Music	++	+	−
Criterion 2: Staff	−	−	++
Criterion 3: Financials	+	++	−

Let's analyze Essack's problem to change the tone of the station. Criterion 1 is to broadcast music that has universal appeal across racial divides. A focus group reveals that Alternative 1—adult mainstream pop or adult contemporary chart music such as Bryan Adams, Celine Dion, Whitney Houston, Michael Jackson, Lionel Richie and Simply Red—is equally loved by white, black and Indian listeners. Alternative 2—1980s synth pop—is liked by some groups but not by all. Alternative 3—heavy guitar rock music—is polarizing and the least liked by all.

Criterion 2 concerns the staff reaction to the changes. After discussing the proposed musical shifts with the team, the music manager is strongly opposed to the all-pop playlist. As someone with a PhD in music, she sees it as her duty to maintain a varied playlist and she personally loves rock-influenced songs, which she says she will insist on playing no matter what.

Criterion 3 would involve some numerical analysis, as with any business decision you will want to factor the potential impacts on the bottom line. Without using any actual numbers from Essack, for argument's sake, let's say that the best result would be a modest adjustment to the playlist, recognizing that continuing along the same path would lead to a loss of listeners and advertising revenue, while introducing a completely new format might spell short-term pain but long-term gain.

Doing this analysis is a way of depicting all the issues at stake, so you have all the critical information you need to make a decision.

5. **Weigh the Decision.** The analysis stage is not meant to lead you by the hand toward a foregone conclusion, with all the plus signs stacked up neatly in one column, so the choice becomes a no-brainer. If that were the case,

then something is wrong with your criteria. You have probably left out some important consideration, because in real life there are usually trade-offs: what one person counts as positive, another person will perceive as negative. Decision-making is a balancing act between the good points and the bad points to reach an optimum solution.

It comes down to the weight you give to your decision criteria. If Criterion 1 is the most heavily weighted, as it was for Essack, then Alternative 1 holds the most sway. Of course, choosing Alternative 1 carries slightly more financial risk than Alternative 2, but that is a judgment call that a manager has to make. Managerial decision-making is often about placing a bet—not a blind one, mind you, but one based on having all the cards openly and explicitly laid on the table. This stage is ultimately about ordering and ranking your criteria to facilitate informed decision-making.

6. **Create an Action Plan.** The last and most important step is to implement the decision. Having identified the key issues as part of a decision-making process, managers can then target their actions accordingly, maximizing the positive aspects highlighted by the analysis while mitigating the negatives.

In implementing the new playlist, Essack took a series of actions to deal with where he anticipated the biggest challenges: the staff. The inclusive playlist would have to be matched by presenters who wouldn't alienate existing audiences and a station environment where everyone would feel comfortable working. He offered training to presenters and recruited new talent to represent diverse cultures and contexts. New issues were presented for discussion at management meetings. Should presenters stop putting on black and Indian accents for fun? Should traffic reports cover roads and suburbs that no one bothered with before, because white people never drove there? Should the sports coverage be broadened to include soccer, which was popular in the townships?

The hardest decision he had to make was to let the music manager go: "She had served the station well for a long time. However, despite repeated requests, she refused to change and adhere to the new playlist. She could not deliver on the key elements that I thought were fundamental to achieving the vision. Eventually, I had to ask her to leave. It was a big shock for staff who had been at the station from its earliest days and the most difficult thing I have ever had to do in my career. But to achieve the transformation we needed, it was important to have change agents in the consumer-facing areas of the business."

This underscores the main advantage of the six-step decision-making process: to force numerically oriented people to deal with the softer issues, and to force the conceptual types not only to do whatever analysis is required but also to make their leaps of faith explicit. Perhaps the greatest benefit of the process in the context of making group-based decisions is that it allows both types of people to communicate with each other in a positive, rigorous way, as Essack attests: "A young manager with little or no experience in managing people but some experience in technical areas can be a recipe for disaster. I encouraged criticism of my methods, so that I could explain why I did what I did. I even encouraged it on air, where I introduced a monthly slot called 'State of the Station' where listeners were encouraged to call in live and challenge the decisions that we had taken or comment on the changing product. It was always risky but also completely empowering for all sides. Even if people vehemently disagree with a decision, there is always value in communicating with them what informed the decision. Our most important stakeholders in media businesses are the audience and the staff/team. It is a travesty that the only ones we pay attention to are the stockholders. Each requires equal consideration and respect."

The result: "We honed the music to emphasize areas of commonality, weeding out songs that polarized any community. We found a perfect mix of pop hits that everybody liked. We brought on new talent, black and Indian, to work with the talent already at the station, so that the station inside represented the new world outside."

Hamlet and Othello: Tragic Decision-Makers

Breaking a decision down into six steps is not to say that decision-making is an easy six-step process. Each step has its own particular challenges, and each person will find some steps more difficult than others, depending on the type of person he or she is. To illustrate two common traps that people fall into during the decision-making process, let's consider two archetypes from English literature: Shakespeare's tragic heroes of Hamlet and Othello.

Hamlet's tragic flaw was his inability to act decisively, encapsulated by his most famous line, "To be or not to be? That is the question." The young prince of Denmark has a lot on his mind: his uncle murdered his father, seized the throne and married his mother, and the country is about to be invaded. The ghost of Hamlet's dead father visits him one night, imploring him to avenge his murder. Hamlet spends the rest of the play plotting his next move. In one scene, he stages a play, which is a thinly disguised reenactment of his father's murder, just to gauge the reaction of his uncle. One minute he is resolved to kill his uncle, the next minute hesitant and confused. This angst-filled cogitation continues for the duration of the play, the longest one ever written by Shakespeare. When performed in its entirety, the full work takes over four hours to perform. That's an awful lot of dithering.

Othello had the opposite problem: he acted first and thought later. Othello is a general in the Venetian army who unwittingly makes an enemy of Iago by promoting another man, Cassio, to lieutenant above him. Consumed by jealousy, Iago sows seeds of suspicion and misunderstanding, tricking Othello into believing that his wife, Desdemona, is having an affair with Cassio. In a fit of rage, Othello smothers her to death. Othello goes from perceiving a problem to taking extreme action with no half steps in between. For example, when he first sees Cassio with his wife's handkerchief, he could have simply asked him where he'd gotten it from, as it was, in reality, a ruse planted by Iago. Instead, Othello jumps to conclusions, assumes the worst, behaves rashly and goes straight for the kill. Even when confronted by the error of his ways, he doesn't use any half measures to express his remorse: he grabs a dagger and commits suicide.

These characters represent two classic approaches to decision-making. Some managers go from Step 1 to Step 6 without passing Go and without collecting $200. There is just an ill-defined problem and drastic action with no steps in between. Others can never seem to make a decision. They struggle with Steps 2 and 3 and never progress beyond Step 4. These are the people who constantly request more data, leading to what is called "analysis paralysis." Most managers tend to be one or the other by nature. Hamlet types need to learn to move toward making a decision, sometimes in the absence of data, while Othello types need to articulate the reasons for their decisions in order to get people to go along with them.

People in creative industries often see themselves as Othellos, recognizing they may need to improve on the analytical, data-gathering side of things, since relying solely on gut instinct can only get you so far. Of course, it's not a case of being either one or the other, but learning how both intuition and analysis need to work together when making decisions in rapidly changing environments. The six-step process for dealing with unstructured problems can help.

Pause for Thought

Am I more of a Hamlet or an Othello?
Do I recognize any of these traits in my teams?

Which steps do I find particularly difficult?

In which steps do I need to focus more of my attention?

Think of a recent decision and try to plot it using the six steps: are there gaps in my decision-making?

How do I resolve to improve my decision-making in future?

Leadership for Uncertain Futures

At the heart of being able to make decisions is knowing what kind of leader you are. Even more important is knowing what kind of leader you want to be and taking the steps necessary to be that leader. This requires a bit of self-reflection and perhaps a retraining of your mind to rid yourself of unhealthy impulses, ingrained prejudices and automatic, reflexive responses to every new situation that arises. It requires taking a more "mindful" approach that learns to think, plan and work backward, from the future to the present. In this way, you will be better able to turn even the most chaotic situations to your advantage.

A good example is C.C. Meyers, a California contractor. On January 17, 1994, Los Angeles was hit by one of its strongest ever earthquakes, causing a bridge of the Santa Monica Freeway to collapse. For a city reliant on its arterial roads and freeways, this represented a major disruption. Caltrans, the state agency responsible for transportation, predicted it could take anywhere from 12 to 18 months to rebuild the damaged section. And then in walked Meyers with a logic-defying bid: not only would he complete the job in six months, but he said Caltrans could penalize him $200,000 for every day he was late [1].

When was the last time you put together a work proposal? Ever thought of promising to do the job in half the time and they can dock your pay for every day late? We wouldn't recommend it—unless you change the way you approach problems and make decisions, the way Meyers did.

When people set out to do something, they usually start from the current state and work forward. They look at the resources presently available and decide the best way to use those means to achieve some future end. You create a five-year plan, with fixed rules and rigid steps that, once set in stone, finally get implemented. And then what happens? The future happens as it happens, and "the best laid plans of mice and men often go astray."

Meyers worked backward. He visited the future and brought it to the present in several crucial ways. Let's explore how.

See Your Future

Seeing the future starts by approaching problems similar to the way a reporter works: "To have a story ready for the 6 o'clock news, I need to file my report by 4; that means I need to be back at the station and in the editing room by 3 at the latest; this requires recording my interviews at 2; the interviews have to be set up in advance, so I have to be making calls and arranging interviews no later than 12; therefore, I need to have the story angle agreed, contact names and numbers, and an editing slot reserved when assignments are allocated at the 10 o'clock editorial meeting." Planning backward reveals your current position and priorities. As such, if it were 1:45 and you still had not lined up any interviews, you would probably start sweating, because your assessment of your current state has been couched in the future. Planning backward also means that if you were calling to pitch a story, you would never call a reporter after 4:00 thinking your event would air on the evening news.

As an experienced contractor, Meyers knew what to expect. There would be lengthy approval processes involving engineers, city planners, approval committees, inspectors and lawyers. But he didn't start by submitting plans to committees and waiting for their replies with fingers crossed. Instead, he forced all the future problems that he knew were bound to surface into his present situation. He invited all the engineers, city planners, approval committees, inspectors and lawyers to be present on site as the work progressed so that problems could be dealt with as they surfaced. All parties worked concurrently instead of consecutively.

If this sounds chaotic, it is—and for good reason. It is far more productive in the long term to deliberately introduce chaos at the beginning of any decision-making or problem-solving process—asking lots of questions and gaining divergent insights—before you pick a path. This means spending more time on problem-finding upfront, less time on problem-solving down the road.

This requires an adaptive mindset, which means you don't act as if nothing will go wrong, but rather you build in the capacity for things to go wrong and correct course as they do.

Another component to this is inviting input rather than waiting for feedback. One of the problems that surfaced during the reconstruction of the freeway was a protest from the community due to the noise level. Meyers could have asked his team to look into it and imposed some solution. Instead, he invited the community to propose their own solutions. They came up with earplugs and sound barriers, which satisfied them. The same happened when employees began to feel the pressure of the tight timetable. Meyers asked them to suggest ways to boost morale. They suggested music and parties on Fridays. In both instances, Meyers could have made lengthy speeches about the importance of meeting deadlines and serving the public good. But more effective than winning the buy-in of stakeholders after the fact (in essence, putting out fires) was creating build-in with stakeholders from the outset (which sets their minds on fire). This reduces future uncertainties.

In business when we refer to ROI we usually mean return on investment. An alternative way of thinking of ROI is relentless ongoing improvement, which will ultimately yield a better return on investment [1].

Figure 5.2 depicts this model of moving from deliberate chaos to reasonable order to new chaos, not by default or neglect but by choice. By inviting varied, multiple, chaotic input at the beginning, we generate divergent questions and move toward convergent answers, which is much preferable to proceeding along a seemingly structured path and ending up with unexpected chaos. However, we never close the door to new questions and potential improvement. As we reach a certain stage of consensus at the end

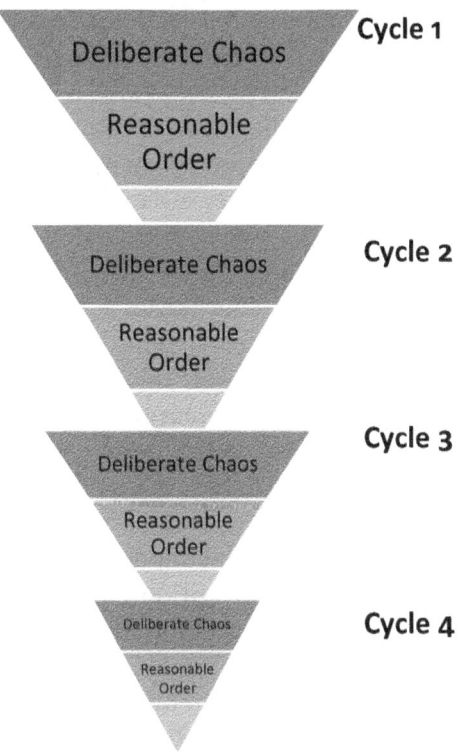

Fig. 5.2 Model of Relentless Ongoing Improvement

of a learning cycle, we enter a new stage of deliberate chaos, but hopefully one that is smaller than the first. We progress in this fashion toward our target, passing through successive cycles of learning and experimentation, trying to be a little bit better every single time.

Pause for Thought

Is last-minute, heroic problem-solving rewarded in my organization?
Are there ways in which I could start rewarding early problem-finding instead?
Which activities could I engage in to get input rather than feedback from my key stakeholders?
Which problem do I face that could benefit from the model of relentless ongoing improvement?

Visit Your Future

Besides helping you to see your future, the process of concurrent perceptions also helps you to visit your future. Think of an apprentice or intern who shadows an expert mentor for several weeks, as happens in certain professions, such as medicine. Spending time with professionals and seeing them in action enable aspirants to experience what their own future will be like. There are many ways that we can go live in someone else's world for a while, getting inspiration for our own future by having a taste of theirs. Seeing the way others have tackled a related problem may yield surprising solutions for your own situation that you never would have thought of for yourself.

Suppose your problem was delivering on time, and you wanted to reduce the operations uncertainties related to meeting delivery schedules or deadlines. To whom would you turn for a glimpse of the future you desire? Another division of your company where they seemed to be slightly better at on-time delivery than other teams were? Why not visit a more distant future, like Cemex did? When this cement producer sought to transform their delivery processes, they didn't go to another cement company; instead they visited Federal Express sites, Domino's Pizza franchises, and fire and ambulance services to experience the future of on-time delivery as they would otherwise never see it. Similarly, when the pharmaceutical company Novartis wanted to come up with a better way of tracking patients, where better to find future inspiration than by visiting a prison system to observe how they reliably tracked and monitored parolees?

The more distant the future from your own sector, the more likely you are to glean better insights. By starting to think this way, a CNN anchor who lamented the coordination challenges involved with dispatching journalists to breaking news scenes suddenly had a Eureka moment: why not go visit Uber, the app developers who have devised a highly effective tool for connecting people wanting rides with drivers of vehicles for ridesharing and car hiring? Might they have cracked the challenge of moving people around locations at a moment's notice without the need for prior investment in infrastructure?

Omar Essack related how he visited the future when recruiting new employees for the radio station that he envisaged: "Finding talent is always difficult. Looking at other radio stations is one way to do it, but there is enormous value, when trying to build something new, to look in unusual places. We've recruited a call center agent, a flight attendant, a newspaper movie reviewer, a travel agent, a stand-up comic, a used car salesman, a sales and marketing guy, and a book buyer for a major bookstore."

Pause for Thought

Regarding the attribute that I am trying to improve, who can help me do it better?

Where are the faraway places outside my own industry that I can visit to glean better insights?

Show Your Future

Inviting chaos into your present situation, in order to see the future, and drawing inspiration from unlikely quarters, in order to visit the future, will amount to little unless you are also able to cast visions of desired states so that people can contemplate the future. A central part of being a manager is getting people to go along with you on a journey from the current state you are in to the desired state of your vision. And for this you need to tell a story that inspires. People in the media and entertainment industry will appreciate the capacity of a compelling story to grab people and move them to action.

Meyers grasped this, which is why he won the freeway contract and saw the job through in record time. He made the objective crystal clear and then empowered everyone to bring their own tools and creativity to solve problems. For example, at one point during the project, a shipment of steel was going to be delayed by five days. The cost of such a delay would amount to $1 million. The supplier offered an alternative shipment on another train, but it would entail an additional cost of $120,000. Suppose you were one of the workers on that construction project and you received the phone call relaying this piece of news. What would be your course of action, in the organizational context in which you currently work? Would you simply go ahead and authorize the shipment, knowing that your boss had empowered you to use your own best judgment and make such decisions so long as they fit within the overall goal? Or would you have to tell the supplier to wait until you checked with your boss and call the supplier back later because you had no authority to make such decisions, even though it risked losing the window of opportunity being offered at that moment, resulting in longer, more expensive delays? Luckily, Meyers had set an unambiguous target and then let everyone get on with doing their jobs within that framework, so the worker was able to exercise his own judgment, accept the alternative shipment and the project proceeded without delay.

Showing the future means that you, as the leader, paint a picture and then step back to let others add their own touches and flourishes. You focus on context more than content. You articulate a sense of purpose and let people surprise you with their capacity for creativity, innovation and self-organization to adapt to the chaos and uncertainty of an unpredictable future. At the global level, you start with statements of grand purpose that expand imaginations and then you give people the authority to solve problems locally. This lets people invest all of themselves—their values and their spirits—in constructing a shared vision of the future.

The Holocaust survivor and psychologist Viktor Frankl contemplated the importance of people being able to construct meaning and find purpose even in life's most desperate situations. He presented the existential tension between failure and success, between despair and fulfillment (Fig. 5.3). Some say that the role of a manager is to help people be successful. The problem with this conception is that you can have success but end up with some very miserable people. Don't aim for success, Frankl said, but search for meaning. Likewise, we would argue that the real role of a leader is to lift people out of failure and despair and move them toward fulfillment by helping them find meaning in what they do; that is true success [2].

Doing this requires two things. First, there needs to be a high level of trust. As a manager, how do you create trusted relationships? Hint: it usually doesn't start by telling your teams not to worry their heads over matters that don't concern them because you're the boss and you've got it under control. Trust starts when you begin to trust other people. Instead of saying, "Trust me," try saying, "I trust you" and see what happens.

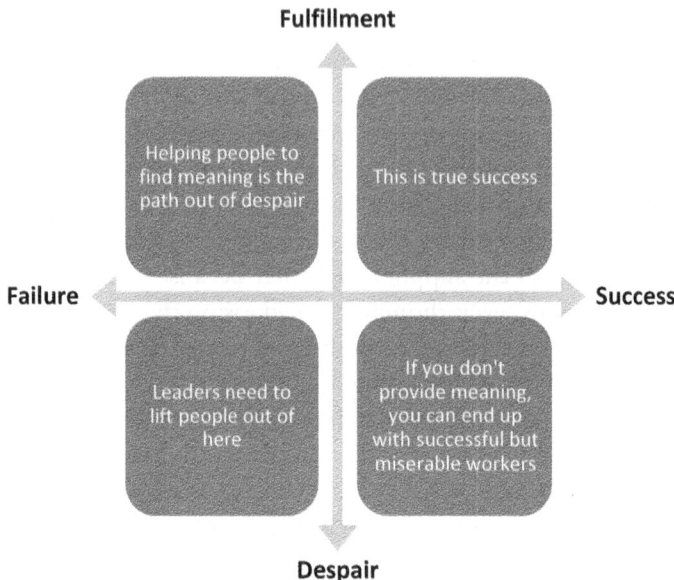

Fig. 5.3 Viktor Frankl's Existential Tension

In putting your trust in other people, they may occasionally let you down. The more freedom you give, the more likely it is they will make a mistake. This need not be a disaster, if you have created the context in which it is all right for mistakes to occur. A second part of helping people create meaningful futures is to use a process orientation rather than an outcome orientation. When we view error as part of an ongoing process, it just becomes part of a continuous revision by which we learn, adapt and move on; when viewed as an outcome, error becomes an endpoint on which we dwell and it cripples us. Being able to learn from failure and assume responsibility for mistakes actually reinforces trust and becomes another strategy for showing the path to the future.

Meyers had shown a clear future—a reopened freeway in six months—and then he allowed all stakeholders to draw meaning from their own personal motivation to achieve that common goal. Some were motivated by the financial bonus promised if they finished the project early; for residents it was the restoration of peace to their neighborhood; for the city authorities it was to restore normal traffic flows and eliminate the gridlocks from traffic being diverted to side streets. People do not all have to be in the project for the same reason. The key is that their individual motivations are aligned with a common future goal. In the end, with all these ingredients in place, the freeway was restored not in 18 months as feared, nor in six months as promised—but in an astonishing 66 days.

Pause for Thought

What is the inspiring story of the future that I am casting for my employees?
Do I leave room for them to run with that story and own it for themselves?
Do I authorize people to act locally within a global framework?
How can I demonstrate my trust in another person?
What is my attitude to failure? What is the culture for failure in my organization? How can I leverage failure to build trust?

A Conversation with Omar Essack of East Coast Radio

Earlier we saw how Omar Essack applied the six-step decision-making process to resolve an unstructured problem he faced. We close this chapter with another story from Essack. As you read Essack's story in his own words, see if you can identify the principles and examples of how he brought the future to the present to show leadership in this case of business transformation.

"To showcase East Coast Radio's new music and talent lineup and new logo, our marketing department thought it was time to make significant expenditure on billboard and television advertising. I resisted. I had a nagging feeling that slapping up a billboard in a segregated suburb and assuming that the people living there would start listening to us was patronizing and exactly the wrong way to win goodwill.

"Instead, I contacted an old acting icon, Alfred, who lived in a Zulu-speaking, black township called Umlazi, the second largest in South Africa. Alfred was a respected community elder who had spent his life using his acting talents as an instrument against apartheid. He was a great storyteller, preserving and celebrating the oral tradition of his ancestors, and capturing the struggle for freedom through riveting theater. I sought his help in learning about the community of Umlazi as only he would know it.

"Alfred suggested I bring my management team to his home where he organized a luncheon meeting with around 20 Umlazi community representatives. There was a bit of trepidation among some of my management team. Many of us had never been to such a township before.

"The people spent most of that lunch talking about their circumstances—specifically the emptiness of their childhoods and the hopelessness they felt about their own children's future. They had hoped to give their children something more than they'd had. Instead, their kids were bored, cooped up in small, corrugated shacks. They worried that their kids would get caught up in alcohol, drugs and gangs.

"Over the course of that lunchtime, our focus shifted from marketing to thinking about making a difference. We went looking for insights to drive our future radio strategy. We emerged with something far more meaningful.

"A week later, we went back to Umlazi, only this time in a double-decker bus with a loudhailer. Blaring a thumping music beat, we drove through every street, inviting the community to bring their children to the King Goodwill Zwelithini stadium because East Coast Radio was hosting a weekend-long soccer tournament. There would be T-shirts, refreshments, local soccer stars and the winning team would win the East Coast Radio trophy.

"Many in our team were convinced that a radio station hosting a soccer tournament for township kids was a monumental waste of time and money—that what we should be doing was sitting in our office strategizing. I felt otherwise. This was the moment to roll up my sleeves and get involved. On the bus, I manned the loudhailer. During the weekend tournaments, I was there from early to closing. If plastic chairs needed to be stacked, I was doing it. When kids were thirsty, I was with the team handing out drinks.

"As the soccer tournaments gained momentum, we began to reach out to community organizations in the townships to understand what other big needs existed. It was apparent that many people were dying in large numbers from HIV/AIDS, leaving behind many young children who suddenly found themselves thrust into the role of provider and breadwinner. We came up with a Christmas campaign called Toy Story, collecting toys from our listeners and distributing them to underprivileged children. This campaign soon morphed into a project to deliver parcels with a six-month supply of food to child-headed households. For many companies, engaging in 'corporate social responsibility' of this kind is reduced to a tick-box exercise. Although we recognized that 'making a difference and spreading goodwill' was a potent marketing tool, we made sure we were never anything but sincere in our commitment.

"When I think back on the moments that made the biggest difference to the success of our radio business, it is surprising how often 'doing the right thing for the consumers, our audiences,' comes up. A sense of purpose—that what we do has a meaningful, positive impact on our communities   invigorated our teams and made East Coast Radio an irresistible force in the region. As our news tagline so eloquently puts it, 'If it matters to you, it matters to us!'

"It is that spirit that defines the next story: I was in a meeting with my management team. It had been raining steadily for a couple of days. During the meeting I noticed that the intensity of the rainstorm had notched up. I rose from the table and went to my office window. Water had begun gushing down the roads and it was clear that the storm drains were struggling to cope. I asked the news editor to check on stories about localized flooding.

The reports back were not good. The Umgeni River was rising and there was a possibility that it could burst its banks. The tone of that meeting changed instantly. My office became a disaster management center.

"On air, East Coast Radio became Storm Watch. Our news team began collecting information from all the emergency services. Our presenters asked listeners to call in if they or people whom they knew were in any difficulty. We became aware of routes that were waterlogged, preventing parents from collecting their kids from school. Animals at a local petting zoo were in danger of drowning. Shantytowns were threatened by mudslides.

"Every team member was mobilized to manage telephone lines and advise people of what to do in cases of emergency. The station stopped playing music and started providing information to save lives. Listeners responded in droves. The animals at the zoo were all rescued and provided with shelter at various homes. People living in shantytowns were helped with tarpaulins to provide better insulation, and various business owners got involved to shore up the foundations to prevent the shacks from collapsing. Meanwhile, bus owners offered to pick up kids from schools, and teachers from those schools that were unreachable because of flooded roads used the station to communicate to parents and reassure them that their children were being looked after.

"I believe this was a defining moment for East Coast Radio—when what we were doing found meaning and resonance as our new country emerged. Black and white staff worked together for a common purpose—a purpose more profound than creating the best radio station in South Africa, yet ultimately delivering that same result as a byproduct of our mission.

"Years later, we canvassed the opinions of black South Africans through formal focus groups. When asked when they started listening to East Coast Radio, many would refer to the bus tour, the soccer tournaments and our role as a community champion. I vividly recall one participant, a 30-year-old professional, saying that his mother first told him about this white radio station that was driving though the township and making a lot of noise about hosting soccer weekends for the kids. That made him tune in and he was surprised by what he heard. The music was different from what he was expecting and there was a presenter with a Zulu name on the air. Astonished, he shared this discovery with his friends, all of whom began tuning in and finding something contrary to their expectations.

"When people speak of business innovation, that conversation often focuses on business models, technology platforms, and more efficient systems and processes. In my experience, the success we had emerged out of an environment that respected ideas; that made it clear that the best ideas emerged from the collective involvement of everyone. When a breakthrough idea emerged, the management committed money and people to make it live, and celebrated the people who volunteered it—sometimes with money, sometimes with their faces on our wall of fame. These acts of recognition and trust created their own momentum. We became a business of ideas, of dialogue, of honest critique, of a lack of fear.

"Some of the most fun we had at East Coast Radio was when we got together in the boardroom to think up the craziest ways to market the station and to surprise and delight our audiences. Above all, we never forgot that what we achieved we got done because we were a team."

Pause for Thought

Who was my best manager ever and why? What can I learn from them in the present situation I am facing?

Who was my worst manager ever and why? What can I learn from them in the present situation I am facing?

What kind of manager or leader am I now?

What kind of manager or leader do I want or need to be, in order to become "a business of ideas, of dialogue, of honest critique, of a lack of fear"?

References

1. M.F. Rubinstein and I.R. Firstenberg (1999), *The Minding Organization: Bring the Future to the Present and Turn Creative Ideas into Business Solutions* (Wiley).
2. V.E. Frankl (1969), *The Will to Meaning: Foundations and Applications of Logotherapy* (Meridian/Plume).

6

Decision Analysis: The "Science" of Predicting Your Next Hit

Miguel A. Ariño, Rafael de Santiago, with Philip H. Seager

During the course of a year, Sarah Noonan travels to four film festivals around the globe—Berlin, Cannes, Los Angeles and Toronto—in search of unique, groundbreaking movies for which she can secure the distribution rights for her region on behalf of her company, Curious Film. With offices in Australia and New Zealand, Curious provides marketing support for the movies it acquires, using a blend of online media and event planning, as well as producing its own indie shorts and commercials. Among the features it has successfully brought to art-house screens in its zone are *Winter's Bone*, the movie that launched Jennifer Lawrence's career, and *Broken*, a modern-day British reinterpretation of *To Kill a Mockingbird*, set in suburban London.

In screening well over 100 movies a year, as well as reviewing dozens of scripts, how does Noonan separate the wheat from the chaff? Obviously, not every pick is a sleeper hit, and her products—small, independently produced features, often in foreign languages, with no household names or A-list celebrity casts—are not likely to achieve the same blockbuster status as, say, *The Amazing Spider-Man*.

This chapter also contains some material from R. de Santiago (2013), "Decision Tools to Keep You on the Right Path," *IESE Insight* magazine, Fourth Quarter, Issue 19.

M.A. Ariño (✉) • R. de Santiago
Managerial Decision Sciences Department, IESE Business School, Barcelona, Spain
e-mail: MAArino@iese.edu; RSantiago@iese.edu

P.H. Seager
IESE Business School, Barcelona, Spain
e-mail: PSeager@iese.edu

© The Author(s) 2017

M. Rosenberg, P.H. Seager (eds.), *Managing Media Businesses*,
DOI 10.1007/978-3-319-52021-6_6

Yet Noonan has to place bets. She has to decide which movies to negotiate hard for and how much would be too much to pay for the distribution rights. But even with all the uncertainties involved, making a decision like this does not amount to "eeny, meeny, miney, mo." There is a clear process involved, one that lies at the intersection of art and science.

In the previous chapter, we outlined a process for making unstructured decisions, which drew heavily on intuition, creativity and a deep understanding of yourself, as a person and as a leader, to work with and through other people to accomplish some higher goal or purpose. It was more about the art of decision-making, whereas in this chapter we will look more at the "science." We put the word "science" in quotation marks deliberately, because even though the decision-making tool we describe in this chapter is a proven methodology to improve decision-making processes, it is by no means foolproof, as we will later explain.

For now, let's start by seeing how Noonan might coolly appraise the risks involved in picking a movie, which, even though it may not give her a guaranteed hit, will at least guarantee that she made the best decision possible at the time and limit the likelihood of making a bad or random decision.

Growing a Decision Tree

Strategic management tools, such as decision diagrams, play important roles in decision-making. They can help managers, like Noonan, to structure complex problems, carefully consider alternatives and calculate the risks involved.

A decision tree—diagraming the sequence of events that could unfold depending on the choices you make—can help to clarify the nature of the problem and evaluate the potential impact of risk on the final decision.

Let's illustrate this process using Noonan's decision of whether to acquire the rights for a movie we'll call *Indie Hit*, about the hardships of a Russian immigrant rendered stateless after being denied citizenship for failing to pass a series of Latvian language tests. On the one hand, the movie generated a lot of buzz at the Berlin International Film Festival for marking the debut of a promising young director from a part of the world not widely known for its cinema; it is beautifully realized in true art-house style: idiosyncratic tone, character-driven, stunning cinematography. On the other hand, it's a three-hour, black-and-white movie in Latvian, starring unknown actors, in which nothing much happens, by a director no one has ever heard of before. Still, the travails of the plucky middle-aged female protagonist might play well with the typical audience demographic for art-house movies in Australia and New Zealand, where immigration is also a hot-button issue.

Noonan has already laid out $4,000 toward this movie in terms of her time, expenses and preparation of the offer she will make to the sales agent to acquire the territorial rights for *Indie Hit*. Based on past experience, the probability of Curious obtaining the rights is 70 percent. If she gets the rights, she can either approach individual movie theaters in Australia and New Zealand directly, which will require additional investment for Curious to do the marketing themselves, or go through a major chain that will show the movie in all the theaters in its network, as well as do the related marketing activities for her.

Depending on how the movie performs at the box office, the net present value of cash flows will vary in each scenario. If going through the theater chain, Curious would receive, say, $125,000. If approaching individual theaters directly, the results are less certain—say, a 30 percent chance of getting $30,000 if the movie doesn't find much of an audience; a 50 percent chance of getting $100,000, which would enable them to recoup their investment and marketing outlay; and if things go very well, a 20 percent chance of getting $200,000.

Noonan begins to draft a decision tree: see Figure 6.1. The first decision is whether to bid for the rights to *Indie Hit* or pass on it altogether. This choice is depicted by a square, indicating that it is a *decision node*—meaning it is the decision-maker (Noonan) who chooses the course of action.

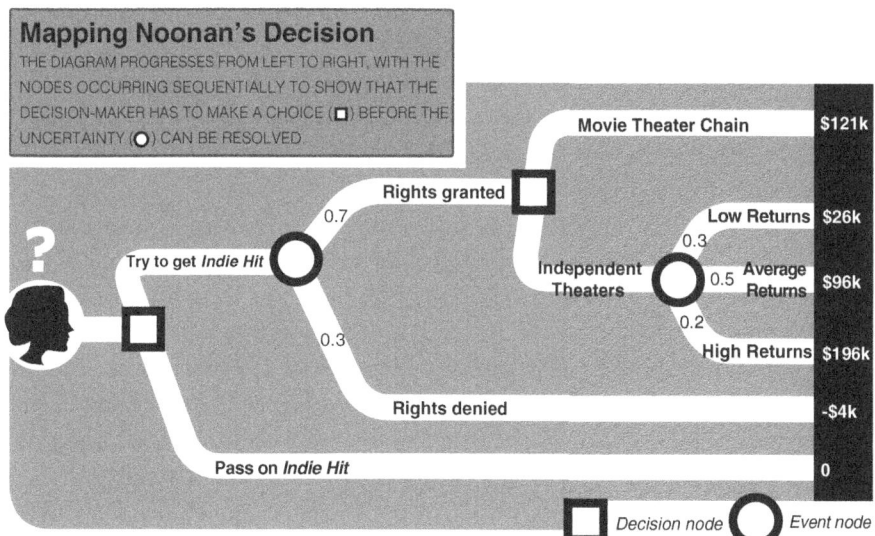

Fig. 6.1   Mapping Noonan's Decision

Cash flows will be contingent on whether the sales agent decides to accept Noonan's offer and to grant Curious territorial rights or not. This uncertainty is represented by a circle. Nodes of this type, where the decision-maker has no control over the outcome, are called *event nodes*. Each branch of an event node represents a possible scenario. An event node should include all possible scenarios, which must be mutually exclusive, in that the occurrence of one scenario excludes all others.

Once she has the rights, Noonan faces another decision node: whether to go through the theater chain owner or deal directly with individual theaters herself. If she decides to go the direct route, then this presents another event node, as then the profits are affected by individual circumstances, marketing outlays and other variables.

Given that decision trees account for time sequences of decisions and events, the diagram should progress from left to right, with the nodes occurring sequentially to show that the decision-maker has to make a choice before the uncertainty can be resolved.

Once the problem has been mapped out this way, the decision-maker can then compute the final value for each branch of the tree. In this example, the net profit may take the following paths:

- If Noonan passes on *Indie Hit*, Curious is guaranteed to get nothing.
- If Noonan puts in an offer but is unable to make a deal with the sales agent, Curious is out of pocket $4,000.
- If Noonan secures the rights and distributes *Indie Hit* through the big chain, Curious stands to make $121,000 (the estimated $125,000 minus the $4,000 originally invested).
- If Noonan secures the rights and distributes *Indie Hit* through an individual theater and box office is low, the net profit will be $26,000 (the estimated $30,000 minus the original $4,000, not to mention the extra marketing involved).
- If Noonan secures the rights and distributes *Indie Hit* through an individual theater and box office is average, the net profit will be $96,000 (the estimated $100,000 minus the original $4,000, not to mention the extra marketing involved).
- If Noonan secures the rights and distributes *Indie Hit* through an individual theater and box office is high, the net profit will be $196,000 (the estimated $200,000 minus the original $4,000, not to mention the extra marketing involved).

While the decision tree has helped to clarify all the potential outcomes, there is one more step that Noonan must take before making her final decision. And that is to calculate the expected values of each course of action.

Calculating Expected Values

An expected value is a weighted average of all possible outcomes, where the weights are the probabilities assigned to each branch of a given event node. Let's consider this with another example. Imagine Noonan's boss tells her that, in terms of salary, she must choose between the following:

- Receive $5,000 every month.
- Go to the boss on the first day of each month and toss a fair coin. If heads, she earns $11,000 that month; if tails, she earns $1,000 that month.

Which option should she choose? If she knew that she would stay with the company for several years, it would make more sense for her to choose the payment scheme with the higher expected value, which is the fair coin toss. That's because, over time, the actual salary she could expect to receive would average out to $6,000 per month.

For expected values to work, there must be an element of repetition involved. This repetition may take place across time, as in the case of a real-estate agent whose past experience tells him that the probability of selling one house a month is 50 percent, two houses, 35 percent, and three houses, 15 percent. So, over the course of 12 months, the agent can count on selling 1.65 houses a month. Some months he will sell three, other months two and other months one (obviously, there will never be a month when he sells 1.65 houses).

Repetition may also take place across business activities, as in the case of a publishing company, which knows that 98 percent of the books it publishes will lose money—say, $30,000 on average—and the remaining 2 percent will be best sellers, each generating average returns of $10m. The average profit will be $151,000, since the best sellers will more than make up for the loss makers.

The second condition for using expected value as the basis for a decision is that a negative outcome will *not* put you out of business. Consider again the situation in which Noonan tosses the coin every month. If the outcome is heads, she gets $11,000 *that month*, and if it is tails, she gets $1,000 *that month*. Then, imagine that she has to make a $2,000 mortgage payment every month. In this situation, even though the expected value over time is $6,000, she could not afford to choose this payment scheme, since if the outcome of the coin flip for the first three months was tails, she would risk losing her home.

Putting Expected Values into Practice

Returning to our earlier example, let's assume that Curious could comfortably absorb a loss should *Indie Hit* turn out to be a flop. Under these conditions, expected value may justifiably be used as a tool to evaluate the different alternatives available and make a final decision.

To identify which alternative has a higher expected value, Noonan works backward, starting with the nodes at the end of the tree. At each event node, she computes the expected value of its branches; and at each decision node, she chooses the branch with the highest expected value. This is called *decision diagram reduction*, and it indicates the best strategy to take at each point.

Figure 6.2 updates the previous decision tree with the expected value of each decision. By computing the expected value of approaching individual theaters (0.3 × $26,000) + (0.5 × $96,000) + (0.2 × $196,000), Noonan realizes that, on average, the node is worth $95,000. This means that if she

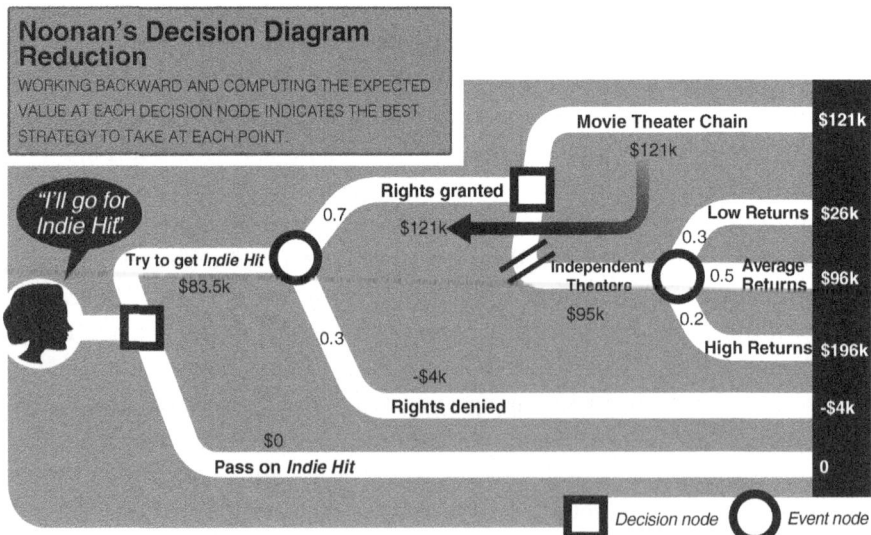

Fig. 6.2 Noonan's Decision Diagram Reduction

decides to acquire the movie, and the rights are granted, she would prefer to go through the chain, because the return ($121,000) is higher than the expected value of doing it directly theater by theater.

Next, Noonan computes the expected value of bidding for the movie. This she does by multiplying *the probability of securing the rights (0.7) by the potential returns of going through the theater chain ($121,000)*, and then subtracting *the probability of being rejected (0.3) multiplied by the resulting losses (−$4,000)*. This produces a total expected value of $83,500. Here, Noonan's decision would be to try to obtain *Indie Hit*.

Know Your Weaknesses

By using decision trees and expected value, Noonan is able to improve her decision-making process. However, such an approach still has limitations. For one thing, on paper the calculations may point her clearly in the direction of the big chain, but the savings in marketing spend and bigger audience need to be factored against the worse deal she will get compared with what she could get from an independent theater, even with having to do her own marketing.

This is where instinct and rationality collide, making human judgment far from infallible. Like Noonan, all managers operate in a world of relative obscurity. Human biases inform most of the decisions we make. It is only by understanding the risks that these biases pose, and then designing systems to curtail their influence, that managers can rest assured that the decisions they make will be as flawless as humanly possible.

To give an idea of the scale of the problem, we highlight three of the most prevalent human biases that play tricks on managerial decision-making. We also present a number of strategies for limiting their influence, both at the individual and organizational levels.

The Anchoring Effect

Anchoring describes the tendency for an estimate to gravitate around an initial starting point. In a famous study, researchers asked participants to state the maximum amount they were willing to pay for a number of products. Before doing so, participants were asked to write down the last two digits of their social security numbers. The researchers discovered a marked correlation between those two numbers and the prices participants gave. Participants with the highest-ending social security digits (80–99) bid highest, while those with the lowest-ending numbers (01–20) bid lowest, showing an irrational propensity to form judgments around a suggested "anchor" without critically assessing the merit of the suggestion in the first place [1]. While most humans may be good at making relative judgments, we have much greater difficulty making absolute judgments. Managers need to be more distrustful of intuition and use as many quantitative references as possible to enhance their decision-making.

Framing: Presentation Is Everything

The way you present information, whether to your company's board or to your team of workers, can have a strong bearing on a final decision or outcome. Organ donation programs illustrate this point well. A study among European countries reveals markedly different participation rates. Why do 100 percent of French drivers opt to donate their organs in the event of their death, whereas only 4 percent of Danish drivers do the same? As the behavioral economist Dan Ariely has pointed out [2], it all comes down to the way people are presented with the choice of whether to participate in the organ donation program. In countries with low participation rates, respondents are asked to tick a box if they want to opt in to the program, whereas in countries with high participation rates, respondents have to opt out if they don't want to participate. Given that in either case most respondents don't bother to tick the box, the way the question is framed makes all the difference. (Having said that, it is worth noting that the founding director of Spain's National Transplant Organization—the world leader in organ donations and transplants—remains skeptical of the supposed effect of framing on outcomes, at least as pertains to organ donation rates in Spain. Although some countries have been changing their legislation to favor the "presumed consent" or opt-out model on the basis that it boosts donations, Dr. Rafael Matesanz insists that adherence to the fundamentals of professional conduct and the transparency of the decision-making process as a whole play decisive roles. This is also good advice) [3].

In her article "Why Do Good Managers Choose Poor Strategies," Elizabeth Olmsted Teisberg elaborates on the importance of framing strategic choices in either positive or negative terms: "One can say that a change in strategy is necessary to avoid losing competitive advantage, or to improve sources of advantage and enhance competitive position. Likewise, new technologies may be considered necessary to avoid falling behind competitors, or attracting new customers and gaining market share" [4]. This is more than a case of trying to present the half-empty glass as half-full. Research has shown that individuals tend to treat uncertainty about possible gains differently from uncertainty about possible losses. So, depending on whether the analysis is framed in terms of losses or gains, people may make different decisions.

Escalation of Commitment

Generally, people are risk averse to gains and risk seekers for losses. Gambling is the classic example: most people find it hard to stop playing when they suffer setbacks and instead double down on their losses. But it's not just gamblers who are prone to this kind of behavior. To save face, employees and managers are just as likely to double down on the losses of a business activity in which they are closely involved. People are reluctant to accept or acknowledge a sure loss. Instead, they take risks that give them the possibility of no loss, but this brings the possibility of an even greater loss. This is known as *escalation of commitment*, and it has been the undoing of many companies.

Escalation of commitment manifests itself in numerous daily decisions, as one of our Media AMP participants attested: "We incorrectly assessed where the market was headed. We should have shut the business down but instead investors preferred to keep it limping along. The company lost $25 million over 10 years." Better to wind down your position before you wind up with an even bigger mess on your hands.

Case in point: Ryan Kavanaugh, founder of Relativity Media, claimed to have cracked the code on predicting a Hollywood hit. The venture capitalist turned movie mogul used a proprietary system of Wall Street-style algorithms, financial modeling and regression analyses to crunch data on everything from budgets to the pulling power of the cast. By simulating a variety of box-office outcomes, he claimed he could pick the winners using math. And for a while it seemed to be working. Investors threw millions at Relativity projects. However, over 11 years of business deals, the flops outnumbered the hits, eventually forcing Relativity to file for bankruptcy in July 2015. The moral of the story may be, as one industry executive warned about Relativity Media back in 2010, "no magic bean" can substitute for discipline, cost control and a careful consideration of your consumer base [5].

How can a company ensure that its executives and employees are not engaging in behavior that could jeopardize the bottom line? The following five measures can help to reduce your exposure to the threats posed by framing and escalation of commitment.

1. **Preserve a healthy balance of risk profiles.** Society is made up of risk-averse, risk-neutral and risk-seeking people. As such, companies need to ensure that these groups are broadly represented in their decision-making teams. Likewise, there needs to be a diverse range of perspectives represented in the analysis of strategy.

2. **Precommit to an exit strategy.** Good decision-making requires constant reevaluation as time passes and situations evolve. Sometimes the best decision for a firm is to revise or abandon a course of action that it had championed previously. As the leading management thinker Peter Drucker recommended, organizations should have monthly meetings to consider "disinvestment" opportunities—ways to halt ineffective programs [6].

3. **Avoid making important decisions on the spot.** Most organizations think of decision-making as an event rather than a process. As such, they attach great importance to key decision meetings, when the real problems often emerge before the meetings take place. The key is to put systems in place to monitor the evolution of programs and the decisions behind them, as well as to encourage people to bring all risky decisions to the table.

4. **Learn to deal with bad outcomes.** Inevitably some decisions—even good ones—may generate bad results. The important thing is to analyze whether these bad results happened even after taking calculated risks as part of an informed process, or whether they were the consequence of poor decision-making habits.

5. **Adopt ranges to describe future possibilities.** Using ranges, rather than single-point forecasts, enhances credibility by avoiding false precision. While this may make it more difficult to pin down potential future revenues, it challenges managers to present a more realistic picture of the future success of the project that they are championing.

Overconfidence: How Sure Are You Really?

Most people tend to feel uncomfortable with uncertainty. As a result, overconfidence is ingrained deep within the psyche, leading us to think we know more than we actually do. This tendency toward overconfidence has vital implications for company decision-making, particularly when it comes to assessing the probability of outcomes.

Going back to the Curious example, the probabilities and sums came from one of Noonan's colleagues. Is it wise for Noonan to base almost all of her decision-making on just one individual's estimates? How reliable is that person's judgment? Could that person be suffering from overconfidence? Perhaps Noonan and her colleague both have a vested interest in seeing *Indie Hit* reach the market (they adore black-and-white movies, for example, or one of them has a Latvian cousin) and, whether consciously or not, they have overestimated the likelihood of everything going according to plan.

To avoid succumbing to this kind of behavior, the first step is to stay on guard. Always be on the lookout for signs of overconfidence. Rely on hard facts wherever possible, and make sure your sources of information are reliable. All assessments should go through a peer review by experienced managers across functions. For example, some banks require that the decision to refinance a loan be made by a different person from the one who approved it. The previous advice of using ranges rather than single-point forecasts to describe future possibilities also applies here.

The main thing is to purposefully challenge your estimates. When evaluating a decision, most people tend to look for evidence that supports their initial predisposition, and fail to consider disconfirming information. To avoid falling into this trap, you need to draw in multiple perspectives during the analysis stage.

This is why Noonan never does the film festival circuit alone, but always with colleagues. They divide and conquer, meeting up every morning to compare notes on the movies they've seen. She scours trade media such as *Variety* and *The Hollywood Reporter* to get a sense of the word on the street and to glean alternative points of view.

"You might say, 'Wow! I loved that film!' but then when you talk to your colleagues they say they hated it. Or you might think, 'There's no audience for this film,' but someone else will point out that the director is a rising star whose last indie film did $3m at the box office. It would be highly unusual for us to buy a film that only one of us had ever seen."

Adopting divergent perspectives not only helps to uncover flaws and plan for contingencies, it also enhances creativity by helping managers to begin their analyses from points of view outside their usual mindset. A proactive devil's advocate persona will also question the role of luck, as well as look for unconsidered opportunities and evidence of cognitive biases in the logic being presented.

You might even second-guess yourself: "I've seen films that I thought were amazing at the time, but then I sleep on it, and the next day I have a completely different opinion." It's always a good idea to build a cooling-off period into the decision-making process.

Learn from Your Mistakes

Yet even having put systems in place to keep your biases in check, and applying an objective methodology to your decision-making processes, there is still no guarantee of getting the exact outcome you hope for. Noonan recalls the case of *The Artist*, the French silent black-and-white movie that took Cannes by storm in 2011 and went on to sweep practically every award ceremony going, including scooping up five Oscars, and grossing $133m worldwide. With that in mind, Curious subsequently obtained the rights to *Blancanieves*, a Spanish silent black-and-white movie based on the Snow White fairy tale that came out the following year and, just like *The Artist*, was hailed as "a love letter to silent cinema." The result? "It tanked in Australia," she said.

So, when weighing up the prospect of pursuing another European black-and-white art-house movie like *Indie Hit*, should Noonan use *The Artist* or *Blancanieves* as her guide? This is when it is important to make sure you have thoughtfully analyzed prior successes and failures, and truly learned from past mistakes.

Ultimately, it is by knowing your, and your team's, biases and limiting their influence on decision-making processes that you will be able to make the right decisions for your company—at least most of the time.

References

1. D. Ariely, G. Loewenstein and D. Prelec (2003), "Coherent Arbitrariness: Stable Demand Curves Without Stable Preferences," *The Quarterly Journal of Economics*, Vol. 118, Issue 1, 73–105.
2. D. Ariely (2008), *Predictably Irrational: The Hidden Forces That Shape Our Decisions* (HarperCollins).
3. IESE Insight (2016), "How to Be No. 1 in Donations," *IESE Insight* magazine, First Quarter, Issue 28, p. 70.
4. E. Olmsted Teisberg (1991), "Why Do Good Managers Choose Poor Strategies?" Harvard Business School Background Note.
5. F. DiGiacomo (2010), "The Theory of Relativity," *Vanity Fair*, March Issue.
6. P.F. Drucker (1980), *Managing in Turbulent Times* (Butterworth-Heinemann).

7

Operations Management: Not Just What You Do, But How You Do It

Philip Moscoso with Philip H. Seager

In May 2014, that bastion of US journalism, *The New York Times*, became the story for two reasons: first, the unceremonious firing of editor Jill Abramson; and second, the leaking of an internal Innovation Report, which was designed to light the path toward a digital future, but instead revealed just how dark the actual journey was for the paper as it moved toward modernizing its operations.

Apart from testifying to the travails of digital disruption, one of the report's recommendations was to do something that should, in fact, be a business no-brainer, but for media companies may come as something of an epiphany. There was real value, it said, in encouraging closer collaboration with the operations side of the business, since understanding operations may hold the keys to innovation and longevity.

Every business has some direct or supporting activities required to make a product or service and deliver it into the hands of the end user: that's operations. However, operations are not just the nuts and bolts of *how* to get the job done. If leveraged well, operations (the *how*) can themselves become a source of competitive advantage, not only in terms of gaining a strong cost position

P. Moscoso (✉)
Production, Technology and Operations Management Department,
IESE Business School, Barcelona, Spain
e-mail: PMoscoso@iese.edu

P.H. Seager
IESE Business School, Barcelona, Spain
e-mail: PSeager@iese.edu

© The Author(s) 2017
M. Rosenberg, P.H. Seager (eds.), *Managing Media Businesses*,
DOI 10.1007/978-3-319-52021-6_7

through greater efficiencies, but also in being able to offer breakthrough levels of service that others can't.

The problem with media companies is encapsulated in the mantra drilled into every journalist for more than a century: the importance of the five Ws (who, what, where, when, why) and "sometimes how." It's the "sometimes how" tagged on at the end that plants the notion that the *how* may be an optional extra, when for business, "effective operations management is absolutely crucial in all aspects of a firm's performance," as David Simchi-Levi, a renowned expert in the field, explained in *IESE Insight* magazine. "There is a direct link between the firm's value proposition and its operations strategy. When operations executives are given an equal seat beside other senior executives, natural synergies emerge" [1].

It's welcome news, then, that *The New York Times* finally saw the light and called for a tearing down of "The Wall" that typically separated the newsroom from the operations side of the business. Fig. 7.1, adapted from page 61 of

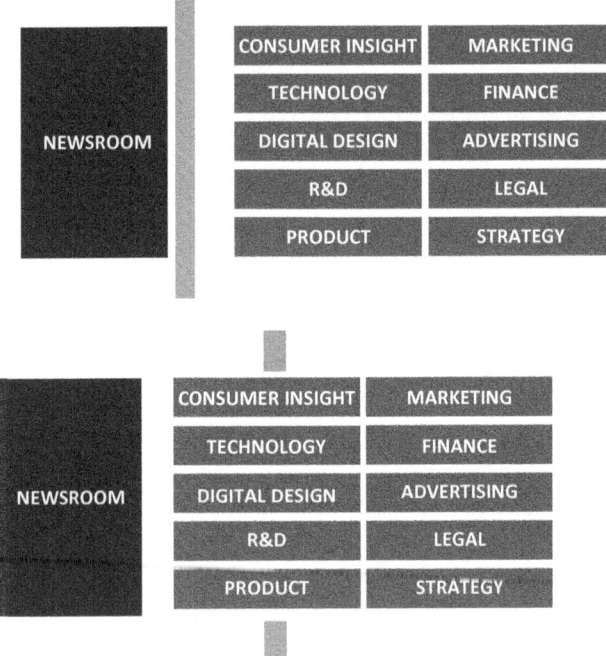

Fig. 7.1 Tearing Down "The Wall"
Many journalists used to picture the organizational chart with the newsroom and business-side functions on opposite sides of a wall. The two sides were generally discouraged from working together to protect the newsroom from being compromised by business-side functions and pressures. In reality, many business-side groups perform vital functions that enhance rather than compromise the reader experience. These groups are coming together to build new products and infrastructure to support journalism in this new media age. (Adapted from *The New York Times* Innovation Report)

the Innovation Report, depicts the integration that the management felt was necessary for any media company to survive.

While some might say, "It's about time," there is a good deal of evidence that *The New York Times* was not alone in being slow to make the vital links with operations as a source of competitive advantage. Many of the theories, tools and frameworks described in this chapter originated in industries—such as manufacturing—that are miles away from the values of media businesses, whose professionalism was historically defined by their ability to remain independent from those suspicious characters on the other side of "The Wall."

Now, we are living in an era when that mentality is as anachronistic as the Berlin Wall. As the report highlighted, it is the BuzzFeeds of the world—those who have embraced the "dry stuff" of operations—that have developed truly powerful business platforms that are extremely difficult to replicate.

First, let's look at some of the fundamental methodologies and tools that can be used to improve processes, consistent with your strategy. Then, we will analyze the peculiarities of processes where you need to engage customers in delivering an experience—very relevant for media and entertainment operations. As process improvements often occur through projects, we will also consider the keys of good project management. Most media and entertainment executives manage a lot of projects, and learning how to do so in a more systematic way is not incompatible with creativity. In the end, you should see that, even though today's new technologies are ushering in radically new business models, the fundamentals of operations management remain just as valid and applicable, whatever your particular business.

Operations as a Source of Competitive Advantage

In Chap. 2 on Strategy, my IESE colleagues Mike Rosenberg and Adrian Caldart stressed the importance of sustainable profitable growth and competitive advantage as the linchpins of Strategy, and that regulating your costs via operational efficiencies was one means of achieving those twin aims. Accordingly, we define the goal of operations management as "to deliver a winning value proposition to customers in an efficient manner." Sometimes, companies develop such great operations that they don't just make the strategy happen, but the operations themselves enable new strategies. Fig. 7.2 summarizes the four main steps to develop winning operations [2].

Your operations model needs to properly align the *who* and *what* with the *how*, and then make it happen through a corresponding delivery system. The problem is, optimizing operations management usually tends not to be a priority for managers who have no direct responsibility for operations.

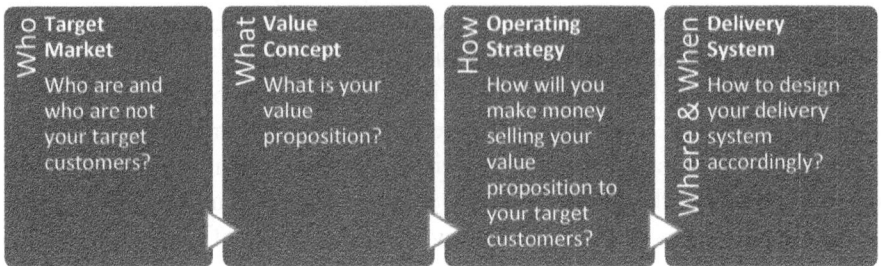

Fig. 7.2 Four steps to develop winning operations (Adapted from Heskett)

Let's think of this in terms of news media. Many editors, for example, embrace the idea of citizen journalism, turning every member of the public with a mobile camera phone into an instant news source and on-the-ground reporter. They hail the cost savings and expanded reach this gives them to cover events from the Arab Spring to the Ukraine rebellion to atrocities in Syria. "What an incredible resource," boasted one BBC journalist, mentioning that after the July 7, 2005 London suicide bombings, the broadcaster received 1000 stills and videos, 3000 texts and 20,000 emails in the space of 24 hours [3].

However, as *The New York Times* Innovation Report makes clear, few thought about the operational implications of editors having to sift through that much incoming material while still doing their jobs with the same resources and without the quality of their output suffering. The report describes the average workday for the editor in charge of both web and mobile reports as "writing headlines, scanning the wires, tracking breaking news and making sure that stories are appearing correctly on mobile. That leaves him with less bandwidth for bigger strategic questions about our digital operations" [4].

"Bandwidth" is the key word. Before embracing a new business activity, you have to assess the ability or capacity of your operations system to process it efficiently.

The Key Elements and Parameters
of an Operations System

Fig. 7.3 depicts the fundamental elements of an operating system. You can picture it as an "operations tube" through which items flow while they are processed by resources. As a manager, you need to analyze your own business in light of this basic sequence, paying careful attention to the most important variables in this "tube"—your items, your activities and your resources.

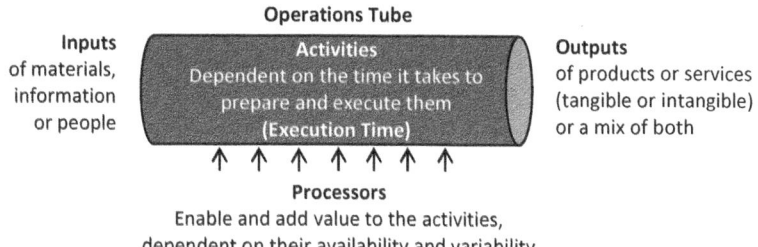

Fig. 7.3 The Operations Tube

An operations system can be described in terms of the following three parameters:

1. **Throughput Rate (Capacity):** This is the quantity of items actually processed per given unit of time. So, for a news organization, it could be the number of filed stories that move through the editorial pipeline and get published per day. The capacity of the system represents the maximum throughput rate a system can achieve if its entire availability is used productively and no processing time is wasted. It is not too difficult to calculate the capacity of any given system, or to evaluate if its resources are balanced, or what the impact of processing in batches or different product mixes would be.

2. **Throughput Time:** Managers should know the *total time* it takes from the moment an item enters the system until it exits the system, along with comparing the *actual* throughput time with the *minimum* throughput time. If there are different processors working in parallel or in succession, they will each have different throughputs and will need to be coordinated. Cycle times, on the other hand, refer to the intervals between the completion of two subsequent items, and should, therefore, not be confused with throughput times.

3. **Work-in-Progress (WIP):** The previous two parameters are related through a third very relevant one: WIP. This represents the total number of items being processed in the "tube." Obviously, throughput time will depend on how much WIP the system carries, on average, and with what speed those WIP items are being processed (throughput rate).

Understanding the dynamics and interrelationship of these three parameters builds the basis for the management of any operations system. Imagine that it takes one hour to vet a story before it can be processed. The throughput time for that story would not be *one hour* plus the time it takes to process the print version; *another hour* plus the time it takes to process the web version; *a third hour* plus the time it takes to process the same story again for social media, and so on. After the story has been vetted once, that initial hour of prep work can be applied to the whole batch of processes—print, web and social media. Unfortunately, in some media organizations where print, web and social media are treated as separate functions—each with separate teams housed in different buildings—such unnecessary doubling-up of effort may take place. Managers should leverage any process that can be reused for different batches, rather than repeating the same step each and every time.

Furthermore, two other closely related concepts are of interest to managers in practice. The first one is bottleneck. The second is batching, as often items are not processed individually, but in lots.

A system's maximum throughput rate (capacity) will be limited by the processor with the lowest maximum throughput rate, which is the *bottleneck*. Anyone who has come up through the ranks of print media will be familiar with operations bottlenecks, particularly in the finishing stages, when the printed sheets had to be shifted from the press to another location for postproduction operations of cutting, trimming, folding, binding, embossing and coating.

Perhaps the biggest bottleneck of all is baked into the journalism profession itself, with its foundational belief that it must bear the mantle as the gatekeeper of information flows and filter which news reaches the public. This existential conceit is perhaps the greatest drag on media operations today, and is something that many are increasingly calling into question as digital operations stretch traditional processes to the limit.

The concept of *batching* is also very familiar to media executives, and was nicely brought to life when, as part of IESE's Media AMP, we visited Sony Pictures' studio lot in Los Angeles where America's Favorite Quiz Show "Jeopardy!" is taped. This game show airs daily—but that doesn't mean they assemble contestants, judges, cameramen, an entire production crew, a 100-member studio audience and the celebrity host, Alex Trebek, every single day of the week to tape each 30-minute episode. Instead, they produce the shows in batches. In one day they tape five episodes back to back. There are two audiences: the first audience watches three tapings, and after a lunch break, the second audience watches the final two. The host and the contestants bring several changes of clothing and switch wardrobes between tapings, so no outfits are repeated on the same day. Episodes are shot two months in advance of when they air, and each has its future air date indicated on a message board, so the host can say, "Have a good Friday, everyone!" even though the taping may be on a Monday. This happens twice a week, so in just two days, ten "Jeopardy!" episodes are produced. In this way, just three weeks of a month, and nine months of a year, are spent producing a full year's worth of daily programs.

Media and entertainment executives would do well to consciously audit their operations periodically and engage in a deeper level of analysis to see which dimensions have the greatest impact on their business. As a basic checklist, they should pay particular attention to the following aspects:

- **Efficiency:** leveraging available resources, aiming at all times to eliminate idleness, waiting or other times that do not add value. This will have a critical impact on costs.
- **Quality:** the ability of the system to process items to customer or market specifications, aiming at all times to minimize waste owing to defects.
- **Agility:** the capability of the system to cope with unexpected changes in the short-term (machine breakdown, for instance). For this, short throughput times are critical.
- **Adaptability:** the capability to cope with changes in the longer term, such as new technologies or new competitors, and to innovate in operations.

Operational excellence, therefore, requires attention to details. And you, as a manger, are responsible for determining where the devil lies in those details. Where to begin?

With technology enabling customers to set the pace and flow of operations like never before, starting with the customer is probably wisest (working right to left in the "tube" depicted earlier). Understand first the customer promise before starting to work on your operations, otherwise your improvement may go against your strategic positioning. Be mindful of the trade-offs and tensions between doing it fastest and cheapest versus delivering customer satisfaction and experience; between standardization and customization; and between throughput and margins. There are a lot of gray areas, but you, as a manager, must position yourself on that spectrum and find the sweet spot between the extremes.

During the Media AMP, an executive director of a national North American broadcaster recognized that one of the biggest challenges he faced was in trying to motivate creative people around process, as they tend to be far more interested in the end result than in reimagining *how* they get there.

Yet some very interesting work is being done related to process. Consider CNN's user-generated iReports. CNN will field at least 500 submissions a day, of which only 40 may get vetted. That's "gatekeeping." However, a growing number of media outlets are revising their operations processes based on a new notion of "gatewatching," a term coined by the media scholar Axel Bruns. They are leveraging web communities to act as "crowdsourced fact-checking engines" to process the vast quantities of incoming information. Proponents of "social journalism" are calling for a policy of "publish first, verify later" by a self-policing community of active users—think *The New York Times* as run by Wikipedia. The more eyes, the fewer mistakes, or so the argument goes. Time would be freed up to do other things. On the other hand, the potential for false stories and hoaxes creeping into the mix is raised, which could be detrimental to quality perceptions and hurt the integrity— and ultimately the profitability—of the brand.

This is a hot debate with no easy answers. "Social journalism" or "crowd-sourced fact-checking" could eliminate some bottlenecks and boost engagement levels with your target audience, becoming a new source of competitive advantage. Alternatively, it could add new operational pressures and hurt your public standing, putting you at a competitive disadvantage. The lesson is you have to analyze your current operations model and then experiment with the dimensions described earlier by carrying out some pilot projects, making continuous improvements as you go. Otherwise, you'll never find out.

Pause for Thought

How important is operations management—the *how*—in your company?
To what extent could the *how* become a source of competitive advantage for
   your company?
What have been the major operational innovations in your industry?
Which of the key operations management variables can you identify for your
   core business processes? Can you quantify the variables?

Managing the Customer Experience: The Case of Secret Cinema

On Monday, August 11, 2014, the world-famous actor Robin Williams was found dead in his home. By Friday, August 15, Secret Cinema, a British events company specializing in live cinema experiences, had pulled off a commemorative screening of the Robin Williams' classic, *Dead Poets Society*, in a London theater, charging £25 a ticket, with all profits going to the mental health charity, Mind.

"We sold 1,000 tickets in five minutes," Secret Cinema founder Fabien Riggall told the Toronto International Film Festival. "I then called every cinema chain in the U.K., because we could have sold 100,000, but none could move fast enough" [5].

At the same time as this happened, Secret Cinema was simultaneously staging a theatricalized production of *Back to the Future* for which a purported 85,000 people paid £53 a pop to dress up and immerse themselves in a re-created 1950s world in order to watch a screening of that other 1980s classic.

How is it possible that an organization can throw together these events so quickly, asking people to pay up front for something without fully knowing what it is or where it will take place, until a few days or even hours before show time?

The answer comes down to clever management of customer operations. This is especially true in situations where companies want to deliver "experiences" to their customers, as media and entertainment companies endeavor to do.

Let's stick with the cinema example. It used to be that you lined up, bought a ticket and watched the movie. This was a fairly simple "customer journey," that is, the sequence of activities and events through which you had to pass, like the "tube" in the previous section. Throughout this process, there were key moments of direct interaction between the customer and the service system or employees—what are called "touchpoints." These interactions would leave lasting impressions, known as "moments of truth," when customers would ultimately make up their minds about what was being offered, with trust and loyalty being the hoped-for result.

Traditionally, companies focused on operational aspects over which they had control in order to optimize the "moments of truth"—in the case of movie theaters, this would be advertising and marketing, cheap matinees (price setting), wait times, cleaning up the popcorn in between showings and comfy seats. Whether the movie itself lived up to the customers' expectations was considered beyond anyone's control, from a purely operations perspective.

Today, however, service delivery has to encompass much more than the tangible elements that a company or customer can objectively measure. As Secret Cinema realizes, any service operation nowadays has to deliver intangible, subjective experiences in which the customer participates in a direct and interactive way, and which almost always occur simultaneously and immediately in time and space.

This throws up a raft of new challenges for companies: How do you control the quality and consistency of what you're offering? How do you match supply with unpredictable demand? How do you design for a high degree of personalization and more human interfaces?

As outlined at the beginning of this chapter, delivering breakthrough service starts by being clear about your target market (*who*) and your value proposition (*what*). Chap. 4 on Marketing delves deeper into the subject of customer segmentation to reach your key targets, but suffice it to say that the broader your customer base, the harder it will be to achieve service excellence, as you will be trying to be all things to all people. With the richness of big data available via Internet-enabled analytics, the means are available, now more than ever, to tailor your operations to specific segments—but it presumes you have given prior thought to who your key targets are, or at least decided who they are not.

When it comes to defining your value concept (Step 2 of the model in Fig. 7.2), the First Law of Services is paramount:

$$\textbf{Satisfaction} = \textbf{Perceived Value} - \textbf{Expectations}$$

Implicit in this formula is that customer satisfaction is dependent on subjective factors. Consider wait times at a movie theater: it's not so much the fact that someone had to wait in line for 10 minutes to buy a ticket that determines their level of satisfaction, but whether they had *expected* to wait that long and if they *considered the wait to be worth it*. So, if an impatient man was not prepared to wait more than two minutes to see some romantic-comedy that his wife had dragged him to, he would likely end up feeling annoyed by the 10-minute wait; whereas if he had fully expected to wait at least an hour to get in to see the premier of the latest *Star Wars* blockbuster for which people were lining up around the block, then 10 minutes would seem nothing.

Owing to the subjective nature of the value concept, researchers Luis M. Huete and Andres Perez have come up with another formula, which deals with the determinants of customer satisfaction on a deeper level [6].

$$\textbf{Perceived Value} = \frac{\left(\textbf{Results} + \textbf{Process} + \textbf{Emotional Value}\right)}{\left(\textbf{Price} + \textbf{Inconveniences} + \textbf{Uncertainties}\right)}$$

The numerator encompasses everything the customer *receives*: the desired results, the positives of the service delivery process and any associated emotional benefits; in short, "what I get" as a customer. The denominator represents everything the customer considers a *cost*—"what I pay"—not only in terms of price but also in terms of personal inconveniences or simply not knowing whether what they get is what they really want.

For Secret Cinema goers, the costs were high—paying £53, in some cases to travel halfway across the country (incurring additional personal costs for transportation and hotel), in order to see a 30-year-old movie in an undisclosed location. On the plus side was the thrill of being part of a once-in-a-lifetime experience, the fun of dressing up, and the adventure of physically immersing themselves in the fictional world of the movie as it was re-created before their eyes, both on screen and with live actors milling about the crowds.

For there to be any perceived value, the numerator has to be bigger than the denominator, and bigger than what competitors offer. As such, in defining the operating strategy (*how*) and the delivery system (*where* and *when*), managers will want to focus on heightening the aspects of the equation they know about and over which they have control, especially concerning the numerator, to boost their chances of achieving service excellence relative to the competition.

"Control" is the operative word. Today the locus of control is increasingly in the hands of consumers—or to put it more accurately "prosumers," those who are both proactive producers and consumers of content. For media and entertainment companies, this means more time, thought and energy have to be devoted to framing the terms of their customer interactions and managing the greater number of variables that enter into the equation when empowered customers participate in the experience.

As such, in considering your own service offering against the value equation, don't just focus on results and price. As the equation makes clear, the customer perspective has a decisive impact on the value perception, and that is where you should take aim in formulating your operating strategy, which will in turn condition the design of your delivery system.

Cirque du Soleil is the supreme example of how to do this, as W. Chan Kim and Renée Mauborgne explain in their book, *Blue Ocean Strategy* (for more on this topic, see Chap. 2 on Strategy). By plotting all the fundamental elements of the value proposition (Fig. 7.4), one sees the very different ways in which Cirque du Soleil leverages the value equation to compete on opposite terms with traditional circuses: it keeps the emotional elements high, while eliminating the big-ticket items that incur costs or are not valued highly enough by target customers to justify the extra costs involved (the stars and animals). This illustrates one way of resolving the inherent tension between cost and quality so that customers still perceive some value from the overall service experience. Price, then, is set as a consequence of the higher value perception.

The same exercise could be plotted for Secret Cinema versus the traditional neighborhood multiplex, revealing how Secret Cinema is able to command five times the price for a ticket to one of its extravaganzas in a way that a local theater never could if it decided to show a *Back to the Future* retrospective.

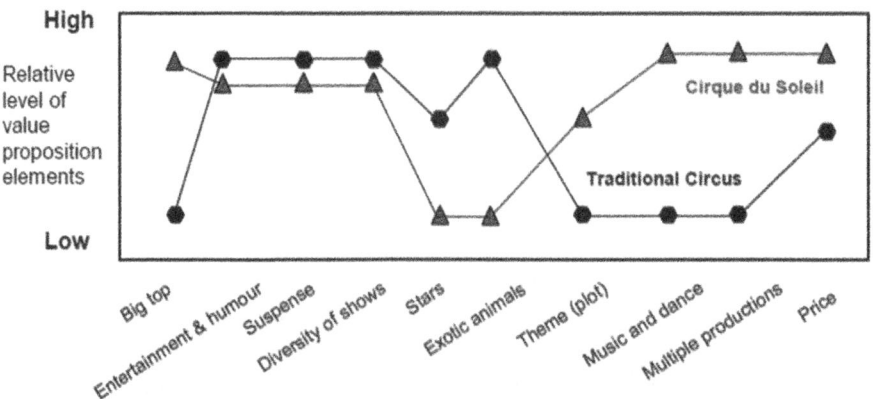

Fig. 7.4 How Cirque du Soleil Competes (Adapted from Kim and Mauborgne)

However, Secret Cinema's operations have not been perfect. Indeed, it has run into the classic problems that arise when allowing too much customer involvement and variability in a company's service system.

Classic Problem 1: Raising Expectations Beyond Reasonable Limits of What's Deliverable

When Secret Cinema staged its first event in 2007, a few hundred people turned up to see Gus Van Sant's *Paranoid Park* projected onto the wall of an abandoned London tunnel. But each and every screening has grown more and more elaborate: 2008's *Ghostbusters* enlisted actors to re-create gags from the movie; 2009's *Alien* issued the audience with space suits and ushered them through a spaceship wreathed in dry ice where they could see "aliens"; 2010's *Lawrence of Arabia* upped the ante with camels, galloping horses, belly dancers and desert sand; and 2012's production of *The Shawshank Redemption* went so far as to put the audience on trial, bused them to a disused school that doubled as a prison, stripped them of their street clothes and made them wear prison uniforms, and then frog-marched them into cells, where they were ordered about by guards and subjected to reenacted scenes of prison violence. For this elaborate piece of theater, the Secret Cinema organizers had just two months, from finding the building to opening night.

This generates enormous buzz, which brings the punters back for more, and sees audience sizes going from hundreds to thousands to tens of thousands. But the bigger they come, the harder they fall. Less than two hours before *Back to the Future* was due to open on July 24, 2014, the event had to be canceled owing to unspecified operational challenges. Riggall has never fully explained what those were, but reports range from the sets not being finished, to health and safety requirements not being met, to issues around animal welfare, to the local council not being satisfied that everything was in order. It took another full week before the issues were resolved, and the show finally opened on July 31—but not before disappointed ticketholders had vented their rage online, with some complaining they had taken off work and traveled from abroad for this one-time event. Secret Cinema broke one of the golden rules of service delivery: don't overpromise what you can't realistically deliver.

Allied to this is cost: according to *Wired* magazine, records show the company to be operating at losses of around half a million pounds per year. In striving to achieve the higher high, each project grows increasingly more capital intensive. Riggall says ticket sales amounted to £3.5 million in 2012, but he won't reveal his operating costs [7], which can only be going up in line with the jaw-dropping scale of each event, involving more paid actors, bands, expensive props, live animals and so on. Ironically, referring back to the Cirque du Soleil graphic, Riggall appears to be competing on the value proposition elements of the traditional circus. How long will this be sustainable?

Classic Problem 2: Managing the Server Side but Forgetting the Customer Side

Secret Cinema owes its success to social media. It uses an online network of millions to spread the word about coming events. People register online and share information via Facebook and Twitter. The locations are kept under wraps until a few weeks or days beforehand, when customers receive an instructional email telling them where to go, what to wear and what to do. From the point of view of the service provider, this is an indispensable tool that reduces costs, eliminates the need for marketing and advertising and adds to the mystique of the brand all at once.

However, the benefits cannot only go one way. Social media tools have to serve the needs of the customers as well. In the case of the *Back to the Future* opening-night fiasco, customers were instructed to leave their cell phones at home, so as not to interfere with them fully immersing themselves in the 1950s atmosphere. That move proved disastrous a few hours later, as social media became the only means of informing customers that the show had been canceled. Customers had no means of seeing the company's eleventh-hour announcements. They were left stranded—foolishly wandering the streets of London in costume—with no way of getting information about what was going on. As one of those affected told the BBC, "It's a big lesson for them to learn: sending 3,500 people to a secret location without their phones" [8].

Classic Problem 3: Focusing so Much on Surpassing Expectations That You Forget About Customer Perceptions

Another operations mistake is not appreciating that production and consumption have to go hand in hand. Even when the service delivery is excellent, providers must not forget that it is how the customers consume the service and their perception of whether it has been excellent that holds sway.

By most accounts, Secret Cinema events have a reputation for excellence. But the more its reputation grows, the more it is being courted by the major studios to partner on movie projects. Ridley Scott, for example, advised on a Secret Cinema version of his movie, *Prometheus*, timed for the same day as its UK premier in traditional movie theaters. Fox Searchlight UK then partnered with Secret Cinema for a lavish screening of *The Grand Budapest Hotel* in advance of its nationwide release. Plans are also under way to take Secret Cinema to the United States, where Hollywood executives are eagerly rubbing their hands together at the prospects of breathing new life into flagging box office sales.

For Riggall, the sky's the limit, and he has voiced ambitions of wanting to hold globally connected screenings involving millions of people. He has also admitted that the bigger the scale, the harder it gets to maintain the same level of interactivity and intimacy that has lent Secret Cinema its devoted fan base [9]. The winning formula until now has been its focus on cult movies and the feeling that fans have been let in on a special secret. The risk now is in biting the hand that feeds it by not respecting how customers perceive what it is they are getting.

Sarah Atkinson, a film and media lecturer at the University of Brighton in England, articulated the problem this way to *The Independent*: "(The new audiences on social media) are getting frustrated because they can't get the information they're used to. They're annoyed they can't take in recording devices, that they don't know where it's going to be. Now it's moving away from its clandestine roots to a more commercial audience, there's a chance it's going to rub up against their values" [9].

As soon as customers start to perceive Secret Cinema as a misnomer—nothing very secret, and just another mainstream commercial product with very little to distinguish it from the multiplex—the danger is they will start to abandon it in favor of another entertainment offering that they perceive as being closer to their needs and desires.

Even though the *Back to the Future* event eventually delivered on its promise, and largely seemed to have recouped the goodwill it initially lost by offering an unforgettable service experience, some customers still complained about the long lines for food, carnival rides and bathrooms, and the high prices for merchandise available for sale on site.

Wait times, crowds, high prices: these are precisely the problems that customers perceive about the current multiplex experience, and for which the Secret Cinema service delivery model is supposed to offer them an alternative. And these issues are service attributes on which any customer will have strong opinions, whereas the quality of the show itself may be harder to evaluate. When this is the case, the denominator attributes will carry more weight in the customer's value perception than the numerator attributes, which brings us to the Second Law of Services, or Classic Problem 4.

Classic Problem 4: It Is Much More Difficult to Recover from a Bad Perception than It Is to Keep a Good One

The effort and cost required to bring the customer's level of satisfaction back up to the level it was before the negative incident (the last-minute show cancelation) are usually much greater than the effort and cost necessary to prevent the drop in satisfaction in the first place. Having said that, it has been shown that a good recovery after a negative incident can result in a high level of customer satisfaction. Customers understand that companies make mistakes, but the decisive factor is how customers perceive them as fixing those mistakes. Given this, the service system should be proactive, rather than reactive.

Service Gaps: Analyzing the Root Causes of Customer Dissatisfaction

The difference between the customer's expectations and perceptions, which was discussed in the First Law of Services, should be managed throughout the delivery of the service—or what we call "the customer journey." Fig. 7.5, adapted from work by A. Parasuraman et al., illustrates the chain of mismatches or

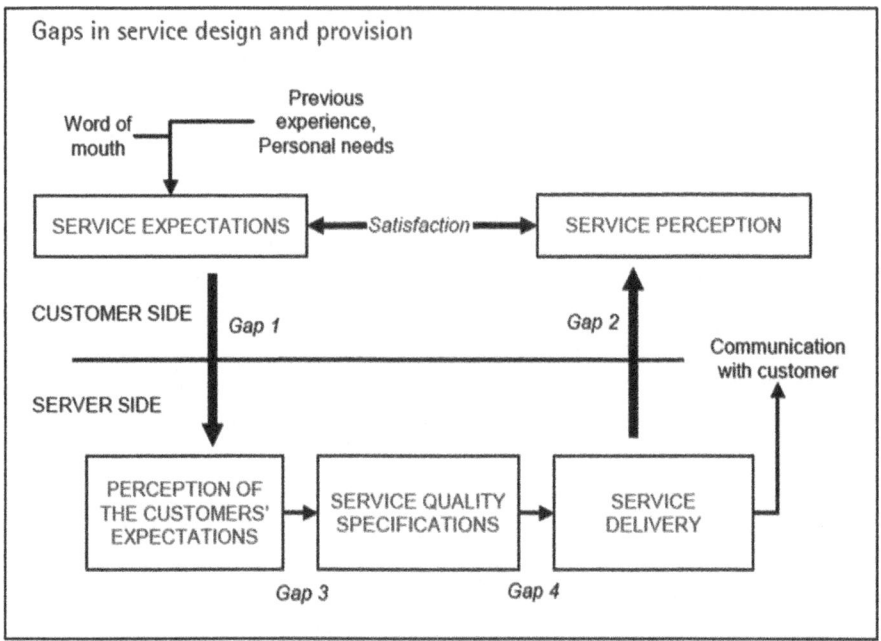

Fig. 7.5 Gaps in Service Design and Provision (Adapted from Parasuraman)

gaps that leads to service quality problems [10]. Managers need to focus their attention on four major gaps where operational mistakes commonly occur. As these gaps are caused by different issues and can be solved in different ways by different people, each must be dealt with separately on its own terms.

Understanding and managing customer service expectations is perhaps where mistakes in service delivery are made most frequently (Gap 1). This is true for the media and entertainment industry. Too many companies are unaware of what the customer really expects of their service or, alternatively, they mistakenly assume that the customer prefers or values certain attributes above others—such as speed over quality of information. Clearly, the way to overcome these errors is by listening to your customers' needs and suggestions. Beyond just understanding their expectations, you should focus on intelligently managing your customers' expectations and adjusting them to what you can realistically offer.

At the other end of the service delivery cycle, you need to manage the customer's final perception of the service (Gap 2). As mentioned before, service providers cannot assume that the customer will fully appreciate their (great) service experience in all its variety. Instead, service providers will have to think about how they can highlight the value. For example, a delivery company that offers money back in the event that a product arrives late does more than just "make good" on a service lapse; it is effectively encouraging the customer to pay much more attention to on-time delivery, which, if normally achieved, will reinforce positive final perceptions.

In addition, there may exist gaps in the service design (Gap 3). This potential error is typically associated with strategic decisions. A manager may deliberately decide to offer a homogeneous service to a very diverse group of customers, but doing so will make it harder to meet everyone's expectations.

Even when the service delivery process has been well designed, it is possible that variations occur and the client does not receive the service as planned (Gap 4). In manufacturing, a product that failed to meet the quality specs, for example, would never reach the customer. In the news business, the speed of online media has led to gaps in quality compared with traditional news channels. This is invariably the case whenever production and consumption are simultaneous: any failure will be directly perceived by the customer and the company has little if any opportunity to get ahead of it.

Pause for Thought

What are the key levers of value in your customer value proposition?
Do you go beyond the traditional "results/price" considerations?
Does the customer contribute significantly to your service provision?
What benefits can you obtain for the customer and the company from that collaboration? Which risks or gaps need to be managed?
What are the root causes of customer dissatisfaction in your case?

Managing Projects Successfully: Bringing Method to the Madness

From an operations management perspective, most of what media and entertainment professionals do can be boiled down to two basic things: they manage *processes* and they manage *projects*. Producing a movie, for example, essentially involves assembling a crew to work together for a specific purpose, over a fixed period of time and within a set budget—the very definition of project management. This does not mean that the resources used for the project cease to exist after the objective has been achieved. Rather, they may be redeployed in a different manner for the next project. So, although movie production processes may be similar, they must be adapted to the needs of each and every new project.

Expert project managers are those who are able to strike the right balance between *scope, schedule* and *budget* in order to ensure positive outcomes for customers, project participants and the business as a whole. If you are put in charge of a project, it's important to frame it in these terms. This will help to concentrate minds on only doing what falls within the scope of fulfilling the unique purpose of the project, sticking to agreed start and end dates, and keeping a close eye on material, labor and economic resources. Then, if there is a shortage of resources, for example, the manager knows that the scope and schedule of the project need to be adjusted accordingly.

There are numerous ways of classifying a project, but the simple matrix of Fig. 7.6 can be useful for project management purposes.

A Projects: If *what* you want and *how* you will achieve it are known in advance, you simply need to deploy familiar activities; these projects are like painting by numbers.

B Projects: If you know *what* you want, but not *how* you will achieve it, the project becomes the means of searching for the best way to achieve the desired result (aka "search projects").

C Projects: These are projects where the solution is available, but you need a problem to solve; in other words, you've got the hammer but you need to find nails for the tool at hand (aka "hammer syndrome").

D Projects: Here you have to determine the *what* and the *how*, perhaps using iterative learning processes, where each phase builds on the one before, and the project takes shape as it evolves (aka "lost in the fog" projects).

Once you have classified the nature of your project, then you can implement a methodology and appoint a project manager or project management office, which could be an entire department, dedicated to making sure the right tools, skill sets and resources are in place, and responsible for keeping the risks under control and the project goals aligned with the strategic aims of the company. When embarking on any project, these two factors are key: the

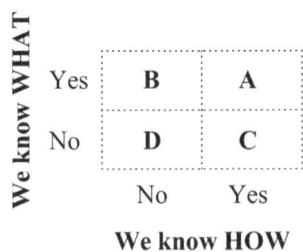

Fig. 7.6 Project Management Matrix

project's strategic fit with overall organizational aims and objectives; and the resources available. These will condition your outcomes.

Though all this may sound obvious, the number of projects that fail—missing their intended targets, going over budget and being late—suggests most managers could do with a reminder as well as a project management methodology.

All projects pass through a similar series of phases, which are summarized in Fig. 7.7. Such a framework forces you to do things in a more systematic way, and not to forget things. Also, as you will have to document work, the methodology can serve for communication purposes.

1. **Project Selection.** This ultimately falls to top managers to decide, as they are the ones who allocate resources of money, equipment, people and time. A studio may get dozens of movie scripts a year, but has to carefully select the one it will bet on next. In deciding which projects to green light, managers need to consider the bandwidth available, particularly related to capacity, and the bottlenecks created by other projects in the pipeline, as described at the beginning of this chapter.

2. **Project Definition.** This is like drawing up a contract to define the parameters of the *what* and *how*. It involves defining the mission, or rationale, of the project, the deliverables, the scope, the stakeholders, the success criteria, the risk assumptions and the economic impact. It also checks that there is a suitable mandate—that there is adequate support from upper management and key stakeholders to keep the project a priority and avoid loss of interest or mission drift.

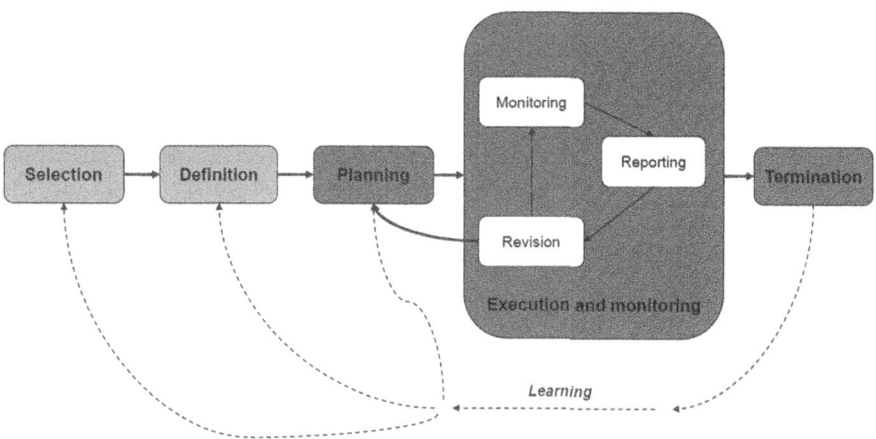

Fig. 7.7 Project Life Cycle

3. **Project Planning.** This step deals explicitly with the *how*. Each phase of the project needs to be broken down into manageable, assignable chunks. If the project were to write a book, you could break it down into activities such as choosing a title, preparing the table of contents, writing the chapters, looking for a publisher, and so forth. One of the biggest mistakes at this phase is not incorporating buffers into the plan to absorb unforeseen changes, or not calculating the probability of certain risks causing the plan to deviate off course, and not preparing action plans to deal with such events. It's best not to be overly optimistic at the planning stage.

4. **Project Execution and Monitoring.** Here you start to put the plan into action. For this, it is vital to have monitoring mechanisms in place. As anyone who has ever worked on a movie will attest, the issue is not whether deviations from the plan will occur, but inevitably when (the director will ask for more money or time), and deciding whether they are significant enough to require intervention. It is often helpful to use a traffic light system to signal difficulties, with yellow indicating "proceed with caution as you could run into bigger problems down the road," and red showing that the project is in real danger.

5. **Project Termination.** This milestone is more than hitting the end date; it entails associated phases of analyzing what went well and not so well, reflecting on the lessons learned that can be applied to future projects (such as next TV show). In journalism, this is known as the post-mortem. Unfortunately, this step is often skipped, and managers rush headlong into the next project, naively believing that everything will go better next time around. *The New York Times* Innovation Report stresses the necessity of learning the lessons and sharing them widely: "No project should be declared a success, or shuttered, without a debrief on what we've learned, so that we can apply those insights more broadly" [11].

Sometimes, projects aim to improve existing operations. During the Media AMP, Dorte Spiegelhauer, a participant, shared several lessons that had worked for her when rolling out a change-management project at the Danish Broadcasting Corporation. At the project definition stage, she was very clear about keeping the scope narrow and time-bound. "We chose a very difficult project with time pressure, in which the managers were worried about it going wrong, so this motivated them to try even harder to make sure it succeeded."

Spiegelhauer also "rewarded people who showed initiative." Generally speaking, every project team needs a healthy mix of personality types and behavioral roles, with some people being more action-oriented, while others are more thinking types. Spiegelhauer made sure she had three managers who could serve as project ambassadors and champions, constantly motivating the team and cascading energy and excitement down to the other members, which would then ripple out across the organization. This, she believed, was crucial for the results to be sustained and provided a solid foundation for building future projects.

Above all, media companies may need to hone their project management skills in the B, C and D categories. Media executives are largely skilled at A projects, where most of the variables are quantifiable and known. They demand full clarity and precision, and are usually prepared to forgo some projects if every "i" is not dotted and every "t" not crossed.

Increasingly, however, in the fast-changing business environment in which we find ourselves operating today, the projects that media and entertainment professionals need to manage are falling into the D category. And this is where we struggle, because these types of projects are undoubtedly more complex, risky and demanding—yet they are also more likely to yield operations breakthroughs.

Pause for Thought

Do you know how many ongoing projects you have in your company?
Do you have a clear definition in your company of what makes a project?
Do you use any methodology for project management?

Some Final Thoughts on Digitization

Although the Internet allows for radically new operations models today, this doesn't make operations management any less relevant. Waiting time will always be present—though rather than a physical queue forming outside a movie theater, the waits now come in the form of buffering problems and cutouts when trying to watch a movie online. To deal with what is essentially a modern variant of a classic operations problem, Netflix has had to sign deals with cable providers to ensure enough bandwidth to its customers' homes, and partnered with Amazon Web Services to be able to quickly deploy thousands of servers and terabytes of content storage on any device anywhere in the world.

At the same time, big data can provide rich customer insights that are highly valuable for the management of operations. Amazon Web Services, for example, leverages Netflix customer insights for anticipating the demand of content, which allows it to optimize content storage on its servers.

So, by all means, play with the business variables. Have a go with the radical new operational models that digital media allow, turning them into new sources of competitive advantage. But don't forget, you will always have a tube to manage!

References

1. D. Simchi-Levi (2011), "Seven Myths to Beat Before They Beat You," *IESE Insight* magazine, First Quarter, Issue 8, p. 66.
2. J.L. Heskett (1987), "Lessons in the Service Sector," *Harvard Business Review*, March Issue.
3. H. Boaden (November 13, 2008), "The Role of Citizen Journalism in Modern Democracy," The Editors BBC blog, http://www.bbc.co.uk/blogs/theeditors/2008/11/the_role_of_citizen_journalism.html
4. *The New York Times* Innovation Report (March 24, 2014), p. 72.
5. F. Riggall (September 19, 2014), "Secret Cinema Founder Fabien Riggall on Future of Cinema," *Screen Daily*, Media Business Insight Limited, http://www.screendaily.com/comment/secret-cinema-founder-on-future-of-cinema/5077742.article
6. L.M. Huete and A. Perez (2003), *Clienting: marketing y servicios para rentabilizar la lealtad* (Deusto).
7. T. Cheshire (June 2013), "The Screen Saver: Secret Cinema's Mission to Save the Movies," *Wired* magazine, http://www.wired.co.uk/magazine/archive/2013/06/feature-the-screen-saver/the-screen-saver/viewgallery/304363
8. BBC News' Entertainment & Arts section (July 24, 2014), "Secret Cinema Cancels Back to the Future Opening Night," http://www.bbc.com/news/entertainment-arts-28471433
9. A. Bland (July 23, 2014|), "Can Secret Cinema Sell 80,000 'Back to the Future' Tickets?" *The Independent*, http://www.independent.co.uk/arts-entertainment/films/features/can-secret-cinema-sell-80000-back-to-the-future-tickets-9621917.html
10. A. Parasuraman, V.A. Zeithaml and L.L. Berry (1985), "A Conceptual Model of Service Quality and Its Implications for Future Research," *Journal of Marketing*, Vol. 49, Issue 4, 41–50.
11. *The New York Times* Innovation Report (March 24, 2014), p. 32.

8

The Digital Economy: It's Not the Technology, It's the Business Model, Stupid!

Sandra Sieber with Philip H. Seager

Think about this: you have to catch a flight, so you pull out your phone. It summons a cab or your driverless car, which automatically knows what the traffic conditions are, and gets you to the airport on time. No need to fumble for your flight information: as soon as you walk through the doors of the airport, your phone pulls up your boarding pass and tells you which gate to go to. When you get on the plane, your drink and food preferences are already waiting, as is the rental car when you arrive at the other end. When you get to your hotel, no need to get in line and check in: the front desk has already been informed of your arrival, and they hand you your keycard. When you get to your room, the door automatically opens for you. As you walk in, already playing are the television shows you want to see or the music you like to listen to, not some hotel dub. The room temperature is set the way you like it. Room service is on its way, as

This chapter also contains some material from E. Káganer, J. Zamora and S. Sieber (2013), "5 Skills Every Leader Needs to Succeed in the Digital World," *IESE Insight* magazine, Third Quarter, Issue 18, and the video "The Digital Mindset" from the IESE Insight Business Knowledge Portal, http://www.ieseinsight.com/fichaMaterial.aspx?pk=119449&idi=2&origen=1&ar=5&

S. Sieber (✉)
Information Systems Department,
IESE Business School, Barcelona, Spain
e-mail: SSieber@iese.edu

P.H. Seager
IESE Business School, Barcelona, Spain
e-mail: PSeager@iese.edu

© The Author(s) 2017
M. Rosenberg, P.H. Seager (eds.), *Managing Media Businesses*,
DOI 10.1007/978-3-319-52021-6_8

135

your movements have been tracked from the moment you left the airport, and the kitchen placed your order so your favorite dish would be delivered as desired.

This is not science fiction. In fact, as one of the world's leading technology experts Greg Harper attests, all this currently exists. It's just that they mostly exist as individual apps that have not been combined together into one total, seamless experience—yet.

Visiting Harper's Manhattan home is like taking a trip to Mr. Magorium's Wonder Emporium. The thermostat automatically adjusts the room temperature according to the number of bodies heating up the room. The smoke detector in the basement talks to the one upstairs. The lights turn on and off as you move from room to room. His music—one of millions of tracks—plays in whichever room he wants, as do any one of the thousands of movies stored in his home server (boasting 80 terabytes of storage), which are all available via any number of portable devices scattered throughout the house. His upstairs features a fully equipped television studio. Running the fiber-optic cabling necessary to turn his house into a state-of-the-art technology palace involved everyone from New York City street authorities, Empire City Subway and even the Secret Service, as the path of all these exceptional works fell along the same route traveled by the president of the United States during official visits.

And when Harper says, "Wearables are everywhere," he's not kidding. His entire body is kitted out with all manner of devices, making him a walking testimony to all the technology of which he speaks in the same hallowed, dulcet tones that Willy Wonka might use to describe chocolate.

"Obviously I'm wearing Google Glass," he says. "I'm also wearing a Pebble watch. I'm wearing a sports sensor here which is a—which one am I wearing?" He has to check his wrist. "I'm wearing the Nike Fuel. On here, I've got the Samsung. This one is—I don't even remember what this one is." You would think he would run out of appendages on which to hang all his tech toys, many of which are not even on the market yet but for which he is first in line to serve as the gizmo guinea pig.

When it comes to wearables, "I have a few of them," he tells the group of media and entertainment executives gathered, wide-eyed, in his living room. And then, as if realizing his gross understatement, he laughingly corrects himself: "Actually, I pretty much have all of them."

"People ask me, 'What is the most interesting of them all?' The answer is none of them. It's still too early. This one has a display that is readable in daylight and also at night without using a lot of battery, but the software is so bad that you can't use it. These guys came up with a very good measurement of how well your body is doing, but when you wear it for a while, you get a rash. This one has more functionality, with a nice big screen, but it's pretty ugly and it runs out of battery. This is probably the best one. That's what I'm wearing more often now because at least this works for five days. But you can't see anything unless you push the button and see the light on."

He waves them aside. "All of these are heading out to my Museum of Computing"—which, he explains, is a barn in Upstate New York where nearly 40 years' worth of his collectibles is being dutifully gathered and will serve as his legacy to mankind, cataloging our head-spinning shift from life as we know it to the brave new world that media and entertainment executives, especially, need to grasp if they are not only to stay in the game but to carve out their own unique space in the future.

Ready for Anything

That information and communications technologies (ICT) are reshaping the media and entertainment landscape, changing the way companies compete and redrawing market boundaries, goes without saying. We have all experienced the changes firsthand, starting with mobile phones, then with broadband, and now with ever greater wireless communications. As Harper says, we take all this for granted, even though none of this was around little more than a decade ago.

My point in this chapter is not to describe the myriad ways in which digital devices are dramatically changing everything we do and every way we work today. Media and entertainment executives will be familiar with most of them and, like Harper, are probably busy finding ways of incorporating them into their personal and professional lives (though perhaps they stop short of implanting a microchip under their skin so they can simply wave their hands to open doors and use the office photocopier, the way that BBC News' technology correspondent Rory Cellan-Jones did for a story on this happening in Sweden) [1].

Instead, I want to focus on understanding the underlying business models and ecosystems on which today's digital revolution is being built. As one executive of an online platform and app for health-and-wellness services observed, ICT are merely disruption enablers—the real disruption comes from rethinking the business models of an industry.

Another executive echoed this sentiment, noting that becoming a dominant player—akin to the Gang of Four that is Apple, Facebook, Google and Amazon, or the Gang of Five if you count Twitter—is the result of smart strategic choices, based on an appreciation of the affordances of new technology.

In this chapter, I will use examples of digital transformation to reveal the fundamental drivers behind them. I will also discuss some of the key trends in online business and try to project their future implications. Most important, given that the landscape is evolving so fast, I will emphasize the need to adopt a digital mindset—because no matter what new tech innovation comes next, you, as a manager, need to have the capabilities and competencies to be ready for anything.

The People Have Spoken: Have You Been Listening?

Let's start by reminding ourselves of the general backdrop against which the digital revolution is taking place. A decade ago, technology was hardly the living-room conversation it is today. In 2005, Britain's *Guardian* made what it considered to be a bold move by christening a new Technology section in the newspaper. Nowadays you would be hard-pressed to find any media outlet that doesn't feature Technology as a stand-alone section, sharing privileged space on the navigation bar alongside the old standbys of News, Sport, Business, Lifestyle and Weather. It seems everyone agrees with the *Guardian*'s justification for giving Technology a promotion: "The Internet is, of course, the driving force behind much of society today" [2].

How has this shift happened so fast? For the simple reason that tech innovators grasped a vital truth that established media and entertainment corporations have been slower to realize: bypass the traditional gatekeepers and go straight to the individual. Not only that, make it easier for the individual to consume your product or service by lowering the barriers to entry and making the interaction quick, easy, relevant, intuitive and—the clincher—free.

Back in 2006, Jay Rosen, who teaches journalism at New York University, gave a stark assessment of this shift, in a blog post that described "the people formerly known as the audience." "The people formerly known as the audience are those who were on the receiving end of a media system that ran one way, in a broadcasting pattern, with high entry fees and a few firms competing to speak very loudly while the rest of the population listened in isolation from one another—and who today are not in a situation like that at all. Once they were *your* printing presses … once it was *your* radio station … shooting, editing and distributing video once belonged to *you*, Big Media … Now video is coming into the user's hands … We're not on your clock anymore." Not only do "the people formerly known as the audience" want media when they want it, they want it "without the filler … way better than it is … publishing and broadcasting ourselves when it meets a need or sounds like fun" [3].

Besides this sense of people empowerment, the other key point to bear in mind about these revolutionary words is that they are not just being spoken by the generation commonly referred to as Digital Natives—those young people who have grown up with technology and can't conceive of a world where the Internet didn't exist. The fact of the matter is, even their counterparts—the Digital Immigrants, those older people who supposedly have a much harder time wrapping their heads around technology—are fast joining the same ranks.

Take my elderly mother: when I first bought her a tablet, she reacted like she needed *that* like a fish needs a bicycle. Visiting her one day and seeing the tablet still sitting there untouched, I gently showed her a few features, and then left her to it, figuring it would go back to gathering dust after I left. Imagine my surprise, then, when not long after my visit I received a Skype message from her berating me for not having commented on her latest travel blog post!

This is just one small anecdote of a worldwide trend: the empowering effect of technology that is not limited to a small subset of teenage computer geeks. Indeed, I believe the entire Digital Native/Digital Immigrant media categorization is a false dichotomy that needs to be shed, because it tries to cast the world into two separate types: the whiz kids demanding new media and the old fogeys on whom we can still palm off the same old products and services. Senior citizens, or mature users, are just as, if not more, thrilled by the intuitive, tactile, user-friendly interfaces of tablets and other portable mobile devices as those babies shown in online videos trying to touch and swipe their home TV screens.

Or take this quote from a participant in a research project by an IESE colleague (Giuseppe Auricchio) who studied technology adoption in executive leadership development programs: "I'd like to believe the Generation X and Y and all this jazz. I see people who are in our generation (older) and who are equally adept at technology as people in the younger generation. I think that the common factor is human nature. My general belief in human nature is we prefer things that are relationship-based and that give us human interaction—and I don't buy the generational argument" [4].

For this reason, I am toying with new terms: Digital Visitors and Digital Residents. Rather than referring to Natives, which you either are or you aren't, I prefer a more inclusive conceptualization that recognizes that all of us—young or old, born or reformed—have embraced Digital; we're just at different places along the same spectrum. At first we might be Visitors, but, just like my mother, we can all soon learn enough technology to become permanent Residents. I think this is an important distinction that media and entertainment executives should consider, lest they labor under false notions of a Digital Divide, fooling themselves into thinking they can still get away with serving a non-digital audience. Such thinking will only slow a business transformation that in many cases may already be too late. Even the pundit who popularized the Digital Native/Digital Immigrant label has since moved on to talk about Digital Wisdom—based on the premise that technology is a universal enabler that helps all kinds of people find "wise" solutions to the individual problems they face [5]. Whatever terms you decide to use, make sure that nobody is left out.

The evidence is all around us, as companies of all stripes are increasingly migrating their operations over to the ICT already being used by the masses. This is another truth that tech innovators got right: "Once the users take control, they never give it back," to quote one of the earliest bloggers, Dave Winer [3]. Gmail, for example, went straight for individual users, and now businesses are adopting it after the fact, in a kind of throwing-up-their-hands admission that they have no choice but to go where the majority of people now are. The same goes for Google apps: everyone is already using them in their mobiles, so it makes sense for companies to follow suit. Facebook, too, started out for personal use for individuals to connect and communicate with each other; now more and more organizations are applying similar social media networking solutions to their own workplace collaborations.

This marks a big change from the old order, when all corporations used Microsoft-based PCs and ignored these "consumer technologies." Now the paradigm has flipped: corporations are accepting these technologies as good enough for them, too, and switching over. This is the major challenge confronting Microsoft: it had business clients all sewn up but now it has to follow the general tide of consumers. This is a much harder sell, especially if you come late to the party and the consumers have already spoken. That leaves you having to play catch-up.

Key Ideas

- For the first time in the history of ICT, innovators are going straight to the consumer rather than via corporations—leaving them as the ones that have to catch up.
- Don't think the next generation of users must necessarily be those young people being born today who'll be the Digital Natives of tomorrow. You

need to open the windows of opportunity to consider the full spectrum of digital denizens. Remember, as the IESE research participant observed, "things that are relationship-based and that give us human interaction" are common to human nature, irrespective of generation.

Zopa, a Case in Point: Don't Ask Why, Ask Why Not

Consider the way Zopa (www.zopa.com) understood the shift and used it to disrupt the traditional paradigm of another sector as entrenched as Big Media—that of Big Banking. Zopa is an online platform founded in 2005 that brings borrowers and lenders together, cutting out the banks entirely. If you were a lender, why would you want to give money to strangers over the Internet? If you were a borrower, wouldn't you feel safer dealing with the established terms and conditions of a conventional bank?

But that's the old way of thinking, typical when confronting change. First, there's a level of discomfort, a lack of trust, and the incumbents dig in their heels to maintain the status quo; after all, they have legacy systems to preserve, and their key success factors are different. Today's collaborative technologies bypass this, enabling Zopa to parcel up loans into multiple microloans, so lenders can give as little as £10 and spread the risk among lots of different borrowers, and borrowers receive lending terms better than typical banks. Once you remove the discomfort, people participate. The more people participate, the more success stories there are, and the more people trust the new system. Plus, there is a feeling of being part of something new and exciting. Or to quote Zopa's own one-word descriptions, to be part of something "honest," "trustworthy," "ethical," "fresh," "rewarding" and "sensible." Now the question becomes: why *wouldn't* you try peer-to-peer lending?

As you think about disruptive innovation in your own sector, this change of mindset is key. Take another case: in 2014, the US Supreme Court ruled against the Internet TV startup, Aereo, for violating the rights of traditional broadcasters by retransmitting their programming to users via tiny antennas. As *The Wall Street Journal* explained, "For broadcasters, the victory preserves traditional and lucrative revenue streams, most notably the fees they charge pay-TV distributors to carry their signals, which could have been undercut by an Aereo win … The growth in fees has helped broadcasters offset a slowdown in advertising revenue" [6].

This is the classic reaction of incumbents: fight to preserve the status quo. However, just because this battle was lost, don't think the war has been won. As we have seen time and again over the past decade, there is no holding back the general tide of people wanting more Internet-based broadcasting alternatives. Does anyone seriously believe that, with Aereo gone, consumers will give up on their demand to record and watch programs anywhere, anytime, on any electronic device? That people will no longer seek to "cut the cord" with extortionate pay-TV providers? And if advertisers and other traditional revenue streams are already flowing elsewhere, how long will traditional broadcasters keep waging costly court battles based on legal frameworks conceived before there was even an Internet? It is time for a complete rethink.

An Inside Look at Bloomberg

From Greg Harper's wired home (and body), let's take an entirely different look at the future, this time from inside Bloomberg's New York City headquarters that lies a short stroll from IESE's own Manhattan campus. We are given a tour of the sleek, horseshoe-shaped space, which features one of the world's few spiral escalators; a "green room" made with 3M privacy glass that goes opaque as you walk past to hide the identities of the guests waiting inside to be interviewed; and all-glass offices displaying the names of cities in all the countries where Bloomberg has a business presence, along with the number of subscribers there, which are regularly updated. We file past fish tanks; fresh food stations, or "pantries" as they call them, laden with free, mouth-watering treats for the employees; and glass cases exhibiting Bloomberg's legendary desktop terminals—which, to the eyes of this group of media executives, look perfectly at home in their museum-style settings. We are escorted to a conference room where we are greeted by a Bloomberg executive, who, in an enlightening, free-ranging conversation, reveals why—despite all the dynamics I described earlier—a seemingly old-school product or service can still survive, provided it gets several critical things right about how information ecosystems and platforms work.

First, one needs to understand Bloomberg's business model. Michael Bloomberg (a former Wall Street trader turned businessman, and later three-term mayor of New York City) founded his eponymous company in 1981 as a tech business to provide financial data to industry analysts, like he used to be. Although the company has expanded its offer over the years to include a wire service, television and radio networks, and magazines such as *Businessweek*, its bread and butter remains its formidable Terminal—a computer system that looks barely changed since its inception, yet remains the coveted staple of the global finance industry. At the time of writing, each terminal cost $20,000 a year and Bloomberg had around 320,000 subscribers. Do the math: that's a cool $6.4 billion a year just from terminals alone, making Bloomberg's other media interests seem like the icing on the cake. The terminal display appears no fancier than a basic Windows application or Excel file. While other media sites are vying for Webby Awards for their all-singing, all-dancing online experiences, the Bloomberg screen, with its multicolored text against a black background, looks positively Stone Age. By all modern standards, this should not still work. Yet it does. How?

To appreciate the robustness of the Bloomberg business model, one needs to go back to the basic economic principle of two-sided, or double-sided, markets or networks. Take the example most familiar to media executives: newspapers. A newspaper is a platform that sits between two distinct markets: subscribers on the one side and advertisers on the other. In a traditional economic model, value creation moves from left (cost) to right (revenue). However, in a two-sided model, value can be created on both sides. In other words, a newspaper both serves and makes money off subscribers, while at the same time both serving and making money off advertisers. Moreover, interactions between advertisers and subscribers are facilitated through the newspaper platform, which amplifies these interactions through so-called network effects. This means the more subscribers there are, the more advertisers; and the more advertisers, the more revenue that the platform can use to improve its offer to subscribers, and value keeps getting generated in a virtuous circle until eventually the winner takes all.

The problem facing newspapers at the start of the twenty-first century is not so much that the model is broken, but rather that newspapers are being beaten at their own game. Google essentially leveraged this model better and became the platform of choice for this double-sided dynamic between users and advertisers, leading Google to become the star of the New Economy. Think how Google did it. It began as the basic model of a media company: I give you information paid for by advertising. In positioning itself as the platform between searchers and advertisers, Google made search free. This meant that one side (searchers) was being subsidized by the other (advertisers), which is a common pricing strategy with two-sided networks. It is also a pricing strategy that can work with Internet-based platforms, because the number of users that can be reached grows at exponential rates. The more users there are on the subsidy side, the more those on the money side are willing to pay to reach them.

Deciding the right pricing strategy can be tricky, requiring some experimentation to capture network effects. Price too high and the money side will balk; price too low and you lose important revenue streams, degrading the platform and losing the very users you need to keep the money side interested. But the beauty of Internet platforms is that they are, by nature, constantly evolving and favor experimentation, so Google was able to do things differently.

Consider the way Google grew by stealth though advertising. Google listed them at the top of search results, which pleased advertisers, but the ads were kept deliberately simple—no distracting colors, just plain text—to maintain the ease for users. Also, when space was a scarce resource (air time, physical pages) you had to go for the "head"—the few big spenders. But there is unlimited advertising space online (infinite search links), so you can afford to go after the "tail"—the little guys and small business owners to whom you can charge less and attract many, many more. So, while traditional media fought over the one advertiser prepared to pay $1 million, online media went after the million advertisers who could afford to pay $1 each: the numbers add up the same.

In Google's case, the numbers add up even better, until the tail ends up wagging the head: the big spender paying the newspaper $1 million suddenly starts questioning why he should pay that much to reach a dwindling audience when for a fraction of that cost he can reach the same or other audiences that are growing much bigger and more segmented by the day. Once you reach a critical mass, like Google did, you disrupt the mainstream market. This becomes a virtuous circle: maintaining ease for users means they are more likely to click on the paid link when it comes up as the top search result, which attracts advertisers; the more advertisers, the more Google can hone its search engine, making it better and better for users, and so it goes on.

No discussion of platform economics would be complete without also understanding the allied issue of public and private standards. In essence, *public* platforms are those in which the intellectual property is publicly owned or administered by a consortium or by industry-wide regulation, whereas *private* platforms are those in which the intellectual property is controlled and owned by a firm. In addition, the platform standards can be *open*, so that third parties are able to develop complementary products and services, or they can be *closed*, where the details are not released but remain inside the firm. Fig. 8.1 illustrates these dimensions, with some of the best-known examples in each field.

With closed standards, firms exploit the uniqueness of their products/services and compete *for* the market by licensing or selling key technologies, and they exercise "control" via monopolistic rents: think Microsoft Windows. With open standards, the playing field is more level, the idea being that

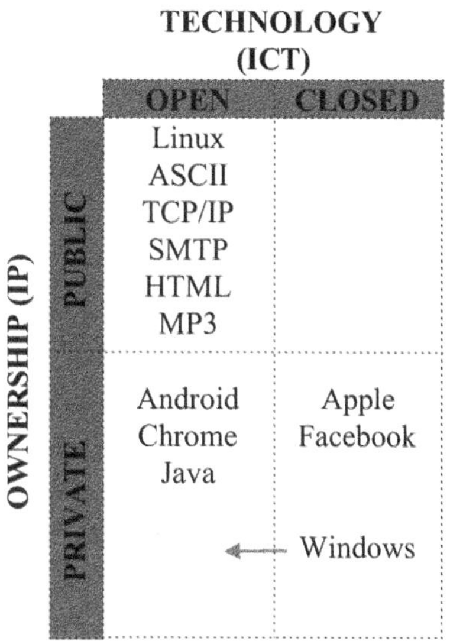

TECHNOLOGY (ICT)

		OPEN	CLOSED
OWNERSHIP (IP)	PUBLIC	Linux ASCII TCP/IP SMTP HTML MP3	
	PRIVATE	Android Chrome Java	Apple Facebook ← Windows

Fig. 8.1 Platform Standards and Examples

keeping the platform open will trigger widespread adoption and the development of complementary assets. Here firms compete *in* the market, going head-to-head against each other using lower cost or superior execution, such as speed to market, innovation, better service and distribution excellence.

The lower right-hand field is an extremely attractive position to be in: Apple has carved out its dominance here. Interestingly, Microsoft used to occupy the same position but has shifted to the lower left-hand space. In moving to docx and open-sourcing more of its software, Microsoft has been trying to switch camps, recognizing that the original means by which it achieved global dominance (proprietary software) will not last forever (given that the HTML browser is the new gatekeeper of choice for users). Even Apple, which exists in this space by design, knows that it has to embrace some degree of openness, for the simple reason that the sheer number of Android devices on the market makes its long-term position here tricky.

While there are legitimate reasons for firms to occupy the upper left-hand space, they, too, may need to change their game, as they will invariably come to rely on some complementary asset in order to make any money. And that is the key consideration for whichever position you occupy: how will you make the money necessary to guarantee your continued survival? Only ever being a complementor can be much more dangerous than trying to compete in a different segment. If you find yourself in this position, you will have to think very carefully about which platform you will choose to support, and assess how openly the platform leader is providing its IP and ICT to complementary producers. Above all, more than just working to enhance the value of the existing platform, you must focus on products/services that the leader is unlikely to offer, continuously innovating and then moving in fast and early, so as not to leave yourself exposed and let the leader beat you to the punch.

The Lock-in Effect: A Hard Habit to Break

Let's return to the Bloomberg story that began this discussion. Where does it sit in the diagram? What is the nature of its double-sided platform? What network effects are at play? Bloomberg has a very robust double-sided platform, with traders on one side and information providers on the other. At first glance, one might scoff, "You want me to pay *how much* for a machine that essentially *aggregates and displays data*, all of which is *publicly available information*?" You'd think in this day and age of countless data management tools that financial institutions would have found much better solutions by now. And yet, they haven't. That's because Bloomberg's terminal is not just another piece of technology; it's a network, and a strong one at that. Crucially, it has more than three decades' worth of user insights under its belt, informing tens of thousands of different features that customers find extremely valuable. For every story on its news feed, users can pull up additional material, charts and explainers ("What is bitcoin?"). If analysts want company information, it doesn't just spew out a list of dry stats, but generates intricate relationship patterns, supply-chain maps and money trails. Click on Carlos Slim, for example, and you don't just find out he's one of the richest businessmen in the world, but you see his entire global footprint (revealing that his sphere of influence is primarily limited to his native Mexico, a piece of contextualized information that could prove useful to a market analyst). Bloomberg's restaurant listings even provide decibel levels for executives who want to steer clear of cacophonous cafés. Bloomberg has entire teams and departments dedicated to sorting through data and then assembling the info in ways that its customers find useful.

Giving customers an unparalled user experience is what keeps them loyal and consolidates the network. So, when a user submits a query, it goes to a group of editors who respond in real time. If anyone hits the Help key twice, they are immediately patched through to a live person to resolve their dilemma. Even the simple screen displays are not lazy design, but are deliberately efficient ways of visualizing data quickly and plainly to a global audience, many of whom are non-native English speakers who prefer unembellished language, unfussy designs and cut-to-the-chase figures to something ostensibly more elegant. (This echoes Google's design philosophy for its search ads: simple, readable, spare on imagery.)

As one executive in our group commented afterward, what makes the Bloomberg platform so powerful is its content, tailored exactly to what those 320,000 customers want (and in some cases didn't even know they wanted but now can't live without). "It just goes to show that even with a customer base as small as theirs, people will pay premium if the content is good, and you can be a money-making machine if you have a laser-like focus on customers," he said. Or, to put it another way, it's not the technology, it's the business model, stupid! And Bloomberg's proprietary platform produces a strong lock-in effect that makes it hard for other media companies to break.

Toppling the Leader

This raises perhaps the toughest question of all for managers of media and entertainment companies: how to overcome an existing market dominance, or how can a dominant platform be displaced?

First, it's vital to grasp the fundamentals of double-sided markets and network effects, as these, not ICT per se, are what truly hold the key to media companies' reinvention and long-term survival. Sometimes one can build market share through complementary products/services or by making one's platform "backward compatible" with older-generation products/services. This may yield a new customer base.

The higher stakes challenge is to change the rules of the game altogether by disrupting a market with an entirely new product/service. Bloomberg's competition is no longer just another company in the same sector, like a Thomson Reuters or a Dow Jones; rather, it's anyone who can figure out better ways of putting information into consumers' hands, exactly as they want it. This opens the field to growing legions of crowdsourced data providers or third-party developers coming up with indispensable apps to help make Bloomberg's financial tools compatible and operable across multiple platforms. Likewise, the competition for television producers is not so much rival TV networks but whoever can deliver quality content to a screen that is consumable whenever and wherever the consumer wants it. Suddenly, the issue of "dominance" becomes an open question. Dominance for how much longer? Perhaps a more accurate way of tackling the competitive battleground of the media and entertainment industry is as an ever-fluctuating landscape of serial monopolies, with the dominant players constantly shape-shifting. Google's reinvention of itself as Alphabet in 2015 is a good example of this tendency: the company now exists as a collection of multiple platforms of various shapes, sizes and business objectives.

Second, in coming up with a new product/service, it has to be an *insanely great* product/service, as only a slightly better alternative to the dominant platform is not going to convince the masses to switch over. And *insanely great* products/services do not happen overnight. They require serious effort, usually coming to light over time. This only happens through endless experimentation. The good news is that today's digital tools are perfect for this job. As the Bloomberg executive recommended to us: "Try new features. If something doesn't work very well, don't necessarily take it down, but understand how those few people do use it. For those who don't use it (or who used to use it but don't anymore) understand why and what else they are using instead. This creates an opportunity. Besides, as it's just an extra feature of a paid service, it's not really costing much to keep it up there anyway."

This kind of thinking is what has been the making of Google. In its famously leaked 2014 innovation report, *The New York Times* admitted that one of the newspaper's flaws was its strict adherence to only ever launching things after they had been polished to near perfection. There was much to learn from digital innovators like Google, it said, mining user data and then refining its offer through cycles of continuous improvement [7]. Start by resisting your own perfectionist tendencies and launch a few experiments. Study how the Googles or Bloombergs of the world operate. It is in studying the underlying dynamics at play that we learn, and perhaps find an untapped gap or niche to exploit.

Third, as one of our media executives rightly observed, for all the disruptive technologies on the market today, the status quo is strong. (The Aereo ruling proves that.) Many of the fundamentals are still with us, and will remain with us for the foreseeable future. In this regard, traditional media and entertainment businesses may have certain advantages, especially if they have already dealt with and, better yet, figured out methods of resolving some of the long-running tensions that new media are now beginning to grapple with. So, you may envy the powerful search capabilities of Google, but the searches are getting increasingly complex for anything, from videos to photos to text to news to maps and who knows what else. Now Google invites users to log in and search through its platform so that it can tailor its searches according to your history. What is this except another form of paywall, the very thing that has stymied the online efforts of traditional media enterprises? What's more, it opens a raft of privacy concerns, which is giving Google plenty of legal headaches.

What about the age-old tension between editorial content and advertising? This, too, is fast entering the social media world. The use of predictive technologies to return advertising results is as aggravating for users as newspapers and magazines coming stuffed full of unwanted advertising rather than the quality content that attracted readers there in the first place. So endemic is this digital-era malady that the British satirical magazine, *Private Eye*, has dedicated an entire section to "Malgorithms" in which it republishes some of the unfortunate gaffes frequently generated by automated advertising that has nothing to do with the accompanying editorial content. (For example, a *Times* article on research showing that people who gave up Facebook experienced a boost in happiness and life satisfaction was accompanied by a web ad for Facebook, obviously generated by technology with no sense of irony.) What did traditional media do to manage this tension, and how should it be managed in a new context? For its part, YouTube has introduced rollover ads to see who skips the ad and who watches through, and then not placing ads for users who skip and targeting those who watch. It can then charge the advertiser more by being able to target ads to receptive audiences. Again, this is just a fancy technological solution to the old advertising chestnut of "targeting" going back to the 1950s.

Of course, it is important to recognize the undeniably powerful affordances of the new media players—namely, Apple, Facebook, Google, Amazon and Twitter—which are, no doubt, conditioning the future prospects of your own business. However, it is equally important not to get blinded by them but to see clearly from a perspective that is able to integrate the timeless business fundamentals behind the content you produce.

Pause for Thought
Think of the platform logic in terms of your own business:

- How might my open platform be displaced? In which directions should I be building and developing now?
- Are there pieces in my value chain that could become a closed standard?
- Is my platform backward compatible?
- What would happen if my platform leader started to behave in a more restrictive fashion and did not carry my complementary products/services anymore? What steps should I be taking now in anticipation of such a move?
- Where are my key customer bases? How am I preparing to move with them if they suddenly decide to switch platforms?

Experiment

During the Media AMP, we divided participants into three or four groups to imagine future trends. (See Chap. 11 on Scenario Planning, by Mike Rosenberg, for a detailed explanation of how to do this.) This is something you should be doing in your own company if you aren't already. Divide management teams into small, cross-functional groups to analyze the platform strategies that may affect your industry over the next three to five years. I recommend short time frames, because the pace of change in the digital realm is so fast.

In one IESE session, we asked managers to forecast the platform strategies of Comcast and Netflix, Disney and Google, and the NBA and Aereo (the startup that is no more, but another similar platform technology will no doubt resurface). Once everyone has had a chance to grapple with questions like those above and postulate on their futures, we reconvene and compare findings. In one of our sessions, some consensus emerged that:

- traditional channels would disappear in favor of more on-demand, multi-screen delivery models;
- monetization models would be content dependent, making content providers, and those who can curate content, more important than ever;
- as the discovery of new content increasingly moves away from the broadcaster and to the market, those who have the most data on the market will emerge as the winners.

The benefit of engaging in such an exercise is that it helps hone your ability to spot disruption and be prepared for whatever is next. As one executive remarked afterward, "Sometimes you can feel helpless, like your fate is being decided by the big, dominant providers. But by taking the time to really analyze the competitive dynamics going on, you realize that the end game isn't decided yet. At the end of the day, they still need content providers. And in this sense we can begin to figure out how to influence the shape and direction of the disruption, and allocate our spending accordingly."

Remember, in the digital economy, timing is everything. Your teams have to be dedicated to reading the signs—for example, if your customer base or the platform leader starts migrating in a new direction—so you know when it's time to stay in and when it's time to get out. Recalling the Zopa example mentioned earlier in this chapter, if "trust" is the key consideration that's holding the market back from fully embracing a large-scale switchover from traditional providers to P2P lenders, and you read headlines that Standard & Poor's has for the first time agreed to start giving credit ratings to P2P lenders, then you have to start asking yourself whether this is the trigger that will give these alternative providers much-needed legitimacy and mark the beginning of a mass migration to these new platforms. In which case, you don't want to be the last one standing when, in fewer years than anyone thinks possible, you wake up one day to find yours is the dinosaur platform.

Exercise

I find the Business Model Canvas (Table 8.1) created by the Swiss entrepreneur Alexander Osterwalder to be a useful way of structuring your thinking according to nine essentials and of visualizing how these business considerations fit together. You can easily draw this on a board and use Post-it notes to brainstorm in each block, or you can download resources from http://www.businessmodelgeneration.com/canvas/bmc, where there are also web-based software and iPad app versions of the same tool. There are also explainer videos online should you wish to incorporate this tool as part of an in-house workshop.

Table 8.1 Business Model Canvas (Osterwalder)

No Time for Sitting Still

Back in Greg Harper's house, he has just released the robots to mingle under-foot of our gathering. "This is a Segway robot. I like this guy. Stick him right here and he'll move around on two wheels and go find things. This is Sparky. These little robots run around and do things. Baxter is a robot that will actu-ally sit in the workplace next to you. You can make this one dance and sing. We're going to see a lot of these robots coming along."

In an unfortunate accident of timing, he lets everyone try out a pair of virtual reality goggles just after a meal break. "I was doing a demonstration of these in Denmark. It felt like being on a roller coaster, and one of the guys actually started getting sick," he chuckles.

In the midst of these antics, you have to admire one thing: Harper's passion for experimentation. There is seemingly nothing he won't try. He breathlessly tells us: "About 11 o'clock last night I said, 'You know, I really should get a second Amazon Fire TV.' So I placed the order last night and it showed up this afternoon, all programmed and ready to go. If we have time, I'll show you how easy it is to just plug it in and you'll see it working."

This eager attitude seems to be rubbing off on his wife, who he says now watches all of her television on a tablet. "My wife used to have a TV in the kitchen. It's gone. There's now an iPad in there. She's not watching linear TV anymore; she's watching whatever she wants. And that's my wife," whom he describes as being much less of a tech freak than him.

Harper's curious nature is something that every media and entertain-ment organization needs to make sure is part of its corporate culture. Media companies, especially those accustomed to enjoying entrenched, privileged positions, have to work on their disruptive skills. Regulation won't favor the incumbents forever, particularly as those who are bringing disruptive ideas to the market are precisely the ones who are pushing our existing regulatory frameworks in untold directions (and perhaps in directions more favorable to their new platforms). Media and entertainment managers urgently need to change their chip, which certainly entails a risk-taking attitude, but more than that, requires what I call a *digital mindset*, and then modeling behavior and taking action appropriate to that new way of thinking.

Uber is a prime example of the digital mindset. It's about looking at your existing business and then applying digital criteria to reimagine new possibili-ties along several critical dimensions:

- **Nature of your product/service:** digital vs. atoms?
- **Relationship with your customers:** direct vs. removed?
- **Regulatory environment:** strict vs. loose?
- **Stakeholders:** which have the strongest influence on your business?
- **Connections:** it's not so much the trends that matter, but rather, what business strategy can you adopt that will connect those trends?
- **Interactions:** it's not just making the connections but deciding what you do with the interactions between those connections, the invisible as well as the visible ones; how are you dreaming your interactions with your customers?
- **Information:** what is the key piece of information you need to answer any of the above?

Think of this logic in terms of Uber: Uber squeezed efficiencies out of idle capacity, thinking in terms of data held on the cloud rather than installed in a device. It took this idea of "idle capacity" and applied it to cars. It then built a business model around it which was not only more efficient but cheaper than the existing alternative (taxis).

Who thinks like this in your organization? Who are your Greg Harpers, the people with forward-looking mindsets who not only love technology but are able to contextualize it as part of a deeper, ongoing mega-shift that is transforming the very nature of our societies and businesses?

I call these people your HEROes, which stands for Highly Empowered and Resourceful Operatives. You need to identify them and embed them as part of a triangulated organizational framework (Fig. 8.2). HEROes are

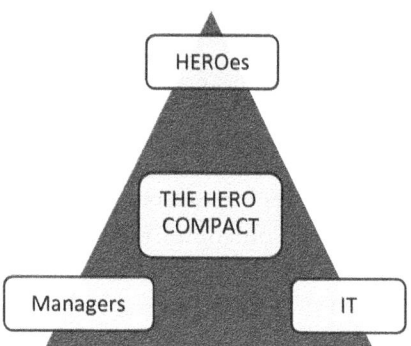

Fig. 8.2 HERO Framework

those who use the latest digital technologies, in cooperation with IT, to know and serve customer needs in line with managerial objectives. Managers are there to make sure innovation becomes a shared priority, and they support the HEROes while working with IT to manage the risks. The IT department provides the tools and must be ready to scale up solutions.

However, don't make the mistake of simply appointing a chief digital officer and thinking that's your HERO. I think the tendency of many organizations to delegate the digital role to a lone individual is misguided, as it reinforces a siloed, or outsourced, approach to problem-solving and innovation. Worse, that person will be made the fall guy for every digital experiment that goes wrong. Instead, companies need to foster distributed ownership. Just as the blending of the physical and digital worlds does not respect boundaries, neither does the imperative for digitally minded leadership reside in one individual. It spans the entire organization, irrespective of departmental and hierarchical lines. Everyone needs to step out of their comfort zones and embrace a digital mindset. What are we talking about? Specifically, digitally minded leaders need to synthesize five seemingly paradoxical or contradictory qualities, practices and approaches.

1. **Provide Top-Down Vision yet Bottom-Up Empowerment**

   - Cast a vision for how the company should evolve, and then translate this high-level vision into on-the-ground action by supporting the grassroots initiatives of your employees.
   - Foster an organizational culture where employees feel safe to experiment with their ideas and where the learning from their experimentation is systematically captured, analyzed and acted upon.

2. **Give Up Control yet "Architect" the Choices**

   - Yield traditional forms of control such as enforcing rigid rules or banning the use of social media or personal devices at work.
   - Instead, seek to influence outcomes through the way you design and present the choices. This is akin to the idea of "choice architecture," as described in Richard H. Thaler and Cass R. Sunstein's influential book, *Nudge* [8]. Make the option you want the default choice. Provide gentle policy nudges, offering positive advice on what kind of content should be shared and where it makes most sense to share it. Offer training and support. Share best practices.

3. **Sustain yet Disrupt**

- Sustain the old to ensure ongoing operations and profitability, as well as providing a foundation for the future business model. This ensures a sense of stability, helping employees cope with uncertainty as they start to develop new skills and capabilities.
- Act as a bridge between the old and the new, mitigating conflicts and internal rifts that will no doubt open up, given that some of the skills and competencies that people have spent their careers mastering may start to feel undermined.
- Shield disruptive transformation efforts from traditional metrics and evaluation criteria, like demonstrable ROI, which opponents will use to try to kill off new ideas.

4. **Rely on Data yet Trust Your Intuition**

- Make decisions based on empirical data and analytics.
- Change the decision-making culture from the turf wars of opinions toward a reasoned conversation based on facts and experimental measurements.
- That said, historical data may not always be accurate predictors of the future, especially in rapidly changing environments. Use intuition to decide which data sets to focus on, and how to combine, analyze and interpret them, based on your hypotheses about the future.

5. **Be Skeptical yet Open-Minded**

- Don't jump on every bandwagon. Recognize the inconveniences that technology brings—not to dismiss it but to yield valuable insights for formulating your vision of how you will do things better.
- Try it and see for yourself, so long as there is a bigger objective—which is to engage in an exercise of sense-making, learning what technology enables you to do. There's no substitute for sharing in the same experiences that your customers and employees are going through.

In his letter to investors prior to Facebook going public in 2012, Mark Zuckerberg described "a unique culture and management approach that we call the Hacker Way. The word 'hacker' has an unfairly negative connotation from being portrayed in the media as people who break into computers. In reality, hacking just means building something quickly or testing the boundaries of what can be done. Like most things, it can be used for good or bad … The Hacker Way is an approach to building that involves continuous improvement and iteration. Hackers believe that something can always be better, and that nothing is ever complete. They just have to go fix it—often in the face of people who say it's impossible or are content with the status quo … We have the words 'Done is better than perfect' painted on our walls to remind ourselves to always keep shipping … Instead of debating for days whether a new idea is possible or what the best way to build something is, hackers would rather just prototype something and see what works. There's a hacker mantra that you'll hear a lot around Facebook offices: 'Code wins arguments.' Hacker culture is also extremely open and meritocratic. Hackers believe that the best idea and implementation should always win—not the person who is best at lobbying for an idea or the person who manages the most people. To encourage this approach, every few months we have a hackathon, where everyone builds prototypes for new ideas they have. At the end, the whole team gets together and looks at everything that has been built. Many of our most successful products came out of hackathons." He goes on to distill these principles into five core values: focus on impact, move fast, be bold, be open, and build social value [9].

Whether you call them HEROes or Hackers, you want them at every level of your organization. And if the CEO is not being a hacker, then the CEO needs to at least understand the need to have hackers—those innately curious people who dare to do something with a system that the creator didn't imagine or intend to be possible. This should also be prioritized in your hiring profiles. For me, the most shocking part of the leaked *New York Times* innovation report was that, in 2014, they were still wrangling over using "tomorrow's front page, the tick-tock for Sunday's paper" as a metric rather than measuring traffic, sharing and engagement [10]. The front page? Sunday's paper? This is a perfect example of how mindsets, processes and metrics need to change. As the saying goes, "It is not the strongest species that survive, nor the most intelligent, but the ones most responsive to change."

Pause for Thought

- Where are the HEROes or Hackers in my organization?
- What needs to change about my corporate culture to release the principles more in tune with a digital mindset?

- Of the five paradoxical qualities of the digital mindset, which are the ones that I find personally most difficult? How can I focus on improving in that area? What training or support might I need?
- Which skills and competencies do I feel most threatened about losing? Which new ones do I need to acquire to stay relevant in the digital economy?

References

1. R. Cellan-Jones (January 29, 2015), "Office Puts Chips Under Staff's Skin," BBC News' Technology section, http://www.bbc.com/news/technology-31042477
2. J. Schofield, N. Passmore, B. O'Neill and C. Arthur (December 16, 2009), "From Old Futures to Modern Technology," *The Guardian* Technology section, https://www.theguardian.com/technology/2009/dec/16/guardian-technology-section
3. J. Rosen (June 27, 2006), "The People Formerly Known as the Audience," http://archive.pressthink.org/2006/06/27/ppl_frmr.html
4. G. Auricchio and E. Káganer (2015), "How Digitalization Is Changing the Way Executives Learn," *IESE Insight* magazine, Third Quarter, Issue 26.
5. M. Prensky (2012), *From Digital Natives to Digital Wisdom: Hopeful Essays for 21st Century Education* (Corwin).
6. B. Kendall and K. Hagey (June 25, 2014), "Supreme Court Rules Aereo Violates Broadcasters' Copyrights," *The Wall Street Journal*, http://www.wsj.com/articles/supreme-court-rules-against-aereo-sides-with-broadcasters-in-copyright-case-1403705891
7. *The New York Times* Innovation Report (March 24, 2014), p. 31.
8. R.H. Thaler and C.R. Sunstein (2008), *Nudge: Improving Decisions About Health, Wealth and Happiness* (Yale University Press).
9. Epicenter Staff (February 1, 2012), "Mark Zuckerberg's Letter to Investors: The Hacker Way," *Wired*, www.wired.com/2012/02/zuck-letter/
10. *The New York Times* Innovation Report (March 24, 2014), p. 72.

9

Managing Creative People: Time to Tear Up the Handbook?

Philip H. Seager

"The first thing managers have to realize is that HR is not someone else's job. It has to be their job, too." So says Dorte Spiegelhauer, a former director at the Danish Broadcasting Corporation (DR) and now a senior consultant, who has learned through personal experience that managing people in the media and entertainment industry is rather special. On the one hand, you need some rational basis on which to manage people. But people, by nature, are not perfectly rational, predictable and controllable, and even less so creative people, for whom straying outside the lines constitutes their job description. As such, you need to read the HR handbook and then tear it up, she says.

This tension is highlighted by comments posted by employees of another public service broadcaster, the British Broadcasting Corporation (BBC). On the HR website Glassdoor (where people post reviews of what it's really like to work where they do), employees describe the BBC as an "exceptionally rewarding" work environment, full of "exciting" and "amazing" projects, with the opportunity to work with "passionate people" and "dedicated professionals who go out of their way to produce a high-quality result." That's the good news. The same employees also report "lots of bureaucracy," "things happen really slowly," and "awful middle management who have no idea about what you do or how you do it. All they care about is trying to appease those directly above them and sit in endless meetings" [1].

P.H. Seager (✉)
IESE Business School, Barcelona, Spain
e-mail: PSeager@iese.edu

© The Author(s) 2017
M. Rosenberg, P.H. Seager (eds.), *Managing Media Businesses*,
DOI 10.1007/978-3-319-52021-6_9

159

This is the crux: creativity is messy, unruly, rebellious and questioning by nature, while managers are trained to impose some degree of logic, order, discipline and routine as part of an overarching organizational framework. Both depend on each other for their continued existence, since the media or entertainment company is nothing without its talent and "passionate people," just as there would be a lot less creative output in the world if someone did not properly manage it and make it an ongoing, profitable concern, which at times requires appeasing the powers that be and sitting in endless meetings.

Understanding what motivates creative people, and then channeling their passions and energies toward some common business purpose, is not an easy balance to get right. This chapter explores what a manger in this situation can do.

First, the Basics: Expectancy Theory

Let's start by understanding some of the basic paradigms underlying human resource management in general. Back in the 1960s, Victor Vroom of the Yale School of Management was the first to systematically explain why people do what they do, so that managers could use that understanding of what motivates workers to design and build satisfactory rewards that reinforce desired outcomes. The assumption is that people will put in more effort if the reward and outcome are tied back to their personal motivations. Called "expectancy theory," it was expanded on by fellow academics Edward Lawler and Lyman Porter, and continues to be revisited and refined to this day [2] (Fig. 9.1).

Here's how it works. The Expectancy derives from linking Effort with Performance. If employees don't believe they can perform a task no matter

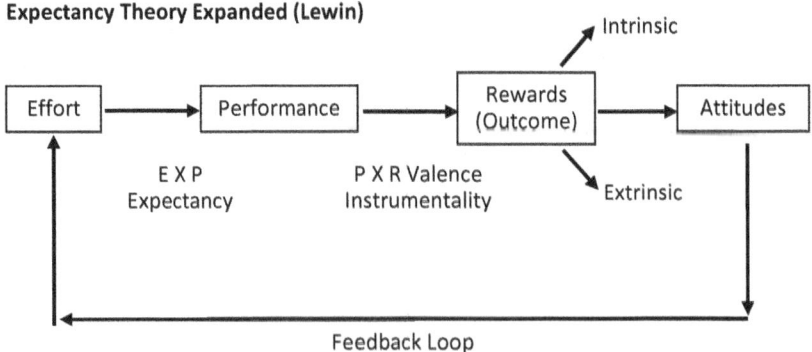

Fig. 9.1 Expectancy Theory Expanded (Lewin) Adapted by David Lewin to include the feedback loop, i.e., motivation, that characterizes the dynamic version of the original model

how hard they try, then they won't see much point in trying, leading to no motivation and therefore low Expectancy. Here, there are many subjective variables, as each employee will have different levels of self-esteem and self-confidence about what they are capable of doing. Your job, as a manager, is to discover what resources, training or supervision may be needed.

Next comes Instrumentality, which links the degree to which employees believe their Performance will affect the Outcome. Again, if employees don't think they can have any influence over the outcome, then there is little point in trying. Here is where managers need to deliver the goods as promised, doing everything within their power to ensure that the process is fair, so that if there is performance, the outcome will result as predicted or be fulfilled as promised. This becomes a mediating variable on motivation.

The third key force is Valence. This refers to employees' emotional orientation with regard to the outcome or reward being offered. How attractive or salient is it to them? What is it that they truly value? This is what you, as a manager, need to find out. If Valence is low, no one cares about the Outcome, and they won't put in much Performance.

One can assign values to each of these variables and calculate Expectancy × Instrumentality × Valence to determine the level of effort an employee will dedicate to a task. The higher the value, the more engaged they are. If one part is zero, the whole value will be zero. This shows the interrelated nature of these variables and the importance of managers gaining a deeper understanding and appreciation of employees' motivational needs in order to achieve the best result.

A crude example of expectancy theory would be the following. You would like to increase your salary, so you work harder, if the expectation is that by working harder you will get a promotion and a raise. If expectations are met, this positively reinforces your motivational state, influencing the effort you are prepared to make next time, in a continuous feedback loop. Conversely, if expectations are not met, managers will have to go back and make adjustments to improve the linkages between Effort and Performance as well as between Performance and Outcome.

What's Wrong with This Theory?

Expectancy theory is a useful formula, not least because it highlights where managers may need to focus their attention in adopting HR strategies that "pull" rather "push" employees in desired directions. It is infinitely more fruitful to harness people's own motivations, desires and values, and then gently nudge or influence them where you want them to go, rather than adopting a command-and-control style of leadership. Creative people, especially, will resist this latter approach.

However, the very term Instrumentality advertises a weakness, in that expectancy theory is rather, um, instrumental. "I do X because I expect to receive X and I do receive X in return." That may work for some, but not for others—and often not for creative types. It is exceptionally rational for a group of people whose motivations may be highly irrational.

As Ramzi Shuaibi, the director of a venue and events management company, attests: "We have a superb art designer working for us who never cares about getting paid. When I chase up his invoice so he can get paid for a project, he insists, 'I don't care, whenever and whatever you pay me is fine. The money isn't important to me. I just love what I'm doing and I'm learning so much.' Not getting paid? At first I couldn't understand it. I thought he was crazy."

Too often, as managers, we assume that employees act out of a desire for reward—usually monetary compensation to fulfill financial obligations. But what about people who do things, like this designer, regardless of the reward? Or maybe the reward is not what we expect. Might we actually be missing out on an excellent motivational tool?

As Shuaibi soon realized, not everyone is motivated by what makes sense from an economic point of view. "My designer simply wants recognition, to feel part of the project, to know that his work has soul. And let's face it: having someone who loves and feels proud of his work will always take you and your business to the next level. Even though it may be hard to understand, we need to recognize that we manage emotions, not soulless companies or projects."

To manage this way implies that we are privy to the inner workings of the creative mind, that we understand what drives them, what their deeply held values are. How do you find that out? Of course, you can come right out and ask them. Some HR managers administer a company-wide questionnaire to do just that. But people may not be able to articulate it for themselves, because this would require a degree of conscious deliberation and analysis that on-the-spot decision-makers and intuitive, artistic types are not known for typically. Yet, without such knowledge, it is difficult to know which key force to tweak to get the desired result.

Taking Time to Motivate Each Employee on a Personal Basis

The following questions are taken from research by Robert G. Isaac, Wilfred J. Zerbe and Douglas C. Pitt, who helpfully summarized the issues that leaders need to consider when attempting to forge strong links between expectations and outcomes [3].

The Effort/Performance Linkage

1. Is the nature of the work assigned reasonable, interesting, attainable and challenging? How does the person feel about it?
2. Does the person feel able to perform the task? Is more education, training and/or experience warranted?
3. Does the person possess the self-confidence required to do the job? Do I need to spend more time with this person to raise the level of confidence?
4. What constitutes acceptable performance, and are we sure we know this and agree? Do we have concrete measures of performance to monitor?
5. Does this job provide the person with feelings of usefulness, involvement and competence? What can I do to reinforce these feelings?

The Performance/Outcome Linkage

1. Do my employees trust me? Do I keep my promises? Do I avoid making excuses and lies?
2. Am I predictable, as well as fair, in dispensing outcomes? While outcomes may vary in each case, are they perceived as being equitable? Am I consistent in their application?

The Valence

1. Are the person-specific goals congruent with those of the organization? Does the person perceive this? What can I do to achieve a greater degree of alignment in these regards?
2. Is the outcome worth the expenditure of time and effort? What constraints on and off the job influence this person? Do we have realistic and mutual expectations and are they current?
3. Am I offering rewards the person really values? What informal rewards can I offer over and above the formal ones sanctioned by the organization? How are they perceived?

Other academics have suggested that the model could be improved by making the variables add up rather than multiplying them. So, if one linkage was zero, the equation would not equal "zero motivation." Instead, Expectancy + Instrumentality + Valence = Some Motivation. This would seem more in keeping with real life, in which employees will make some effort even if there are no guarantees that the hoped-for reward will ever materialize.

And what about media and entertainment professionals who work on a project or two not because of a guarantee of seeing an immediate reward but because of some longer-term payoff—a stepping stone to a bigger success down the road. This is a different motivation that is trickier to calculate in the case-specific formula. The big-picture reward may have nothing to do with the reward being offered for the project at hand, in which case any alignment of motivation to boost outcomes would be misplaced and irrelevant.

The Limits of Extrinsic Motivations

What this points to is a need for taking account of intrinsic as well as extrinsic motivations. Sure, some media professionals, particularly those in the movie and entertainment business, may be moved to get out of bed in the morning for "the easy money—the champagne, the Cadillacs, the glamour and glitter lifestyles," in the words of George Rose, executive vice president of People & Organization at Sony Pictures Entertainment. But those types of motivators have limited viability and are partly responsible for the current state of the movie and entertainment industry. "This industry is considerably populated by people who have been working in it for a long time," Rose told IESE Media AMP participants during a visit to Sony Pictures' studio lot in Los Angeles. But times are changing—and fast. "So we have to address that change of culture and mindset, in a way that allows us to be around in five or ten years' time."

Rose has had a long and varied career in human resources working for Cigna, Allied Signal, Honeywell, Alpharma, Ogilvy & Mather and, since 2009, Sony. He believes the HR function has a key role to play, and it starts by expanding your repertoire and tapping into a wider array of motivational drivers better suited to the realities of creative enterprises.

Top 10 Tips for Motivating Change

Like many companies in the media and entertainment sector, Sony has undergone significant restructuring in recent years to make sure "those critical jobs have a contemporary mindset and look across the landscape and know how to go about changing, so we get a different kind of profile," says Rose. He admits it is a delicate thing. "As HR managers, this is what we spend most of our time asking ourselves: how do we gracefully manage through this transition, maintaining a profitable company while at the same time setting our company up for the future?"

The following tips emerged through a discussion with Rose and David Lewin, the Neil H. Jacoby Professor of Management, Human Resources and Organizational Behavior at the UCLA Anderson School of Management, involving a group of Media AMP participants.

1. **Appeal to Intrinsic Needs**

As mentioned previously, managers will rarely see better results simply by throwing more money at creative professionals. Winston Fletcher explained it this way in his book, *Tantrums and Talent: How to Get the Best From Creative People*: "Creators' attitudes tend to diminish the importance of remuneration as a motivating factor. That is not to say creators are not interested in money, far from it. They most certainly are. However, there appears to be no correlation whatsoever between the money they are paid and the resulting quality of their work. Unlike pieceworkers [work done by the piece and paid for at a set rate per unit], they cannot be incentivized to work harder by being paid more; their productivity cannot be geared to their wages. Yes, the best creators generally get the most money. But it happens that way round. The money is paid to them for their talent, not to motivate them to do better" [4].

If you want to see change, you have to get people excited about the possibilities. "People have to believe that what you've got on your mind is actually something that can work, if they can figure out a way to get it to happen," says Rose.

He explains that Sony has been actively trying to recapture the original venturesome spirit of the founders, Akio Morita and Masaru Ibuka. As stated in the Founding Prospectus (1946):

The first and primary motive for setting up this company was to create a stable work environment where engineers who had a deep and profound appreciation for technology could realize their societal mission and work to their heart's content … Thus I began to conceive of ways for these motivated individuals to be united on a personal level, to embrace a firm cooperative spirit and unleash their technological capacities without any reserve. If this could be accomplished, the organization would bring untold pleasure and tremendous results, regardless of the meagerness of its facilities or the limited number of employees [5].

Media and entertainment managers need to "get people excited about the intrinsic proposition: discovering that, exploring that, digging into it and seeing the potential combinations and synergies." This is what motivates people, insists Rose. Fortunately, "being passionate about what you do" tends to form an inherent part of creative media and entertainment environments, so it helps that HR managers can appeal to this common base as a launchpad for change.

2. Understand Your Culture

"Culturally, you have to be sophisticated about how you manage a global enterprise," says Rose. By "culture" we mean national identities as well as companies' idiosyncratic ways of doing things. In the case of a Japanese multinational, like Sony, both understandings are at play.

Sony is a 150,000-person company. Around 50,000—a third—are Japanese, with 1,600 expatriated Japanese around the globe. "What can we learn from that?" asks Rose. "What can other people appreciate about living outside their own country?"

The general resistance to change and the job-for-life mentality that typify many Japanese corporate cultures bring a different set of challenges to the process of change management—"different" being the operative word, as it is vital to treat these cultural factors on their own terms, rather than judging them as either "good" or "bad," "better" or "worse." As Rose counsels, "you have to be very sensitive and smart about understanding your culture, its limitations as well as its opportunities."

So, Japanese culture provides continuity, stability and security, which may be precisely what is needed as the world changes at breakneck speed. At the same time, such a culture implies that one's ability to dramatically change things may be somewhat constrained. Similarly, a familial, social culture in which "we love all our people" may be just what the doctor ordered as you hold people's hands through change. At the same time, such a culture, where churn is low, makes it that much harder when painful decisions have to be made, regarding redundancies, for example.

The real question for managers is: how do you work with as well as around your workplace culture?

3. Work Collaboratively, Not in Silos

Sony has a number of autonomous units—the publishing business headquartered in New York, the movie business headquartered in Los Angeles—each with its own infrastructure. In such case, there is obvious opportunity to look at that structurally and say, "Couldn't we share more about what we're doing and facilitate a better cost structure than what we have independently?"

Part of the HR task and role has to be "to think about ways of integrating some of what happens there [in Japan] and make intentional efforts to develop your people to become global citizens," explains Rose. "How do we become a global organization that is integrated, not siloed, thinking about the concept of 'networked performance' as opposed to just linear, individual contributions? That is one of the areas that we are really exploring."

He adds: "While historically we were isolated and only thinking about our own P&L, what we have done is try to become a bit more transparent about the opportunities and the successes—or the shortfalls—of what is happening organizationally and get people excited [about the possibilities of working together]."

To generate that excitement, Rose says it all comes down to the way you, as the manager, sell it to people, so that they see it is in their own interest to change. You present it as: "Hey, you have to pay attention everywhere, because if these three parts don't perform so well, it's not like your life is going to be great, either. We are all part of the same enterprise and we have to have a viable future. If we can find ways to partner with each other to introduce some of those things, we are all going to be better off."

4. Tap into Younger Creatives

Most media and entertainment businesses are sitting on a veritable goldmine of underutilized talent in the form of 20-somethings with no positional power but loads of cutting-edge knowledge and capabilities vital for the future viability of these businesses. But how do we treat them?

Rose describes an all-too-familiar scenario: "If you think about most workplaces, we provide linear contact in interactive settings. Most of the world today is interactive: people take their mobile devices with them everywhere, connecting with everybody and everything. So, how can it be that the workplace is one of the few places left in the world, other than airplanes, where they say 'Turn off your device'? That attitude is counterintuitive to the generation coming through." According to Rose, the question that needs to be thrown back at media managers is: "How about you tell me to turn that device on? How about we find a way of using that technological capability to make an interesting experience?"

If you really want your colleagues to think about the future, Rose recommends upward mentoring: "As part of our diversity and inclusion effort, we have a very active process of connecting people to a Millennial affinity group, who are critical for giving us feedback about what we need to be paying attention to. They tell us what they watch, how they behave, how much they deal with their online devices, giving access to and awareness of content that otherwise people might not know about."

Table 9.1 summarizes ways in which companies can provide personal and professional development and support, based on an appreciation of the values and motivations of the four generations that make up today's workforce [6].

5. **Educate Your Workforce**

The media and entertainment industry is considerably populated by people who have been working in it for a long time. Such low churn is not necessarily healthy when these businesses get threatened by the Googles and Amazons of the world, which operate with a much different mindset. The challenge for HR managers is clear: how to rapidly evolve your workforce in an analog-based industry that doesn't have a lot of churn? Allied to this is: how do you manage your retention effort against the need to change the workforce?

For Sony's part, it ran a series of workshops to make employees more savvy about digital distribution, social media marketing and other disruptive industry trends, so that "from the moment when you have an idea about a film until the time it goes to the movie house or the television set or as home entertainment, you are always thinking in terms of a digital strategy."

6. **Don't Have Boring Meetings, Have Stimulating Conversations**

Being a manager is a tricky balancing act, regardless of your industry, as Rose explains: "You have to have exceptional people and you have to build great teams. At the same time, you have to be realistic about the future, about what the challenges, the strategies and the issues are."

What distinguishes the management process in creative industries versus other sectors is that "few creators accept that organizational hierarchies are an unavoidable fact of life" the way that others might do, as Winston Fletcher states in his book. "If a manager is to lead them he must get their respect, and to get their respect he must earn it. It will not be bestowed upon him merely because of his status in the hierarchy." As such, management phrases such as "The boss won't go for it" or "Let's form a committee" will be welcomed like a red rag to a bull. Managers need to remember that their primary role is to enable, not stifle, creative expression. "Producing great creative work should be playful fun," writes Fletcher, "and the good manager must not expect, worse still try to insist upon, the creators being deadly serious while they are working" [4].

Table 9.1 The values and motivations of today's workforce require that companies rethink their approaches to talent development

Generation	Over 60s	50s	30s–40s	Teens and 20s
Attitude to work	Work comes first	Live to work	Work to live	Live first, work later
They define success as	Reaching the top, thanks to hard work; Achieving status within the hierarchy; Financial security	Having a defined path within the organization; Enjoying status within the organization, including enhanced social status; A strong work ethic; Supporting a good cause	Promotion; Learning opportunities; Overcoming challenges; Money to cover financial obligations, with pay on a par with what others earn in similar situations; Time to devote to personal and family needs	Finding employment, especially their dream job; Exploring their own capabilities; Earning enough money to live on; Experiencing other cultures and countries
They are motivated by	Formal workplace structures; Moving up the corporate ladder; Being rewarded for years of service	Self-motivation, which may at times be compromised; Social justice and fairness; Stable and secure jobs; Visibility	Clarity in their assessment and expectations; Diversity of tasks and duties; Flexibility; Independence; Visibility	Opportunities for learning; Variety of tasks; New challenges; Contact with people from whom they can learn; Promotion
They leave if	They are forced to, because they generally expect to have a job for life	They feel that the company has broken contractual relationships	They feel ignored; They perceive incongruent values; They are assigned tasks unconnected to what they have learned	They perceive that they are stagnating

Based on research by IESE's Mireia Las Heras as part of the International Center for Work and Family (ICWF) and the IESE Family-Responsible Employer Index (IFREI)

Rose recounts his experience working with R&D personnel at Honeywell: "If you gave them a fact that you thought was based on science and told them this was what was necessary for them to pay attention to, they were on it. You had process-driven thinking and very disciplined ways of going about your people practices." At Sony, however, "to make sure you are getting the most out of your talent, you have to present it in different terms. You say, 'What do you think we ought to do about that?' as opposed to, 'We have a key session coming up next Tuesday at 4 o'clock and we are going to take three hours to go through each of your disciplines, organizational structures and succession plans.' We don't have that kind of rigidity. Essentially we are trying to get at the same thing, but doing it in an interesting way that isn't necessarily dry and engineering oriented."

7. Respect Their Intelligence

Following on from the previous point, Rose reiterates: "Make sure you convey respect for what they are doing and understand them—that you are curious about them and interested to know what makes for a creative vibe in the interests of having to differentiate what we do compared with what our competitors do. You want everyone in your group adhering to that kind of standard and working through that conversation together."

Having tough conversations is sometimes made easier in creative industries, believes Rose. "In contrast with working in another industry where it may take a long time to figure out if something is working or not, the beauty of working in a creative industry like the movie business is that you know right away whether something is working—the movie opens on a weekend and you immediately know if it succeeds or fails."

This generally predisposes people to grasp what you are talking about straight away—they cut to the chase, they are on the same page, they are prepared to "be realistic about the future, about what the challenges, the strategies and the issues are," because they want to get to success as quickly as possible, too.

8. Make Sense of Bad Behavior

Ever since Vincent van Gogh severed his ear, creative types have earned a reputation for being weirdos, prone to erratic behavior. While studies have shown that creative types tend to be "more independent, assertive, introspective, radical, experimental, non-conformist and high in self-esteem," as Fletcher stresses in his book, this does not make them all out-of-control egomaniacs suffering from psychiatric disorders [4].

Rose recalls a high-profile episode involving a well-known actor who shall remain nameless. "We occasionally get into the business of having to sit with some of the more eccentric and extreme behavioral types who occasionally populate this industry. Every once in a while we get people who don't behave in the right kind of way. We have to get into counseling mode. 'Tell me about what just happened or what I just heard and let me make sure that I understand it.' When it repeats itself, that is when we step in and try to resolve it. And if it can't be resolved, we have to talk to the director, and the network usually gets involved. It gets tricky and sticky, but we have to be very thorough and diligent and make sure that we create a safe, nondiscriminating, secure environment for people to be able to perform."

No matter what happens, "never treat them as oddballs," adds Fletcher, quoting the advice of former Channel 4 British television executive Michael Grade, who found that egocentricity usually masked deep insecurities: "We are all insecure in some ways, and our insecurities manifest themselves differently. Some of us are temperamental, some of us are depressive, some are bad at paperwork. And in each case you have to understand why. You have to understand what the job is you want the creators to do, and find a way to get the best out of them" [4].

9. **Handle Feedback with Care**

This leads to another key point when it comes to managing creative personalities: they tend to be more sensitive. As such, they may react more negatively to criticism than they should, and they may not take constructive feedback so easily or put it into perspective. This requires that managers adopt a different approach when it comes to feedback conversations. "Looking backward and saying, 'On a 5-point scale, I'm thinking you're a 3,' a creative type will go, 'Oh my God!' Instead, we create a plan—looking ahead so that we are constantly thinking about the idea of development," says Rose. "We decided that the best thing we could do for people is to talk about what's really going on—to have a conversation about what's working and what you are struggling with—and connect with them on that level, so that you and I are in the same place."

This approach seems to work much better. During an appearance at IESE Business School, Sheila Heen, author of *Thanks for the Feedback*, elaborated on this issue of how the way we give and receive feedback is inextricably bound up with our personalities. Many people simply don't hear what is being said, because they are either too sensitive or too insensitive. As such, managers need to understand this and adapt their messages accordingly [7].

10. Reconsider How You Offer Learning Opportunities

The belief that creative professionals are less likely to sit through long, rigid classroom sessions holds implications for the way that learning and development opportunities should be offered. Thirty years ago, the Center for Creative Leadership (CCL) came up with the 70-20-10 rule based on research into how executives learn and grow. This framework still serves as a handy rule of thumb [8]. At Sony, each executive has a development plan that is broken down as follows:

- 70 percent of learning happens on the job, via challenging stretch assignments and projects where you learn through the experience of doing.
- 20 percent of learning happens via developmental relationships with other people: these can be with your boss, role models, mentors, coaches, communities of practice and other forms of work-related networking.
- 10 percent of learning comes via training courses and reading.

Structuring development plans like this gives more weight to learning by doing and to informal, relational channels, and less weight to formal classroom settings. Even in those settings, the learning experience can be enhanced by employing dynamic tools such as apps, social media and Massive Open Online Courses (MOOCs), which are completely transforming the way media and entertainment executives approach workplace learning today.

11. Pursue Continuous Learning

As the musician from the 1984 spoof documentary *This Is Spinal Tap* would say, this Top 10 list needs to go to 11! There is one more overarching tip for media and entertainment managers. True to the nature of creative enterprises, all of the previous 10 activities must be revisited on a continual basis. "I don't think you ever fully resolve these issues," says Rose. "You are always looking to find ways to improve and overcome challenges."

As it should be: the best work often arises out of a profound sense of dissatisfaction or disaffection with the status quo—like the insomniac anxieties of the author or filmmaker to produce an even better sequel next time. This restless attitude resonates with the often perfectionistic tendencies of creative personality types. Manage your people the way Antoni Gaudi managed construction of the Sagrada Familia cathedral in Barcelona—as a work in progress that began in 1883 and continues to this day, each generation interpreting and adding to the codevelopment of a masterpiece. Robin Sharma spoke about the importance of continuous learning during an appearance at IESE Business School: "Work like Picasso painted. Bring your best game when you go to work. Put a smile on your face and radiate positive energy. Geniuses practice every single day. Practice is the price champions pay to be called champions. Most people go to work every day without practicing. It's really important to think about your goals, think about how you can improve, and read or listen to inspirational material before you go to work. If you're in business right now, you're in show business, and when you get to work, you're on stage" [9].

Performance Management and Appraisal Systems

One thing Rose noted in the previous section is that creative people are not huge fans of rating systems. Indeed, few people like them. But what's the alternative? Most people don't oppose, in principle, the need for some mechanism to evaluate employee performance, one that recognizes the different endowments of skills, talents, innate traits and learned behavioral characteristics, as UCLA Anderson's David Lewin points out in a chapter on "Appraisal and Reward" from his book *Human Resource Management: An Economic Approach*, coauthored with Daniel J.B. Mitchell. The "performance appraisal" is, at heart, the HR profession's attempt to formalize this process. But every man-made system, however well-meaning, has its faults, and performance appraisals are no exception.

First, there is the question of the person doing the appraisal. How qualified are they to be rating or ranking those below them? Might they have less than pure motives and abuse their position to extract "rents" and "favors" from subordinates? Simply acquiescing to supervisors' demands is no answer, as Lewin writes: "A rule that to get ahead, you should 'please your boss' is fine for the employer if what pleases the supervisor-boss is congruent with advancing the employer's agenda. But congruence of interests between employer and supervisor is not always perfect and certainly is not guaranteed" [10].

It is to avoid or reduce the scope of supervisory abuse that performance appraisal systems have become surrounded by formal rules and procedures. But this does not mean that "perverse incentives" don't persist. Here Lewin summarizes the vicious cycles of performance appraisal trade-offs that will no doubt be familiar to most managers.

Problem Employees: Too Much of a Bad Thing

1. Supervisors accurately report mistakes and misconduct.
2. Employees might complain, fomenting an unpleasant work climate in which morale and output suffer. Disgruntled employees take their grievances higher.
3. Upper management might think that persistent problems within supervisors' jurisdiction stem more from supervisors' inability to manage.
4. Therefore, supervisors may feel it is in their own best interests not to advertise too many problems, so they avoid giving too harsh a rating.
5. Supervisors downplay subordinate deficiencies in formal documentation. They attempt to handle difficult or incompetent workers on an informal basis.
6. This may lead to bigger problems down the road if the problems are left unchecked and the unofficial route fails.
7. The situation blows up, and supervisors are left holding the bag: why was the incompetence hidden? Why is there no official record of known deficiencies?
8. As such, perhaps it would be better to accurately report mistakes and misconduct. Which takes us back to step one, and the cycle repeats itself.

Excellent Employees: Too Much of a Good Thing

1. Supervisors sing employees' praises.
2. Employees are happy and don't complain, even about things that should be brought to someone's attention.
3. Upper management might regard high ratings as a positive reflection of supervisor efficacy, giving rewards accordingly.
4. However, supervisors may start to worry that too highly rated subordinates will eventually outshine them.
5. To protect themselves, supervisors introduce artificially low ratings to block progression, not giving credit where credit is due.
6. Upper management continues to attribute team success to supervisor efficacy, giving rewards accordingly.
7. Potential backlash from subordinates and possible lodging of grievances against supervisors for unfavorable ratings or for taking credit for others' work.
8. As such, perhaps it would be better to sing employees' praises. Which takes us back to step one, and the cycle repeats itself.

As these scenarios show, there are numerous "perverse incentives" built into the performance appraisal process that often skew results to the artificially high end of the scale. At root:

- Nobody likes to be the bearer of bad news, particularly when dealing with fragile egos, as mentioned earlier.
- Nobody likes conflict, particularly when dealing with oversized egos and volatile personality types, as mentioned earlier.
- Nobody wants to develop a reputation for being a bad manager, particularly in the cutthroat media and entertainment business, where a younger, hungrier manager is always ready and waiting to take your place.
- Nobody wants to put their budget in jeopardy, particularly when the costs required for actors and directors are not in line with what the industry can afford, meaning managers are going to fight tooth and nail to maintain their stranglehold on whatever stake they currently have.

Although some might argue that encouraging a happy workplace environment in which "everyone's a winner" lowers voluntary turnover, "scoring high on HR outcomes does not necessarily result in better organizational performance; in fact, it may worsen it," says Lewin. "Therefore, a strong argument can be made for more realistic performance appraisals."

The Performance Appraisal: A Necessary Evil?

Firms are not blind to these perverse incentives, but most are prepared to accept them, to a greater or lesser extent, for the sake of decentralized efficiency. The fact is, the larger the organization, the more necessary it becomes to delegate authority to middle managers and supervisors; not to do so would prove too costly. "Of course, you try to minimize those misincentives as much as possible," acknowledges Lewin, "but you cannot eliminate them entirely."

Consider
How does your firm deal with this trade-off?
How do you balance the need for accurate information about your creative people and talent, with the need for managerial delegation and decentralized organizational efficiency?
What monitoring mechanisms do you have in place to distinguish between poor supervisors and poor employees?

Practice	Pros	Cons
Documentation: Back up ratings with tangible, verifiable criteria and concrete examples, sometimes written in essay form to fully capture and explain "critical incidents"	Makes it clear to all involved which types of behaviors are being sought, and justifies high or low ratings Requires more thought and care, making it more meaningful than a last-minute, box-ticking exercise	Time-consuming, particularly the time of typically higher-paid employees who perform the rating function
Ranking: Grade employees on a curve	Avoids the problem of giving absolute ratings and the tendency to rate most employees as "above average"	Artificially forces employees into upper and lower camps Pits employees against each other, when cooperation may be more desirable
Reviewing the Review: Get HR reviewers to scrutinize the ratings and question supervisors' ratings against past reports	Provides an impartial perspective to minimize misleading ratings	Monitoring the monitors adds another layer of bureaucracy It is not HR's job to be constantly criticizing and interfering with the work of line managers
Self-Review: Invite employees to designate the criteria by which they will be judged, a technique called "management by objectives" Have rated employees review completed form and add any relevant comments	In setting their own criteria or rating themselves, employees have greater incentive and pressure to deal with self-confessed weak points Prevents false negative information from becoming part of the record without challenge	Employees are less likely to correct false positive information Supervisors with distaste for confrontations may be less willing to challenge employees' self-assessments
Peer Review: Have coworkers do the rating rather than supervisors	Takes onus off supervisor Removes the perverse incentives inherent in boss/subordinate relationship dynamics Improves fairness of process	Cliques of coworkers may be less forgiving than a supervisor and take advantage of the process to punish substandard performance by a colleague that has affected the team
360-Degree Feedback: Solicit feedback from myriad sources—from coworkers and wider staff, to customers, clients and other peer groups—to supplement that of the supervisor	Adds a much wider array of information Good for identifying development opportunities, as it is likely to yield a much more holistic picture of the individual's true capabilities	As the sources of the other feedback are usually anonymous, the employee may not be able to clarify or challenge poor ratings coming from unknown quarters Time-consuming and labor-intensive, due to the multiple people involved Casting the net wide is only effective if tied back to strategic organizational objectives

Practice	Pros	Cons
Measure Team Performance: Take the focus off the individual entirely and instead measure group dynamics using indicators related to the effectiveness of work processes (working together, reaching consensus, running meetings) and work results	Can be effective in organizations with a high-performance culture, where the only thing that matters is demonstrated results Useful when everyone essentially has the same job and collaborates together on a joint effort	Research on creatives and innovators finds they may perform better when left alone, working in privacy and solitude, so measuring "teamwork" in this context may be barking up the wrong tree Some would even argue that "teamwork" actively stymies creative output
Continuous Performance Appraisal: Replace the last-minute, once-a-year appraisal with on-the-spot feedback and coaching as and when issues arise, to be constantly taking the pulse of employee performance	Especially relevant in creative industries, where there is a greater need for constant encouragement and praise: "lots of verbal cuddles" in the words of one publishing manager Also, given the nature of creative pursuits, it is vital that supervisors stay on top of projects as they progress, to make sure employees are working in desired directions, so no unpleasant surprises surface when it is too late to do anything about them	Constant feedback is only welcome when the supervisor has earned the respect of the creative person, and it is offered in a spirit of good humor; otherwise, it will be taken as interference or micromanagement, demoralizing everyone involved
No Performance Appraisals: Scrap appraisals altogether	Surveys of creatives, particularly younger ones, reveal their huge dislike for regular performance appraisals or any system that would try to reduce or categorize them This works well in startup settings, where the market ends up rating your performance with either success or failure	Unless replaced by some informal mentoring or coaching, it is doubtful whether supervisors, if left to their own devices, would adequately fulfill the right development functions for their direct reports to the same extent and professional degree that a formal system was designed precisely for

No matter how imperfect your answers to these questions are, there is one overarching reason to retain performance appraisal systems: "Because of the signaling effect they provide," says Lewin. "To not have a system, however imperfect, might signal to employees that the employer does not place much weight on quality performance. Having a system, even if all involved understand its deficiencies, at least communicates that performance is important to the employer." To reduce the perverse behaviors that undermine a performance appraisal system, Lewin suggests the following practices.

Sony's Rose says: "We threw out all of our rating systems. We don't rate people anymore." Could you get away with that in your organization? Indeed, this seems to be a growing trend for many organizations. How are these questions handled in your organization? No matter what you decide to do, the most important thing to remember is that any appraisal data should be used for competency development, and not just for the determination of rewards, specifically pay rewards, Lewin reminds managers.

Lewin offers this final thought: "Creative people need a challenge. More than scoring consistently high on performance appraisals, perhaps what they really need is less satisfaction in order to motivate them and push them harder." This echoes Rose's earlier comment about the restless nature of creative personality types. Simply giving people high scores so as not to hurt their feelings may lead to worse performance in the long term. Maybe in the media and entertainment industry, we need to read the HR handbook and then tear it up, like Dorte Spiegelhauer said at the start of this chapter.

However, if you do end up doing away with the annual performance appraisal rating system, Lewin urges that you find some alternative, but no less conscientious, way of providing the requisite correction and coaching that all people, no matter what their business, still need to succeed.

A Conversation with Dorte Spiegelhauer

"We are all trapped in our own particular frames," says Dorte Spiegelhauer, echoing a thread throughout this book. "A finance person might be motivated by being told he was a 4 and here is what he needs to do to become a 5, because those are terms he understands. But using that same kind of performance measure would kill a creative person, because their frame is different. I would say 50 percent of my time as a manager is spent translating or reframing organizational measures, like this, into messages that will be listened to and understood by creative people. Getting people to understand each other across categories—legal, financial, HR—and serving as this constant filter so that organizational goals are put in terms that have real meaning for the people you work with. This is an essential part of being a manager. It's also the biggest challenge."

For Spiegelhauer, the challenge is twofold. First, whenever you have a corporate message or directive, you always have to put meaning into it. Why are we doing this? The "why" is extremely important for creative people, she says.

Second, the "whys" for management are often quite different from the "whys" for creatives, which brings us back to the need for getting people to understand each other across categories.

Consider musicians: they may have done nothing else since the age of seven except train to play the violin or flute. It has been the sole focus of their life. But in stressing this one single competency so much, they are not trained to understand much else outside of music.

"As a manager dealing with this type of personality, I have to think about the best way of presenting what needs to be said to get the desired results. What motivates these people is their passion, and any message coming from outside will be interpreted in terms of how it affects their ability to pursue that passion. As such, I need to do whatever I can to reduce anxiety levels and reassure them that this change is going to enable them to focus on doing what they are good at and doing it even better."

Creative people, Spiegelhauer finds, need a lot of high-touch feedback. She recalls, "When I first came to this organization, I thought, 'Wow! These people really know how to express their feelings. This will make the job so much easier.'" However, she soon realized that there was a big difference between effusive banter and honest communication. "You think they're talking, but it's often about each other rather than to each other. You think they're highly self-confident, but they actually need a lot of reassurance to make them feel stable and secure—maybe because the environments they work in tend to be so unstable and insecure."

One thing DR did to improve the quality of their feedback conversations was to change the way they approached performance management. They used to use balanced scorecards—a structured method for setting goals and then tracking them over time using quantitative measurement tools. Each and every quarter, managers would meet to set their key performance indicators (KPIs). There always seemed to be lots of high-level discussion about KPIs that had very little connection with ground-level realities, and everyone left the meeting room feeling that very little of substance had been achieved.

While they didn't ditch their rating systems entirely, what they did do was try to turn their quantitative metrics into qualitative leadership development conversations, which happened every two months. Instead of trying to present everything as a number, they focused more on sitting down with people and discussing the challenges they faced over the next one to three years. From this, they derived six competencies specific to that person's job and used that as a basis for goal setting. Subsequent evaluations were done by both sides—the reviewer and the reviewee—and they compared notes on progress, providing support and development plans according to needs as they arose.

They piloted this assessment program among a small group to inspire people and show them how it worked, before rolling it out more widely across the organization. Interestingly, the unions, intrigued by the success of the pilot cases, started to ask for a similar kind of assessment tool, as they saw there had been an important shift from target-setting and box-ticking to genuinely trying to develop people and help them in their professional growth paths.

Admittedly, the power dynamics inherent in boss/subordinate relationships are ever-present, which is why Spiegelhauer insists on honest conversations. "There's nothing worse than being afraid of hurting someone's feelings. If there is something you are not happy about, you have an obligation to tell that person what you are not happy about, and turn it into an opportunity for learning. This is basic leadership."

One learning opportunity that DR created to prepare their employees for the digital disruption happening in the media industry was to set up a social media academy. This is a cross-organizational group run by six of their best people with social media capabilities, together with key departmental managers and a project leader from HR. Thirty employees made the first cut to go through the initial training, having passed a prior assessment to get into the group. These forerunners then served as champions to encourage others to go through the training program.

In launching such an initiative, Spiegelhauer admits that the first reaction is fear—from old dogs who have to learn new tricks, from overworked people who worry about how much time this is going to take away from their passion, from the existing social media manager who wonders why everyone in the organization is suddenly being trained to do her job.

But Spiegelhauer insists you have to push past the pain barrier: "As a manager, you have a responsibility to be clear with people about where you want them to be and what they need to do to get there—because you always want your people to develop. If they get mad at you, well, so be it. That's part of your job, too: to be that person whom they can be mad at. I would rather that than to think my job is to protect people from the outside world or apologize for saying uncomfortable truths. That would be doing everyone a huge disservice. If you really want to help people, you will prepare them."

And in preparing them, you will break through to the next reaction, which should be what every manager desires for his or her employees, as Spiegelhauer explains: excitement, empowerment and developing people as tomorrow's leaders.

References

1. Glassdoor, BBC Reviews, http://www.glassdoor.co.uk/Reviews/BBC-Reviews-E5847.htm
2. V.H. Vroom (1964), *Work and Motivation* (John Wiley & Sons).
3. R.G. Isaac, W.J. Zerbe and D.C. Pitt (2001), "Leadership and Motivation: The Effective Application of Expectancy Theory," *Journal of Managerial Issues*, Vol. 13, No. 2, 212–26.
4. W. Fletcher (1999), *Tantrums and Talent: How to Get the Best from Creative People* (NTC Publications).
5. M. Ibuka (1946), "The Founding Prospectus," http://www.sony.net/SonyInfo/CorporateInfo/History/prospectus.html
6. M. Las Heras (2011), "Multiple Stories to Career Building," *IESE Insight* magazine, Fourth Quarter, Issue 11, p. 27.
7. S. Heen (2014), "Feedback Tips for Less Grumbling, More Growth," *IESE Insight* magazine, Second Quarter, Issue 21, and S. Heen (2014), "Feedback: A Game of Give and Take," IESE Insight Business Knowledge Portal, http://www.ieseinsight.com/fichaMaterial.aspx?pk=115187&idi=2&origen=1&ar=9&
8. Center for Creative Leadership, www.ccl.org
9. R. Sharma (2013), "Show 'Em What You're Made Of," *IESE Insight* magazine, Third Quarter, Issue 18, and R. Sharma (2013), "Robin Sharma: Leading Without a Title," IESE Insight Business Knowledge Portal, http://www.ieseinsight.com/fichaMaterial.aspx?pk=103781&idi=2&origen=1
10. D. Lewin and D.J.B. Mitchell (1994), "Appraisal and Reward," in *Human Resource Management: An Economic Approach* (South-Western Pub).

10

Corporate and Entrepreneurial Finance: Moving Your Business from Back of the Envelope to Front of the Class

Ahmad Rahnema Alavi, Jan Simon, with Philip H. Seager

On the face of it, Fiction Entertainment was a profitable, solvent company. In just four years, this TV and radio program producer had more than doubled its turnover. Sales had leaped 58 percent and were forecast to rise another 30 percent when the managing director, Stephen Lazaro, approached his bank about extending his line of credit to finance the next stage of the company's phenomenal growth. When the bank refused, Lazaro was stunned. He asked another bank; again the answer came back no. Stumped, he went back to look at the company's financial forecasts. Fiction Entertainment had a strong client base with committed contracts for the next three years. So why did the banks deny his loan request?

This chapter summarizes the financial context of business decisions. At times, media managers like Lazaro may have only a hazy idea of their company's finances, regarding financial management as the exclusive purview of the CFO. This is a fallacy. Indeed, just as most managers wouldn't think twice about the need to coordinate production to match sales, the coordination between financial management and operational management is equally essential. Unless you can accurately diagnose the situation, operational issues might spiral out of control, leading to cash-flow problems and eventually suspension of payments.

A. Rahnema Alavi (✉) • J. Simon
Financial Management Department, IESE Business School, Barcelona, Spain
e-mail: ARahnema@iese.edu; JSimon@iese.edu

P.H. Seager
IESE Business School, Barcelona, Spain
e-mail: PSeager@iese.edu

© The Author(s) 2017
M. Rosenberg, P.H. Seager (eds.), *Managing Media Businesses*,
DOI 10.1007/978-3-319-52021-6_10

Let's examine some critical financial decisions, first with existing companies and then with startups—an area of growing importance, given the plethora of new ventures in the digital media and entertainment space. As the legendary US venture capitalist Alan Patricof told Media AMP participants during a gathering in IESE's New York Center, "I've never seen the startup world as buoyant as it is today." Apart from the fundamentals of financial analysis that we will describe in this chapter, Patricof reminds readers of the other important tool to employ when it comes to corporate and entrepreneurial finance: common sense.

Physician, Heal Thyself

Earlier in this book, Hillel Maximon showed how accountants approach the balance sheet. His aim was to equip media managers with the right questions to ask to get to the story behind the story. This chapter is about how to interpret that story to improve managerial decision-making. The manager's job, in the media business or otherwise, is to find an optimal combination of resources—whether technical, human or financial—to achieve strategic goals and objectives. And of these three resources, the one that is decisive in differentiating your company is the human one, which is why the leadership you show in managing and coordinating financial efficiencies is so vital.

That said, one must recognize that any achievement on the human and technical dimensions requires a minimum amount of financial resources to keep going. You must be able to look at any set of financial statements over a period of time and draw some conclusions about a business's strategic objectives. You must also be able to forecast financial statements under different scenarios and draw some conclusions about the outcome of certain decisions.

Try this exercise: take a moment to examine the following balance sheets and income statements of Fiction Entertainment over a four-year period. Try to analyze why the banks would decline increasing Fiction Entertainment's credit limit from $2 million to $3 million, just based on the financial story being told here (Fig. 10.1).

To go about this task, you need to think a bit like a physician. What do doctors do when someone goes to them complaining of a headache? They ask a series of questions, to build up a picture of that person's history and hopefully get at the root of the problem, so they can make an accurate diagnosis that treats the causes and not only the symptoms. Does this person need glasses, suffer from the flu or have a brain tumor?

Balance Sheets of Fiction Entertainment from 2013 to 2016

ASSETS				
Fixed assets	2,597,280	2,821,268	3,781,646	3,839,520
Intangible assets	300,987	411,410	533,295	593,698
Property, plant and equipment (net)	2,277,603	2,391,168	2,688,551	2,686,021
Other fixed assets	18,690	18,690	559,800	559,801
Current assets	5,174,219	8,204,588	11,668,214	14,222,351
Inventories	1,487,407	2,478,451	3,057,079	3,143,194
Accounts receivable	3,470,366	5,441,384	8,276,523	10,992,832
Cash at bank and in hand	216,446	284,753	334,612	86,325
TOTAL ASSETS	7,771,499	11,025,856	15,449,860	18,061,871
EQUITY AND LIABILITIES				
Shareholders' equity	1,121,107	2,058,509	3,411,194	3,985,180
Capital stock	120,000	120,000	120,000	120,000
Reserves	1,001,107	1,938,509	3,291,194	3,865,180
Long-term liabilities	1,700,502	1,344,498	1,085,808	927,118
Non-current payables	1,700,502	1,344,498	1,085,808	927,118
Other LT liabilities				
Short-term liabilities	4,949,890	7,622,850	10,952,857	13,149,573
Bank borrowings	3,630,190	5,228,399	7,295,347	8,378,440
Trade payables	1,026,372	1,640,348	2,394,269	3,389,088
Other ST liabilities[1]	293,328	754,103	1,263,241	1,382,045
TOTAL EQUITY AND LIABILITIES	7,771,499	11,025,857	15,449,859	18,061,871

[1] Includes payables corresponding to other operating expenses and unpaid taxes.

Income Statements of Fiction Entertainment from 2013 to 2016

Sales	11,741,598	18,610,432	27,413,167	8,977,812
Less: Cost of sales	-10,722,948	-16,331,441	-23,848,022	-7,791,032
Change in inventories	563,166	991,044	578,628	86,115
Work done by third parties[1]	-6,093,459	-9,216,855	-12,640,421	-4,045,330
Wages and salaries	-4,135,911	-6,207,366	-9,017,499	-2,925,058
Other operating expenses	-1,056,744	-1,898,264	-2,768,730	-906,759
Gross operating income (EBITDA)	1,018,650	2,278,991	3,565,145	1,186,780
Depreciation and amortization	-194,185	-334,590	-387,584	-97,347
Operating income (EBIT)	824,465	1,944,401	3,177,561	1,089,433
Financial income	4,610	7,119	10,038	3,150
Financial expenses	-359,019	-509,363	-645,006	-209,529
Net financial income/expense	-354,409	-502,244	-634,968	-206,379
Income before taxes	470,056	1,442,157	2,542,593	883,054
Taxes	-164,520	-504,755	-889,908	-309,069
Net Income (NI)	305,536	937,402	1,652,685	573,985
NI/Sales	2.6%	5.0%	6.0%	6.4%
Interim dividends paid	0	0	300,000	0

[1] Equivalent to the purchases in a manufacturing company.

Fig. 10.1 What do you see in these financial statements that would give you pause?

In Lazaro's case, he needs more cash in order to invest in future program-making. In addition, the initial investors in his company are threatening to sell their shares unless he pays dividends—something he had promised at the start (10 percent of annual profits in dividends, with a minimum payout of $200,000, profits permitting). Is this the cause of Lazaro's "headache" or is it a symptom? It could be either, so we need to probe further.

Pause for Thought

How much time do I spend diagnosing the causes of a problem in relation to the time I spend prescribing solutions?

Diagnostic Tools

You don't have to be a CFO to use the following basic diagnostic tools of financial management.

Ratio Analysis One of the most commonly used tools is ratio analysis. It allows you to compare the financial statement ratios of one company with the same ratios of other companies, benchmarking one company versus others.

For example, cash is best measured in terms of the proportion of the company's short-term debts, rather than its absolute value. In other words:

$$\text{Cash ratio} = \text{Cash} / \text{Short-term liabilities}$$

Now refer back to Fiction Entertainment's balance sheets (Fig. 10.2). Four years ago, it had $216,446 in "cash at bank and in hand" and now it has $86,325. A decline, for sure, but that figure is meaningless unless it is put into some kind of context. Using ratio analysis, we see that the ratio of Fiction Entertainment's cash to its short-term liabilities is 0.66 percent today compared with 4.4 percent four years ago. That represents a drop of 60 percent—a much more worrying decrease.

There are many ratios that one can use like this, depending on what you are trying to evaluate and also the characteristics and circumstances of each individual company, country and industry context. They are useful tools to deepen your perspective of a firm's performance over time, indicating trends, raising red flags and providing telling clues to strategic-level concerns that you, as a manager, ought to be addressing.

ASSETS				
Fixed assets	2,597,280	2,821,268	3,781,646	3,839,520
Intangible assets	300,987	411,410	533,295	593,698
Property, plant and equipment (net)	2,277,603	2,391,168	2,688,551	2,686,021
Other fixed assets	18,690	18,690	559,800	559,801
Current assets	5,174,219	8,204,588	11,668,214	14,222,351
Inventories	1,487,407	2,478,451	3,057,079	3,143,194
Accounts receivable	3,470,366	5,441,384	8,276,523	10,992,832
Cash at bank and in hand	216,446	284,753	334,612	86,325
TOTAL ASSETS	7,771,499	11,025,856	15,449,860	18,061,871
EQUITY AND LIABILITIES				
Shareholders' equity	1,121,107	2,058,509	3,411,194	3,985,180
Capital stock	120,000	120,000	120,000	120,000
Reserves	1,001,107	1,938,509	3,291,194	3,865,180
Long-term liabilities	1,700,502	1,344,498	1,085,808	927,118
Non-current payables	1,700,502	1,344,498	1,085,808	927,118
Other LT liabilities				
Short-term liabilities	4,949,890	7,622,850	10,952,857	13,149,573
Bank borrowings	3,630,190	5,228,399	7,295,347	8,378,440
Trade payables	1,026,372	1,640,348	2,394,269	3,389,088
Other ST liabilities[1]	293,328	754,103	1,263,241	1,382,045
TOTAL EQUITY AND LIABILITIES	7,771,499	11,025,857	15,449,859	18,061,871

[1] Includes payables corresponding to other operating expenses and unpaid taxes.

Fig. 10.2   Balance sheets of Fiction Entertainment from 2013 to 2016: Look closely at the rows "cash at bank and in hand" and "short-term liabilities"

Here are four of the most common ratio sets:

1. Profitability ratios

Gross margin ratio = Gross margin / Sales

Net return on sales (ROS) = Net profit / Sales

Return on equity (ROE) = Net profit / Shareholder equity

2. Liquidity ratios

Cash ratio = Cash / Short-term liabilities

Cash in days of expenses = $(Cash / Annual expenses) \times 360$

Current ratio = Current assets / Current liabilities

3. **Financial structure ratios**

Solvency ratio = Shareholder equity / Total liabilities
Fixed asset coverage = Permanent funds / Net fixed assets
Leverage = Debt / Equity

4. **Operational ratios**

Average collection period = (Accounts receivable net of sales tax / Sales) × 360
Average pay period = (Accounts payable net of sales tax / Purchases) × 360
Raw materials in days of purchase = (Stocks of raw materials / Purchases) × 360
Finished goods in days of sale = (Stocks of finished goods /
Cost of goods sold) × 360
Stock turnover = Cost of goods sold / Total stocks

From the above list, current ratio (Current assets/Current liabilities) is widely used. Doing the current ratio for Fiction Entertainment (14,222,351/ 13,149,573) yields 1.08. Is that a good or a bad ratio to have? Again, it depends. Some guides say that a current ratio of 1.4 is good, 1.25 is average and 1.10 is bad, though in practice it's not quite so simple. You have to bench-mark the ratio against the industry average to judge whether it's good or not. In some industries, a lower ratio like 0.5 could be better, whereas in media and entertainment, the current ratio could be as high as 3 and you could still be having cash-flow problems.

While ratios give managers some helpful indicators, they are not enough on their own. We must do further tests.

Working Capital The next tools in the manager's arsenal are working capital and working capital requirements, two distinct yet complementary concepts that are helpful in understanding the financial implications of operations.

Working capital (WC) is the equity plus long-term debt less net fixed assets. In short, it's the money or financial resources that the company has available to finance its day-to-day operations. In the balance sheet, this is equal to current assets minus current liabilities.

But just knowing how much capital you have available is not enough: more important is knowing how much capital you actually *need*, what's called your working capital requirement (WCR). This is calculated, or estimated, as operational current assets minus short-term liabilities without interest charges (spontaneous funds), often coming in the form of suppliers who provide a product or service in which you typically have 30, 60 or 90 days to pay.

The problem arises when WCR ≠ WC, meaning the money you need is not equal to what you have available. To obtain the difference, you usually have to borrow, either short term, as just mentioned, or from the bank, which entails interest.

The challenge for management is keeping a close eye on this gap, because the wider it gets, the more you have to borrow. What then?

- First, you might say, "Okay, I'll borrow more." But you have to remember that each business has a certain capacity to borrow; if you saturate this capacity, nobody will lend you any more.
- Second, even if you have the capacity to borrow, the lending may not be available. This was especially the case during the credit crunch of recent years.
- Third, if you have the capacity and manage to get the funds, don't forget you will have to pay it back with interest, which is an additional expense, just like labor, raw materials and other costs, which can reduce your profitability.

This gap must always be controlled. To put it simply, if you don't get the money required to work, you cannot work, and this is when the company starts having problems, experiencing financial distress or eventually filing for bankruptcy.

How often should you track these numbers? Large companies usually issue monthly financial statements; small and medium-sized enterprises tend to be quarterly. Whether monthly or quarterly, you have to watch the gap between WC and WCR to spot if something is not behaving in a normal way. "Normal" will mean different things to different types of businesses. If you are in a seasonal business, you may require more or less WC, depending on the season (low or high).

When Fiction Entertainment found its WCR was growing at a faster rate than available WC, it tried to get a loan. But with the WCR ≠ WC trend lines opening like a pair of crocodile jaws, it's obvious why the banks would refuse this loan. Alternatively, Fiction Entertainment could try to:

- *Get long-term debt financing*—though this is unlikely if it has already been refused short-term debt financing, especially since it is looking for financing to cover short-term needs.
- *Reduce fixed assets*—though being a production company, it would be loath to sell off any productive capacity.
- *Reduce costs by collecting faster*—which may be easier said than done if more powerful business partners or clients choose not to pay on time or delay payment.
- *Not pay others*—but then it risks damaging vital business relationships with suppliers, which is potentially self-destructive if they are unique suppliers, as then the company will have a supply-chain problem besides.
- *Charge more for its products or services to raise more money and at the same time grow slower*—however, this could undermine its entire business model and alienate customers.
- *Raise WC by raising equity*, perhaps by bringing in a new partner or finding venture capital (VC). (This is, in fact, what Fiction Entertainment finally had to do.)

What this exercise highlights is that there's no one simple solution. Rather, a constellation of management issues has to be navigated with creativity and, as we will state again later, with common sense.

Many media companies with fixed assets—that is, physical infrastructure like a TV studio with lots of equipment—are more limited in what they can do to resolve their capital requirements, because their margin for flexibility is very low. Even though the financing decisions are ultimately taken at the C-level, when it comes to WCR, all the decisions taken at the operational level of the company will have an impact on the amount of money you need for day-to-day work—making this the job of everyone in the company.

The decision to buy something. The decision to sell something. The decision to find a new client. The decision to sign a new contract. The decision to hire anyone. The decision to fire anyone. The decision to go with a new supplier. The decision to change operations. A client who decides to pay in 60 instead of 30 days. A client who pays late. All these decisions, either directly or indirectly, hold financial implications for WCR.

At the very least, you have to be aware of the financial implications of your day-to-day decisions. You also have to "mind the gap" so you don't run into problems down the road. And returning to the doctor analogy, remember that prevention is always better than the cure.

Valuation: A Rough Guide

In addition to making sure a business has enough money to finance its ongoing operations, one also needs to make sure it has enough money to grow. How does one get money?

One can take out loans like Fiction Entertainment tried to do, but as we just discussed, that's not always possible. More important than increasing the size of the balance sheet is building a sustainable business characterized by an innovative, differentiated product or service that fills new or unmet needs. This kind of growth is derived from creating value for customers.

Value rests on three pillars—growth, profit and control—all of them working together and supporting each other. Profit feeds growth and vice versa. But without good management control systems, one might soon run into trouble. This holds true for any business but especially for growing businesses, because at each stage of growth one needs different managerial talents. Attention needs to be paid to all these pillars working together (Fig. 10.3).

Value should not be confused with price. The price a person agrees to pay for some goods or services can be distinct from its inherent value. Facebook's jaw-dropping purchase of the mobile messaging service WhatsApp for $19 billion in 2014 is a case in point. At the time of the deal, WhatsApp's ad-free revenue model was based on charging its users a subscription fee of $1 per year, so assuming there were 450 million users at the time of the sale all paying $1, a crude calculation of 1 × Sales might put the company's asset value at $450 million.

But Facebook's Mark Zuckerberg saw lots more value in WhatsApp than what was on its balance sheet—namely, the ability of Facebook to dominate mobile messaging, to remain relevant as user trends shift and to wipe out the competition, all in one fell swoop. As he told the Mobile World Congress in Barcelona, he considered the app to be worth even more than what he paid for it [1]. And that perfectly illustrates why "value" can sometimes be "priceless."

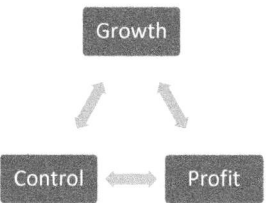

Fig. 10.3 Value rests on three pillars: attention needs to be paid to growth, profit and control

This also underscores the importance of seeking to value your own business, not just to remain solvent, but so that you have some measure by which to gauge your performance over time. This helps for strategic planning, knowing which products, business lines, countries or customers to maintain, grow or abandon.

It also helps in determining compensation schemes for certain executives by quantifying the value they create. Moreover, you never know what the future might hold: one day you might just want to sell part or all of your business operations, merge with or buy other companies, or issue shares on the stock market to fund the next stage of your growth.

There are several ways to value a company, all of them more art than science. Here are the three main valuation methods.

1. **Balance-sheet-based methods.** These methods measure a company's value based on the balance sheet: the difference between total assets and liabilities, yielding the net asset value (also called equity value, net worth or shareholder value).

Balance-sheet-based methods can be calculated as book value, adjusted book value, liquidation value and substantial value; however, they all share the same basic weakness of the balance sheet, which is that it measures value based on the value of the assets rather than on the value that these assets, in combination with management, can create.

Any information that is not apparent in accounting statements—organizational problems, the state of the industry or human resources—will not be reflected in this valuation method. As such, one needs to keep in mind that any valuation based on the balance sheet ignores the future and hence hardly ever matches the market value.

2. **Income-statement-based methods.** Due to the weaknesses of balance-sheet-based methods, the next set of methods turns to the income statement to determine the company's value using other indicators such as multiples of sales and price/earnings ratios.

For example, based on valuations of similar companies, Fiction Entertainment might choose to calculate its value by multiplying its annual sales by 2. There are two main issues with this methodology: one is determining which metric to use (in our example: x Sales); the other is deciding which companies to use as "comparables" or peers.

This issue arose when Amazon was being valued. Was its "market comparable" its chief bookstore rival, Barnes & Noble, a brick-and-mortar operation? Or did being an Internet-based direct retailer put it in the same category as Dell, a computer technology company? Neither seemed quite right, and either would change Amazon's valuation dramatically.

The same goes for sports companies. Is their "comparable" another sports category? Or should they be classed as entertainment, which might put Barça in the same category as Disney?

This is hard enough for existing companies to calculate, let alone when trying to find "comparables" for industries that don't even exist yet, as in the case of assigning a value to a trailblazing startup for which there is as yet no industry peer. This is why experience in these matters becomes vital. More on this issue later.

3. **Cash-flow-discounting-based methods.** A third set of methods estimates the cash flows that a company will generate in the future and discounts them at a suitable rate (taking into account real economic growth, inflation and risk). Cash-flow-discounting-based valuations are increasingly favored because they capture the time-value—though these methods also have shortcomings.

It is important that all managers are involved in calibrating risks as well as analyzing and projecting how the strategy of each business unit will affect cash flows, so that critical factors are not missed during the valuation process. Though the numbers may be crunched by the CFO, forecasting the strategic and competitive factors that will have an impact on the evolution of a business's balance sheets, income statements and cash flows has to form part of every manager's responsibilities. *Question: does it form part of yours?*

Although no valuation method is perfect, doing so is an essential part of corporate finance and gives you a rough guide for future decision-making. Referring back to the growth, profit and control triangle, valuation informs each pillar. It helps you:

- Calculate your profitability
- Evaluate your growth potential
- Identify success factors, value drivers and synergies
- Calibrate risk
- Define the characteristics that create revenue
- Recognize the determinants of capital inflows and outflows
- With such knowledge, implement the management control systems that best mitigate or leverage these dynamics

At some stage, you might be involved in a merger-and-acquisition decision, where the value of the target company will be one of the central issues. The same valuation techniques will apply.

What About When a Company Doesn't Exist Yet?

So far in this chapter we have discussed how to value a business that has assets, sales and cash flows. But what happens when the business is hardly more than a team with an idea—when there is no balance sheet and income statement to evaluate?

This is where we turn to the experience of Alan Patricof, hailed as the god-father of VC, having been in the business since the 1960s. He was one of the first to set up an independent VC firm in the United States—Apax Partners, based on a wordplay of his own name—with which he earned the reputation of being the man who "knew how to spot 'em," famously investing in and helping to grow such ventures as America Online, Office Depot and a little-known computer company you might have heard of called Apple. He started Apax with $2.5 million, and today it is one of the world's leading private equity firms, with more than $40 billion under management.

Perhaps because it got so big, Patricof stepped back from Apax to set up Greycroft, which focuses exclusively on small, early stage investments in Internet and mobile companies. Greycroft makes comparatively modest investments of between $100,000 and $5 million at inception, and growth investments of up to $20 million.

A look at Greycroft's portfolio (http://greycroft.com/portfolio/) reveals the occasional household name (*Huffington Post*) but most are for ad tech, video aggregators, e-commerce, gaming and publishing sites, the likes of which you have probably never seen or heard of before. Yet make no mistake: these are all genuinely disruptive businesses.

There's an entrepreneurial movement sweeping the globe, says Patricof, suggesting that high unemployment due to the global economic crisis may be pushing jobless people, particularly young people, to try new things, not just in the United States but everywhere from Iceland to Estonia, where he is busy making deals.

On a typical Monday morning, Patricof finds himself listening to yet another eager entrepreneur giving him a pitch for the latest business idea that's going to take the world by storm. The week he came to IESE's New York Center to meet with Media AMP participants, he'd heard 26 new business plans in New York, 16 in Los Angeles and 104 contenders were still alive on his list as potentials for investment.

Suppose you are in one of Patricof's Monday morning meetings, either as an entrepreneur making a pitch or as a Greycroft partner trying to figure out whether the project on the table in front of you is going to move the needle. How do you assess if what is presented to you is merely an idea or a great opportunity? This is what we will look at next.

Business Opportunity Assessment

An important point to make—whether you're approaching the business proposition from the standpoint of the entrepreneur or the investor—is that any startup is highly risky. It's true that every business activity is risky, but this holds especially true when it comes to startups. Where possible, it is your task to assess these risks, understand their nature and manage them. In some cases, they can indeed be mitigated. At times, by understanding the sources of the risks, you may actually be able to turn them into value drivers.

Here are some typical sources of risk:

- Lack of revenue
- Cost overruns
- Timings
- Competition
- Capabilities, whether technical, human or financial
- Competence of the team

Each of these can be turned around when you can demonstrate how to address or compensate for associated risks. Show you have done your homework, with thorough analyses of market trends, demographics, target populations, market growth potential and so forth.

To mitigate operational risks, you can build in incentives or penalties for every target hit or missed. You can offer stakes in the company. The founder might sink his or her own cash into the business. Given the notoriously high failure rate of startups—with one in ten not surviving past their first year of operation and only three in ten lasting a decade, on average—having some mechanism that signals the seriousness of one's personal commitment to the venture will inspire confidence in others.

It's important to have experienced, competent people in positions of leadership. It's also essential for the team to have complementary competencies and share similar values. Patricof makes the following point: "Sound management is key. If the product doesn't work, great management can change it. But if you have management that doesn't work, that's a lot harder to change, no matter how good the product."

For this reason, he looks for someone who comes with a team of people: "We always ask: how many of these people have worked with you before? We have found this to be the highest predictor of success. A person who starts a business in a similar field, and who attracts people who have worked for him or her before, shows that the other people who follow are betting on that manager and the idea, because it's clear this person knows the business they've been in. They're giving confirmation that the idea is good and the person is good, too."

Having said that, Patricof stresses that the experience factor is not the only factor. There has to be a sound business plan underneath it all. You have to consider what's happening more widely across the industry as a whole. There has to be some basic differentiation and competitive advantage. He sees too many look-alikes, citing a recent pitch for "yet another disruptive business taking coupons to the digital world." Despite being "an interesting team," when it comes to couponing, "you need enormous numbers because you only get a fraction of a percent on returns. There are so many obstacles. You add all these factors together and you realize it's too high a risk."

With this in mind, here are six key question areas for assessing a business opportunity. Being relentless on these six differentiators will help you no matter whether you are trying to make your own business project attractive for investment, or whether you are a venture capitalist making an initial assessment of a new business idea.

1. Is There a Market/Demand?

- Do we have to create the market? How large is the market?
- Why will there be demand? Is there proof of concept?
- Who are the buyers? How can the company identify them? How will the company reach them?
- How will sales be made? Will there be follow-on sales?

2. What Is the Competitive Advantage?

- How compelling is it? Is it game-changing?
- Who is, or who will be, competing in this same space?
- How will competitors react? Substitutes? *Do not underestimate this!*
- Is the competitive advantage sustainable? What will it take to sustain it?

3. Is the Timing Right?

- Is the market ready for this? Is the company too early/too late? How long will the window be open?
- What is the status of the product/service? What remains to be done?
- Any breakthroughs required? How long will they take?
- How long will it take for sales to build?

4. How Can It Be Scaled?

- What is the economic model?
- How big can the business be?
- How profitable can it be?
- How valuable can it be?
- Can we afford the scaling requirements?
- Will the effort be worth it?

5. Who Are the People Behind It? *This is the most critical factor!*

- Can they make this business work? Can they sell? Are they capable of growing the business?
- What is their objective? Might they be too in love with their own product?
- Do they have the right team? How will they fill any gaps?
- Is the chemistry right for working closely together with these people?

6. What's the Exit Strategy?

- How do I exit from the deal?
- Are there many likely buyers?
- Could the company lend itself to an IPO?
- Is exit achievable in a reasonable time frame?
- Will an exit fit with the team's goals?
- Will they push for top value?
- Is my required return (hurdle rate) achievable?
- Will the sector pay up?

Valuation Techniques

Now that we know how to assess a business opportunity, we need to know how to value it. Earlier we learned that when assessing an existing business, operating cash flows can be used as an indicator of present value. We can also use "comparables" and weigh them against a metric to extrapolate future earnings potential.

But in the absence of fixed assets, of like-for-like comparisons or of relevant metrics to make cash-flow projections, we need to have some other basis for valuation. So for startups and early-stage companies, venture capitalists employ different valuation methods. These take into account the specific nature of startups.

The VC method of valuing startups and early stage companies is a variation on discounted-cash-flow methods, based on the VC investment and the expected internal rate of return (IRR). Using the minimum IRR and the projected exit valuation, the business parties determine the various ownership stakes in the venture that will be given in exchange for the funds being invested today.

Pre-financing Valuation First, you have to decide the value of the business idea today, before VC financing (Vpre). Here's where one needs the seasoned expertise of someone like Alan Patricof. He'll be the first to tell you that "this is not something you learn in school. It's an art form. You learn by doing."

According to the experts, any new idea, with the exception of technology and biotechnology, cannot be worth more than $1 million to $5 million. The dot-com area is illustrative of what happens when the VC-industry structurally ignores this principle. Anything more than that may lead to the situation of the dot-com bubble, with people making outlandishly high valuations. Every time VC people don't stick to this rule of thumb, risk is not correctly assessed. Remember, these business ideas are just that—ideas—so keep it real. If a valuation seems unreasonable, it probably is.

Patricof worries about another bubble in the making. For instance, Greycroft's founding philosophy was that every company in which they invested would get sold for less than $100 million, predicated on five years' worth of data showing that Internet and media businesses sold for an average of $70 million. Since 2013, however, Patricof has noticed those averages shooting up beyond reasonable expectations. "We're going through crazy times again," he says, wondering if we are "about to hit an air pocket and drop from 40,000 to 20,000 feet."

Think of this valuation stage as securing initial funding to prove the concept works with real consumers and the market. There's no point purposely trying to inflate the value of the business idea. Propelled by Steve Blank's "lean startup" idea (http://steveblank.com/), initial capital serves to achieve a "proof of concept." Once the entrepreneurs can demonstrate that their product or service finds recurring paying customers, a business plan is formed and more capital is raised. A decade ago, you would start with a business plan; now you end up with one. Once you've got some empirical data behind you, then you can fine-tune the valuation during subsequent rounds.

For argument's sake, let's say someone makes a seasoned judgment that the business idea, as it stands today, is theoretically worth $2 million (Vpre). Most investors look for deals that can deliver ten times their investment. So, an investor who provides $200,000 is thinking he or she might get $2 million at exit. With this in mind, the investor will formulate an ownership position.

Using Greycroft's rule of thumb that an Internet business sells for an average $70 million, the following formula is applied:

$$\text{Investor's exit amount} (\$2m) / \text{total exit value} (\$70m) = \text{required ownership share} (3 \text{ percent})$$

However, bearing in mind there will be subsequent rounds of funding involving various other parties, the investor will want to boost this ownership share to compensate for future dilutions. But at least this provides a baseline for negotiation.

Post-financing Valuation Continuing the calculation, the post-financing valuation (Vpost) is determined by taking the Vpre and adding it to the amount of capital that the company needs at this stage (C).

$$\$2m (\text{Vpre}) + \$200,000 (C) = \$2.2m (\text{Vpost})$$

To determine how much equity the investor should require, divide $200,000 (C) by $2.2 million (Vpost) to get 9 percent (%E). This means 9 percent of the common shares should be allocated to this venture capitalist in exchange for his or her investment, leaving 91 percent of the equity to be distributed among other investors and management.

Note the variance between the Vpre and Vpost valuations, of between 3 percent and 9 percent. This gives investors a range in which to negotiate, making sure that one does not overpay nor underpay for deals. It also gives parties a reference to measure against, as the company grows and builds greater value. Every time new financing is required, investors should repeat the same Vpre and Vpost valuation process. If the business goes well, then the Vpre in subsequent rounds should keep getting higher than the previous Vpost.

If, on the other hand, the business does not develop as expected and the Vpre of posterior rounds is lower than the Vpost of the previous round, value has been destroyed as time progresses.

Suppose after a year the company is only worth $1 million and needs to raise another $200,000:

$$\$200,000 \, (C) \, / \, \$1m \, (Vpost) = 20 \text{ percent} \, (\%E)$$

In this case, the present owners end up giving up 20 percent of the company for a mere $200,000 (compare this with the 9 percent in the earlier example). One can soon come to understand the importance of things like "proof of concept," "recurring paying customers" or "accelerating cash flow." They all point to increasing valuations and hence increasing shareholder value.

Remember Stephen Lazaro at the beginning of this chapter? Part of his "headache" derived from the fact that he had pre-committed himself to pay out a percentage to his investors that he could not pay—yet he desperately needed more money or else his business would go bust. Sometimes if you are desperate, and this is your last resort, you are in a take-it-or-leave-it position—and you unhappily give up 20 percent of the company for a mere $200,000. Always remember, though, that equity is the most expensive form of financing.

As such, one of the top lessons of business in general and entrepreneurial finance in particular is don't overpromise what you can't deliver. Being too generous may also limit your possibilities going forward.

Of course, for great opportunities that execute what they set out to deliver, this often works the other way. In the previous example, if, between rounds, the business had nicely established itself with increasing sales and customers, a different valuation of, say, $3 million Vpre might have been established, with the $200,000 capital increase only leading to a give-up of 6.25 percent of capital:

$$\$200,000 \, (C) \, / \, \$3.2m \, (Vpost) = 6.25 \text{ percent} \, (\%E)$$

Due Diligence

For most startup ventures, this need for capital is unavoidable. The more rounds, the more financing, the more investors—and the more complicated this whole process becomes.

Anja Mellage, managing director of Berlin-based startup, admitted during the Media AMP that she finds a lot of her time is spent acquiring new investors and taking care of existing investors. Unfortunately, there are no ways around this. (Read the interview with her at the end of this chapter.)

That's why, as "simple" as the VC method might seem, the reality of assessing the terms of the financing offer (stated in the term sheet), and the effects on the development of the business and the value of the company, can be complex and time consuming. What seems a great valuation may not necessarily be a good deal. But when the need for cash is high, an on-the-face-of-it "good" valuation might be the excuse for a starting entrepreneur to do no further due diligence or to do so superficially. This is an error.

Although Patricof personally loves subscription-and-database-based businesses "because they get stronger every year," he knows, too, that love is blind—and that poses dangers.

For example, the growth prospects of Internet startups are often based on what they can prove their traffic and reach are according to Facebook and Google analytics. When Facebook and Google suddenly change their algorithms, a lot of businesses, and hence valuations, are left vulnerable. Things can change very quickly, Patricof says, so you have to be able to react very quickly. You have to understand the subtleties of financing structures and instruments; if not, you'll come to some wildly inaccurate valuations and conclusions.

For Patricof, this means being willing to miss some deals. Besides being one of the early investors in Apple, he is also famous for passing on Federal Express and turning down Starbucks: "I was living in New York where we have at least one coffee shop on every single block. I couldn't understand who would want a coffee shop business?" You win some, you lose some.

Above all, there comes a time when the previously described valuation methods and rules of thumb are no longer useful. Once the early stages are past, and the startup breaks through to the next phase of its business life, managers must revert to the traditional financial analyses and valuation methods described at the beginning of this chapter. This is another aspect to the art of financial management: knowing when to make the switch, understanding which instruments to apply and when. This is when your company moves from back of the envelope to front of the class.

To Recap

Before committing cash, have I been relentless on the six keys?

Am I valuing the right things: "comparables" and discounted cash flows for established companies; realistic benchmarks for startups?

Have I applied due diligence? Gone to the most experienced people? Structured wisely? Although the new money and investors set the terms, are there ways I can ensure those terms are optimal for me?

A Conversation with Anja Mellage

Anja Mellage worked for the largest publishing house in Europe, Axel Springer, for 13 years before switching to become the managing director of a digital media startup (called Niiu Publishing at the time) whose star product was a customizable news app for the iPad enabling readers to consume all their favorite media on one platform. Here she talks about the new challenges she faced going from a traditional publishing industry to a startup environment, and the skills needed to help a small company grow.

"All of the traditional skills of organizing and managing operations and processes certainly still apply, but one thing that is definitely different in a startup environment is that you constantly have to prepare your company for growth. Simply having a really good idea, being very creative and innovative, is not enough. You have to be ready with answers to those six key differentiators mentioned in this chapter. As managing director, I review our strategy on a regular basis, looking exactly at those six points. I look at the market. The timing. Is our product ready? Things like this.

"One of our investors once told me that startups needed to change their strategy every month. I don't know if I would go so far as to say that, but you do have to review your strategy and business opportunities quite often. It's not like sitting down and having a one-day annual strategy meeting like I would have done before at a more traditional company.

"With a startup, it happens as a matter of course when talking with investors or customers. As we're still in the growth phase, we need to talk to a lot of investors to get additional financing for the next round and the round after that. We also have to convince publishers to license their media for our product. And as we have these meetings, we invariably go over those six points. They challenge you. They ask specific questions: 'Are you sure it's working?

Are you sure you're addressing the right customers? Are you sure you're in the right market?' We have to have answers ready for everything.

"The good thing about digital media is that they are excellent for enabling the exchange of ideas and information with other people, especially with your customers. With digital newspapers, we are able to gain a lot of information about our readers or users. We know when they are making their purchase decisions, when they are using the product more often, and which parts of the product they are using a lot. You can evaluate this and adapt your business to the demand of the market very easily. We try different business models, different markets, and adapt the business to the opportunities ahead.

"Granted, to be constantly adapting like this has its pros and cons. On the one hand, there are so many changes going on all time, all around the world, from Africa to Australia, which may well affect us, but we can't keep changing every single time. This is impossible, even though some of those other business models might be better. On the other hand, having this fast-changing media landscape is good for being able to see what others are doing and benchmarking yourself in relation to them, even if you can't always change your business model in response.

"This makes my job hugely challenging, but I also believe it makes my job the greatest, most fascinating and interesting one that anybody can have right now on the planet. One day I might be trying to secure new financing; the next day I might be defining new product features, doing HR and general accounting, or meeting existing investors. Many, many different things. Obviously, this adds to the challenge of being a manager in the media industry today, because you have to focus on so many different things in parallel. And being a startup, there are fewer resources and people available, so you have to jump into the job that needs you most urgently. But it's great fun!

"There's another aspect to having to do a lot of different things at once. You also need to be looking ahead – very far ahead – because, for example, our market doesn't fully exist yet. So, although there's a huge print subscription market behind us, the digital newspaper market is still relatively small. At some point, this will change. We count on this. So in addition to everything else, you have to be preparing yourself to address exactly the right way to eventually get all these customers to your business.

"Jan Simon and Alan Patricof are right when they say the team – the people behind your business – is critical. It's much easier to convince investors if you have a really innovative and creative team to back up your great idea. We generally find people via word of mouth. Being Berlin-based helps, because there's every kind of talent coming from around the world who would like to work in Berlin right now.

"One of my first tasks as managing director was to change the office language from German to English, so we are able to integrate every nationality – from Britain to Iceland to the United States – in our team. We even have developers and quality assurance people in India, and they are part of our team. When I say India, most people think outplacement, but it's not like that for us. We're one team together. The head of our India team is also our art director, and we always have one of our CTOs in India taking care of business. We have regular media conferences. Nowadays it's easier to manage with Skype and all those kinds of communication. And the time difference is just five hours. We definitely have a great team.

"Alan Patricof was also right when he said you learn by doing. The more you go to investors and have these types of conversations, the more you begin to develop this sense, this intuition for assessing business opportunities.

"Even if you don't work for a new media startup, in every company you will have owners or investors. They might be institutional investors or a private person or another huge company that owns part of your company. You always have shareholders and other stakeholders whom you have to take care of – you have to recognize their needs, and translate those needs into your business model, and answer to those people. Even though, being in a startup, I'm now much closer to the actual investors who give the money than I was before, in the end, no matter where you work, you have to be able to do the things described in this chapter: assess the opportunities, anticipate the risks, and do the math to ensure a profitable, solvent company."

Reference

1. C. Rahn (February 25, 2014), "Mark Zuckerberg Says WhatsApp Worth More than $19 Billion," Bloomberg Technology, http://www.bloomberg.com/news/articles/2014-02-24/zuckerberg-seeks-phone-partners-in-quest-to-connect-billions

11

Scenario Planning: Your Playbook for the Future

Mike Rosenberg with Philip H. Seager

"There's no playbook for this." That's what CEO Michael Lynton told Associated Press following a devastating cyberattack in November 2014 that crippled Sony's computers, stole its data and nearly scuppered the release of its controversial movie, *The Interview*, which was purportedly the focus of the hackers' unbridled rage. Likening Sony to being "the canary in the coal mine," Lynton said, "you are in essence trying to look at the situation as it unfolds and make decisions without being able to refer to a lot of experiences you've had in the past or other people's experiences. You're on completely new ground."

"We were so taken by surprise by the events…that we didn't have a plan at that moment to go forward," he added [1].

Stories like this should serve as a wake-up call to all managers, no matter if they are in the media and entertainment industry or not. But the response should not be one of hand-wringing, hoping and praying your company won't be next. There are actions you can take so that you *do* have a playbook—not

---

This chapter also contains some material from M. Rosenberg (2012), "Using Scenarios to Plan for Tomorrow," *IESE Insight* magazine, First Quarter, Issue 12.

M. Rosenberg (✉)
Strategic Management Department, IESE Business School, Barcelona, Spain
e-mail: MRosenberg@iese.edu

P.H. Seager
IESE Business School, Barcelona, Spain
e-mail: PSeager@iese.edu

© The Author(s) 2017
M. Rosenberg, P.H. Seager (eds.), *Managing Media Businesses*,
DOI 10.1007/978-3-319-52021-6_11

just for eventualities like a cyberattack but to envisage your future business environment more clearly so that you make better strategic choices. Scenario planning, the subject of this chapter, is a helpful way of future-proofing your business.

Why Scenario Planning Is Better

"One of the things I realized on the Media AMP was that the broadcasting industry, in my point of view, is dying—slowly but it's dying. Content will still be important, but you are going to distribute that content via other types of devices—not through traditional broadcast television as we know it today," says Martin Breidsprecher, COO of Azteca America, a Hispanic broadcaster based in Los Angeles. "I realized this by trying to imagine what might happen in the future, based on different premises. As managers, we really need to think not just about today or tomorrow but over the next 10 years. Ten years is a very long stretch, and technology is evolving so quickly. How do you plan for 10 years' time if you really don't know and can't be sure what's going to happen next?"

There are ways, one of which is to develop tremendously flexible business models and capabilities, so that you can change or pivot, depending on how things go. Many firms, for example, have outsourced aspects of their operations to buy themselves some additional flexibility, so in the event of a sudden downturn in one area they can scale up quickly in another. (Chap. 7 on Operations Management and Chap. 2 on Strategy delve into this subject more deeply.)

Yet operational flexibility has limits, especially in industries in which fixed assets with significant useful life spans factor heavily. In businesses where investments must remain viable for at least a decade, managers have to place relatively large bets based on a reasonable approximation of what they believe the future will look like.

Moreover, developing new capabilities takes time, while consumer behavior changes constantly and at an ever faster pace. The media industry, in particular, faces unprecedented change as a result of digitization, but it is still far too early to tell what the industry will look like in the not-so-distant future.

Business planners may resort to forecasting, using formal statistical methods to estimate outcomes at some future point in time, but this, too, has limits. Although forecasting methods do try to incorporate, or at least acknowledge, some level of uncertainty in their calculations, they are not very reliable guides for the long-term future. Computer-model forecasting has its place: it can be useful for making short-term budgetary decisions. But once you start projecting 50 or 100 years into the future, so many variables enter into the equation that your guess becomes as good as mine.

Think of some of the truly game-changing tectonic shifts in the business landscape over the past several years—from the ubiquity of smartphones, tablets and apps to the financial crisis of 2008. None of them was forecasted.

Or take another timely example: oil prices. Any business that had predicated its future strategy on a price forecast made in 2014 ("If X continues to grow at current rates") would be dazed and confused by 2016 when prices had dropped by more than 70 percent. This highlights the chief limitation of forecasting: it assumes tomorrow's conditions and context will be pretty much the same as today's, which they never are.

The idea that the future *cannot* be known is scenario planning's starting point. Rather than trying to predict the future, scenario planning requires managers, like Breidsprecher, to imagine what *might* happen, so they can better prepare and position themselves in anticipation of plausible alternative futures.

Scenario Planning: How It Started

Royal Dutch Shell is widely acknowledged as being one of the first companies to use scenario planning effectively. In the late 1960s, Pierre Wack, a French executive based at Shell's London headquarters, was experimenting with unconventional ideas about "seeing the future," which seemed more the preserve of mystics than managers.

Wack and his team began by looking at the facts before them, but they didn't let those facts point them in straight lines to foregone conclusions. Instead, they used those facts as creative jumping-off points to imagine different worlds, or scenarios, beyond what the facts said.

With no serious disruption in oil supplies since the Second World War, the facts said there would be continued, sustained expansion and growth for years to come. Wack's team imagined something quite different: a changed geopolitical context, leading to a disruption in oil supplies, a subsequent rise in oil prices and various knock-on business effects.

Of course, this is exactly what did happen in 1973, when the Arab members of OPEC declared an oil embargo in protest against the West supporting Israel in the Yom Kippur War. Within weeks, the price of oil skyrocketed from $3 to $12 a barrel.

Thanks to scenario planning, Shell found itself one step ahead. Managers in different parts of the company had already made a number of strategic decisions and investments to diversify into other energies, such as coal and nuclear power, and to other oil fields in the North Sea, to be less dependent on the Middle East. Such measures enabled the company to emerge from the shock in relatively good shape.

This initial success lent credence to scenario planning, and the Shell team was empowered to take these ideas further. Since then, Shell has become a leading example of how an organization can use scenario planning successfully.

Besides Pierre Wack, Shell has given rise to a number of influential business thinkers over the years, including Peter Schwartz, whose books *The Art of the Long View* and *Inevitable Surprises: Thinking Ahead in a Time of Turbulence* have become required reading on scenario planning. It was during Schwartz's tenure in the 1980s that Shell anticipated the collapse of the Soviet Union and positioned itself for the eventual opening up of Russia and Eastern European markets nearly a decade before that actually happened.

Shell regularly publishes its scenarios (www.shell.com/scenarios). Some of the ideas for this chapter are distilled from Shell's sophisticated work in this area, as well as my own professional consulting work and custom programs developed for multinational companies.

Experimenting with Scenarios

There are many possible approaches for developing scenarios. The process for a specific company should be chosen in light of the objectives of the exercise and the time and money available.

For firms interested in experimenting with the concept but not yet ready to embark on a major effort, I would recommend the following process, which can be done effectively in one day or two half-day workshops (Fig. 11.1).

1. **Convene scenario-planning team**. You first have to select which members of the company are going to be involved in scenario planning. The process should include, at the very least, the senior management team. It is vital to have significant commitment from the top, as well as members who are personally convinced of its value, which will ensure active engagement in the process. It is also important to have diversity among the participants so that the scenarios will be as rich and complete as possible.

Breidsprecher assembled a special team made up of the CEO, CFO and the heads of programming, planning and research, along with an outside consultant who was hired to help crunch the numbers and do the homework associated with analyzing all the different scenarios. More on that later.

If possible, the process needs to be pushed further down in the organization. Breidsprecher planned to roll out the process through televised events at town hall meetings with all employees in the cities across the USA where

Fig. 11.1 Scenario-Planning Process

Azteca America has a presence. "We will try to explain what we are doing, where are we heading, what is our vision, what's our plan, what we want to do, so everybody gets involved in this mentality and everybody is focused on what is our goal," he says.

2. **Divide into groups**. Once you have a core team, divide the participants into groups, again paying attention to the diversity of each group. Each will work separately on developing scenarios for the future. One way is to work in two groups, one optimistic and the other pessimistic. During the Media AMP, we divided participants into four groups to imagine future media scenarios for the world in 2025 based on a more or less digital and globalized business environment (Table 11.1). Choose the groupings that are most relevant for you.

3. **Identify issues/drivers**. Next, each group needs to identify which are the issues or drivers that will most affect the future environment for their business or sector.

4. **Take to extremes**. Work out the time frame of the exercise, which needs to exceed the normal planning horizon of the business. You need to look far enough into the future that you can freely use your imagination and not be overly bound by your assumptions about the past or present. For some, this might be 10 to 20 years; in a rapidly changing sector like media and entertainment, this would likely be three to five years. Whichever time frame is chosen, just make sure it is long enough to get out of your day-to-day thinking.

Then, take the previously identified issues or drivers to extremes for the given time period. If divided along optimistic/pessimistic lines, each team would imagine either the best or worst case scenario, thinking in terms of consumer behavior, macroeconomics, regulation, technology and so on.

5. **Work out the best possible result**. The next step is for both teams to work out the best possible result for the company or business unit in the positive or negative environment they have created. This can be done to different

Table 11.1 Divide into Groups

	Less digital	More digital
More global	Group A	Group C
Less global	Group B	Group D

levels of detail but should include, as a minimum, sales volume, key customer segments, geographic reach and so on.

6. **Develop key lines of action**. Each team needs to identify and develop key lines of action that should be undertaken by the organization in order to achieve the results discussed. If you were certain of the future environment that you have just described, what specific steps or actions would you take—starting today—in order to secure the best possible result?

For example, in the Media AMP exercise, Group D imagined a world that was highly digitized but less globalized than today. All traditional media were gone and all content was delivered via digital platforms. But there was little cooperation: lots of firewalls around zones and regions, markedly differing standards and solutions, independent ecosystems and the focus was on delivering highly localized content in niche markets wherever they were found. If that future were to come to pass, one participant said, "I would have to start selling off stations and producing more local content starting from today."

7. **Regroup**. Once all these steps are done, the final part of the process is to bring the teams together and discuss their findings together. What emerges from this discussion is a common understanding of the key issues that are driving the business, a rough idea of the range of outcomes that might be expected, and a potentially complete list of the lines of action that the group, as a whole, could consider over the medium term.

When the Media AMP groups reconvened, even though their future scenarios all looked different, several common threads emerged: more localized content, more personalization, and a shift to mobile devices. This gives some clear, shared lines of direction to be working in, regardless of which of the four scenarios eventually materializes.

Break for Data, Call in Experts

One issue that often arises during this process is the availability of data. When discussions stray outside the normal competence levels of the management team, it may be impossible to project the evolution of critical issues that are such big unknowns for those involved. Or it may be that one participant has much more information than any of the others.

There are various ways of handling this. One is to break the workshop into two parts, allowing some time for data collection before deciding on your key lines of action.

Outside experts can be called in. These could be experts on specific issues such as legislation or technology. Their insights can add richness to the discussion and fill in any missing details. Or they may be skilled facilitators who help to guide the whole scenario-building process.

"It takes time," says Breidsprecher, whose team has decided to work on five different future scenarios at a time. To do that, he brought in a dedicated person who can go away, gather more data and continue working up new scenarios in light of new, incoming information. The scenario-planning group touches base every two weeks to review where they are and how they may need to reposition themselves as new scenarios take shape. "This way we can stay flexible, changing our assumptions or premises as we go forward."

While this is more thorough, others may choose simply to recognize and accept the limits of having incomplete data. For some, the main benefit of doing this exercise is the shared learning experience and building consensus on the various issues confronting your company, rather than banking on the actual accuracy of the scenarios being developed.

For Shell, the most valuable outcome is that executives' assumptions about the future are made explicit. Incorporating multidisciplinary viewpoints serves to broaden management perspectives. They begin to see the business environment in which they operate as a complex system, and they realize that they need to allow for nonlinear effects [2].

Or as one Media AMP participant remarked after going through this exercise, "Even though our business is doing well now, it forces you to become forward-looking, thinking much more strategically about your future positioning and about future impacts."

Be Prepared for the Challenges

Some words of warning: this is not something to be undertaken lightly. As Breidsprecher acknowledges, developing in-depth, meaningful scenarios requires considerable time and effort. However, companies must ask themselves whether they can afford *not* to do scenario planning, given that it is the ideal tool for helping managers consider strategic options for just such uncertain times as these.

Another challenge is using scenarios in planning decisions. Actually letting a what-if scenario hold sway over a concrete decision you need to make today does require taking a leap of faith. Yet there's no point developing alternative visions of the future if you then do not let those visions have any bearing on day-to-day decision-making and practice.

That means making decisions based on incomplete information, as Breidsprecher explains. "But you have to have a belief and go through that. You have to say, 'Okay, this is what I think is going to happen in the next three years, five years and 10 years.' And you plan toward that goal, all the while remembering that if something changes drastically, you can change tack very quickly."

Finally, think carefully about how you share your scenarios internally. While they can be helpful in preparing people for change, those who have not gone through the process for themselves may come away feeling confused or threatened, especially if they see a future organizational vision with them or their business unit downgraded or unrepresented. That's why it's important to include as many people as possible in the process from the start.

What Are Your Plausible Futures?

The more I read about emerging trends, and the more I work with executives from a wide variety of industries and countries, the more I am convinced that we are living through an unparalleled period of fast change happening on multiple, complex levels. We can't change the fact that the future is, by nature, uncertain and unknown. But that fact should prove why it is all the more urgent and necessary for managers to take the time to engage in scenario planning, to prepare for some of the great unknowns.

Going back to the example that opened this chapter, it seems unfathomable that Sony could not have imagined such an event. As one business expert reminded the BBC, Sony had been hacked before [3]. The 2014 cyberattack was the "worst ever," insofar as each and every cyberattack that Sony has suffered on its Playstation network going back to 2011 has gotten progressively worse each and every time it happens.

Sony's make-it-up-as-you-go-along decision to release *The Interview* through on-demand video is equally surprising. "You would never take a movie of this size and do what we did with it in the end," Lynton told AP. "It's true, it proved to be that kind of experiment, but it certainly wasn't planned. Had this not come along the way it had, we would've proceeded exactly the way we planned to do it, which is to put it out on 3,500-plus screens" [1].

We don't know to what extent Sony engages in scenario planning, but if you were the CEO, you would probably want to go through the exercise as described in this chapter with your senior leadership team. It should not be such a stretch of the imagination for a media and entertainment company to plan for a future in which a movie or drama series skips theaters or television completely and is released online first (Netflix and others are already doing it). Or a future in which controversial content may invite attacks from fanatics (apart from the alleged North Korean hack against Sony, we also have the 2015 attacks against *Charlie Hebdo* magazine in Paris, which echo similar threats made against the *Jyllands-Posten* newspaper in Denmark going back to 2005). You should have a playbook for events like these. After all, these are not future scenarios like, "Aliens invade Earth and take over all communication channels." These are highly plausible futures.

Breidsprecher says, "What I'm doing is planning not just one scenario, but five different scenarios. So I have the flexibility to change as I see things evolving through time. For instance, there's going to be a spectrum auction. Is there any impact on Azteca America? What is the impact on the overall industry? What happens if the auction is successful? What happens if the auction fails? All those different scenarios I have to put into my business model to plan what I'm going to do with Azteca America during the next 10 years."

The following comment by Google Chairman Eric Schmidt when Lynton contacted him for help in his hour of need is highly revealing: "This is what we've been waiting for," Schmidt reportedly said [1]. Google was more than ready and willing to distribute Sony's movie via Google Play and YouTube, while Microsoft's X-box and Apple's iTunes also stepped forward to help get the movie out online. "Sony became an unintended test piece in a new film release strategy of putting out streaming video at the same time as a theatrical release," stated AP [1]. I'm willing to bet that someone had been working toward that scenario for years—and if they hadn't, they should have.

Media and entertainment managers must do all they can to forecast specific trends and gather as much data as possible. And this must be allied with a scenario-planning process, which for me remains the best way to develop the mental agility that is needed to cope with whatever lies ahead.

References

1. Associated Press (January 8, 2015), "Call to Google Got 'The Interview' Out: Sony Pictures CEO," http://hosted.ap.org
2. *40 Years of Shell Scenarios (1972–2012)*, http://www.shell.com/energy-and-innovation/the-energy-future/scenarios/new-lenses-on-the-future/earlier-scenarios.html
3. K. Rawlinson (January 9, 2015), "Sony Boss: 'No Playbook' for Dealing with Hack Attack," BBC News' Technology section, http://www.bbc.com/news/technology-30744834

Index

© The Author(s) 2017

M. Rosenberg, P.H. Seager (eds.), *Managing Media Businesses*,

DOI 10.1007/978-3-319-52021-6

Printed and bound by CPI Group (UK) Ltd, Croydon, CR0 4YY

23/04/2026

02095636-0006